Effects of Fishing Gear
on the Sea Floor of New England

EDITED BY

Eleanor M. Dorsey
Conservation Law Foundation

Judith Pederson
Massachusetts Institute of Technology Sea Grant College Program

PUBLISHED BY THE

Conservation Law Foundation
Boston, Massachusetts
1998

FRONT COVER

Background image generated by
Rich Signell and Ed Roworth,
U.S. Geological Survey

Inset photographs from top to bottom:
- Page Valentine and Dann Blackwood,
  U.S. Geological Survey
- Derek S. Davis
- Jon Witman
- Les Watling
- Jon Witman

MIT Sea Grant Publication 98-4
ISBN 1-892787-00-8

DESIGN & PRODUCTION
David Gerratt/DG Communications, Acton, MA

PRINTING
Puritan Press, Hollis, NH

Additional copies of this volume are available from:
Conservation Law Foundation
62 Summer Street
Boston, MA 02110
617/350-0990

Contents

Preface

This book began with a conference that we chaired on May 30, 1997 at the Warren Conference Center in Ashland, Massachusetts. The purpose of the conference, convened by the Conservation Law Foundation and the Massachusetts Institute of Technology Sea Grant College Program, was to present available information about effects of fishing gear on New England's sea floor and on fishing productivity, benthic habitats, and biodiversity. We were motivated by a concern that widespread and intensive use of fishing gear that contacts the New England sea floor may be damaging fish habitats and threatening biodiversity. A paucity of information about the effects of fishing gear, however, dictated that the first step to addressing the issue must be to gather the available information. Hence the conference and this volume.

Important information about the topic resides both with scientists who study the sea floor and with fishermen who derive their livelihood from it. Most of the contributors to this volume practice one of these two professions, as do most members of the steering committee that we convened to help plan the conference *(see following page)*. Fishermen were selected to include users of diverse bottom tending gear types, including both mobile and fixed gear. The steering committee helped select topics and speakers for the conference and recommended that fishermen be asked to talk only about their own gear types, in order to avoid the conflicts and antagonism that sometimes surface between users of different gear types.

This book contains all of the papers delivered at the conference, but we have not limited the book to a simple reporting of what was presented that day. We have requested from the speakers clarifications of their presentations, we have invited them to expand and update where appropriate, and we have sought additional illustrations for the topics presented. We have added two papers that were not presented at the conference—an initial overview of the geology of New England's sea floor and a final "Short Take" by an invited speaker who could not attend the conference. To conclude this volume, we provide a summary of the discussion session with which the conference ended. A full discussion of management implications and options is, however, beyond the scope of both the conference and this book.

In our editing, we have preserved differences in voice and style among the diverse speakers, and in order to avoid the cumbersome addition of scientific names to papers of nonscientists, we provide an index to scientific names as an appendix.

The views expressed in this volume do not necessarily reflect the views of the funders listed in the Acknowledgments.

Eleanor M. Dorsey
Judith Pederson, Ph.D.
Editors

Conference Steering Committee

Eleanor M. Dorsey
Conservation Law Foundation, co-chair

Judith Pederson
MIT Sea Grant College Program, co-chair

William Adler
Massachusetts Lobstermen's Association

William H. Amaru
F/V Joanne-A III
New England Fishery Management Council

Peter Auster
National Undersea Research Center
University of Connecticut

Roland Barnaby
University of New Hampshire Cooperative Extension

Fred Bennett
F/V Sea Bag III

James H. Churchill
Woods Hole Oceanographic Institution

Jeffrey Cross
National Marine Fisheries Service

James Kendall
New Bedford Seafood Coalition
New England Fishery Management Council

Jonathan M. Kurland
National Marine Fisheries Service

Richard Taylor
F/V My Marie
Gloucester Sea Scallop Project

Steve Welch
F/V American Heritage

John Williamson
Former commercial fisherman
New England Fishery Management Council

Jon Witman
Brown University

Acknowledgments

This volume and the conference from which it originated were made possible by funding from the following sources, whose support we gratefully acknowledge:

- Center for Marine Conservation
- Conservation Law Foundation
- Gulf of Maine Council on the Marine Environment, and the U.S. Environmental Protection Agency
- Massachusetts Environmental Trust
- Massachusetts Institute of Technology Sea Grant College Program NOAA Grant Numbers NA46RG0434, NA86RG0074
- National Fish and Wildlife Foundation
- Regional Marine Research Program for the Gulf of Maine
- Rockefeller Brothers Fund
- The Pew Charitable Trusts

We wish to thank the contributors to this volume for their willingness to share their thoughts and experience both at the conference and in this volume. Some speakers traveled considerable distances in order to make their presentations. In planning for the conference, including the selection of topics and speakers, we had the benefit of thoughtful advice from a steering committee whose members are listed on the preceding page. We are grateful to the following individuals for ably moderating sessions at the conference: William Amaru, Roland Barnaby, James Churchill, and Maggie Raymond. The Warren Conference Center of Northeastern University provided excellent and attractive facilities for the event. The conference ran smoothly because of logistical support from Jennifer Atkinson, Priscilla Brooks, Megan Gamble, and Shelley Hoak. We greatly appreciate the significant administrative support provided by Christine Cristo and Megan Gamble both for the conference and for this volume. This volume's designer, David Gerratt, provided much useful and sage advice about its production. Finally, we would like to thank Chitrita Banerji, Madeline Hall-Arber, Peter Shelley, and Bruce Stedman for a variety of helpful advice and support.

Eleanor M. Dorsey
Judith Pederson

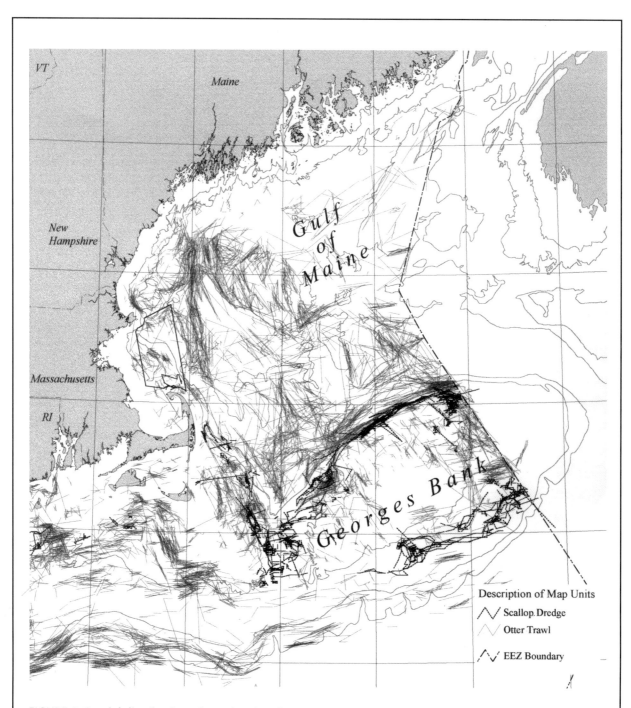

FIGURE 1. Spatial distribution of trawl and scallop dredge tows from NMFS Sea Sampling database for 1989 to 1994 (April). This indicates the location of 14,908 tows, which is less than 5% of the total tows during this period. Note that the spatial distribution of fishing effort is not homogeneous, but is aggregated in productive fishing areas. From Auster and Langton (in press).

Introduction

Eleanor M. Dorsey and Judith Pederson

Habitat alteration by the fishing activities themselves is perhaps the least understood of the important environmental effects of fishing.

COMMITTEE ON FISHERIES
OCEAN STUDIES BOARD
NATIONAL RESEARCH COUNCIL (1994)

Fishing gear makes contact with thousands of square miles of New England's sea floor each year while targeting fish and shellfish that live on or near the bottom. Fishing effort increased dramatically in the region after 1976, when the U.S. declared exclusive rights to fishery resources within 200 miles of shore. Effort in some bottom fisheries has declined in recent years as a result of regulations to address overfishing, but still remains high. No one questions the impact of heavy fishing on the species that are targeted, like cod, haddock, and scallops: too much fishing has caused serious declines in their populations, with resulting disruption of New England's fishing industry.

What about the sea floor itself? How has the ocean bottom been affected by repeated passes of trawls and scallop dredges? These gear types disturb the sea floor and remove many untargeted species that grow there. Is fish productivity reduced by bottom habitat damage from fishing? Is New England's marine biodiversity threatened by fishing activities?

This book presents currently available information about these questions in a collection of papers by scientists and fishermen. The first five papers set the stage by describing the sea floor of New England—its topography and substrates, the organisms that inhabit soft and hard bottoms, natural disturbance to the sea floor, and bottom habitat requirements of groundfish. The next paper describes and illustrates the major types of bottom tending fishing gear used in the region—bottom trawls, scallop dredges, lobster traps, sink gillnets, and bottom long lines.

The following three papers are by scientists studying fishing gear impacts, who summarize the results of research in New England, eastern Canada, and Europe. Fishermen who use different gear types offer their understanding of how their gear works and interacts with the sea floor, in the next section of papers. Options are presented for minimizing gear impacts to the sea floor, and the provisions on essential fish habitat (EFH) in the 1996 Magnuson-Stevens Fishery Conservation and Management Act are reviewed. A section of short observations by fishermen and scientists addresses a variety of other topics relating to the effects of fishing gear. The book ends with a summary of the discussion session that concluded the 1997 conference at which most of the papers were first presented.

The information presented in this volume is directly relevant to one of the important new requirements of the Magnuson-Stevens Act. Fishery management plans are now required by law to "minimize to the extent practicable adverse effects on EFH caused by fishing."

This introduction references specific papers in this volume by the last name of the author(s).

EXTENT OF SEA FLOOR CONTACTED BY MOBILE FISHING GEAR

Bottom tending gear is either towed (bottom trawls and scallop dredges) or fixed (lobster traps, sink gillnets, and bottom longlines) during fishing operations. Fixed gear rests on the bottom while fishing and may be pulled over it for short distances during retrieval or storms. Most of the concern about fishing gear impacts and most scientific studies have been directed at mobile bottom gear, because the area of sea floor contacted is so much larger than with fixed gear. This volume considers both types of bottom gear.

Two sources of data document the widespread use of mobile bottom gear in New England. One source is the plots of tows of known location (*Figure 1*), which represent a small fraction of the total tows, those made with a fisheries observer on board. The other source is data on number of days fished, a measure of fishing effort, collected by the National Marine Fisheries Service (NMFS) for each gear type and attributed to approximate location. These fishing effort data have been combined with assumptions about vessel speed and gear dimensions to derive estimates of total area swept by mobile fishing gear. Each year in recent years, bottom trawls and scallop dredges swept an area of sea floor in the Gulf of Maine equivalent to the size of the gulf (65,000 km^2), according to these estimates. On Georges Bank, these gears covered an area estimated at more than three times the size of the bank (41,000 km^2) (see summary by Collie).

This means that, on average, every square inch of the sea floor was contacted by mobile fishing once a year in the Gulf of Maine and three to four times per year on Georges Bank. The towing does not occur evenly over the sea floor, but is concentrated in areas that produce better catches for fishermen and contain no impediments to towing. Thus some places are swept by fishing gear more often than average and other places are swept less often or not at all.

Improvements in fishing gear and electronics during the last few decades have allowed bottom towing to occur in places that were previously too rough or too deep, so the extent of sea floor protected from mobile gear by natural features has been shrinking. Precise positioning instruments and electronics that improve visualization of the sea floor now allow fishermen to tow closer to bottom irregularities that may damage trawls and dredges. Scallop dredges are heavier and stronger than in the past and can fish on hard bottom that was off limits before the late 1960s. Bottom trawls can now be towed over much rougher terrain because of the innovations of rollers, rock hoppers, and, just recently, "street sweeper" gear.

These and other trawl configurations are illustrated in this volume by Carr and Milliken. Lighter and stronger lines, combined with more powerful hydraulics, now permit towing at depths that fishing gear could not reach previously.

Technological advances have also improved our ability to understand the geology and ecology of the sea floor and the impacts to it from fishing gear. Underwater video cameras, side scan sonar, computer-driven mechanical grabs, manned submersibles, and remotely operated vehicles now allow observations and experiments that were previously impossible. Many papers in this volume are based on these new technologies. Because of its versatility and low cost, underwater video is particularly widely used, both by scientists and by fishermen, to view fishing gear and the sea floor.

INFORMATION FROM SCIENTISTS ON FISHING GEAR IMPACTS

Research on the effects of fishing gear has been conducted on a wide variety of sea floors, differing in depth, substrate type, benthic fauna, fishing gear, and degree of human and natural disturbance. Some studies have compared fished areas with unfished areas of similar depth and substrate, while other studies have looked at the same area before and after fishing disturbance. The most rigorous studies are planned experiments with fishing gear that make both kinds of comparisons. Such experiments have been performed in Canada and Europe, but not yet in New England. Research on fishing gear impacts in New England has been impeded by the paucity of unfished areas to use for comparison with fished areas, as well as by the high cost of conducting research on the sea floor.

One of the few general conclusions that can be drawn from the various studies to date is that mobile fishing gear reduces habitat complexity on the sea floor. This effect has been documented on various substrates in New England, eastern Canada, and Europe, as well in other parts of the world. It results from the tendency of fishing gear to (1) smooth out structures on the bottom and (2) remove bottom fauna that contribute to sea floor complexity. Reduced habitat complexity is expected to reduce shelter for juvenile fish and thus increase their mortality rates due to predation from larger fish. At the same time, removal of benthic fauna may reduce the availability of food from invertebrates for fish of all sizes. The loss of benthic fauna from fishing gear is expected to be greater on stable sea beds with long-lived benthic organisms than in sediments that are frequently disturbed by natural processes, such as the shifting sand dunes on Georges Bank and Nantucket Shoals.

The three major studies conducted in New England on fishing impacts to bottom communities are reviewed in this volume by Collie. One study found significantly greater habitat complexity on cobble-shell and sand-shell bottoms inside a conservation area closed to mobile gear, compared with outside the area. In another study, scientists reported a substantial reduction in sponges and other invertebrates on boulders on a deep bank where trawling was observed and had apparently moved the boulders. A third study found significantly lower abundance, biomass, and species diversity of invertebrates living on gravel in a heavily fished part of Georges Bank, compared to unfished areas of similar depth. This study also documented a partial recovery in the benthic community 18 months after one site was protected by the groundfish closure that began in late 1994.

Studies of communities inhabiting hard and soft substrates in the Gulf of Maine offer further insights into the resilience of these communities to the type of disturbance caused by fishing gear. Witman has observed markedly slower recovery of natural and experimental clearings on hard substrates at depths below 30 meters in his long term studies of disturbance and colonization. Soft-bottom communities, which are described by Watling, have not been the subject of comparable long term studies. However, long lifespans and infrequent reproduction in some of the dominant mud-dwelling organisms in deeper water (sea pens and tube-dwelling anemones) suggest that they would take years to recover from one-time disturbance and may never return to areas that are trawled frequently.

Bottom trawls create clouds of muddy water as they move over the sea floor, and the mud clouds help to herd fish into the net. Sensors deployed on the sea bed in southern New England have detected turbidity that was apparently caused by trawling,

and modeling indicates that trawling is the principal cause of sediment resuspension in the deeper waters of the outer continental shelf, whereas storms and currents are the principal cause in shallower waters. Churchill speculates on some possible implications of these findings, one of which is that phytoplankton productivity may be increased by trawling because of the release into the water column of nutrients trapped in sediment. This in turn may lead to increased productivity of invertebrates and fish at the ocean bottom. Another possible effect of trawling-induced sediment resuspension, not discussed in this volume, is reduced survivorship of juvenile bivalves and fish due to clogging of their gills.

Other research from New England reported in this volume sheds light on fishing gear effects on the sea floor. Moderate harvesting of an estuarine oyster bed with a dredge very much smaller and lighter than the dredge used for sea scallops resulted in fewer large oysters, better recruitment of small oysters, and no changes in the associated benthic invertebrates (*see Langan*). Lindholm and colleagues stress the importance of shelter provided by undisturbed bottom habitat in the survivorship of newly settled cod. Results from their model suggest that protection of sea floor habitat from fishing disturbance may significantly improve cod recruitment at current low population levels.

The Canadian government has undertaken a major research program to investigate the impacts of mobile fishing gear on benthic ecosystems in eastern Canada. After developing technology to sample and image the sea floor, researchers have begun experimental studies of different gear types. Gordon and colleagues report the initial results. Trawling on sandy substrates in the same spot on the Grand Banks over three years reduced the biomass of several invertebrates (snow crabs, sand dollars, soft corals, and brittle stars), but not that of hard-shelled mollusks. The complexity of sediment structure was reduced and an influx of scavengers occurred, but the consequences for harvested species is unknown.

In northern Europe, research on the effects of fishing gear has a longer history than in either New England or Canada. The paper by Rogers and colleagues summarizes many different studies from the eastern North Atlantic. One experiment with beam trawling in the Irish Sea showed a significant reduction in invertebrate numbers and species inhabiting stable sediments of sand, gravel, and shell, but no effect on invertebrates in nearby mobile sediments. Another study found slower recolonization after fishing disturbance for large long-lived clams than for small polychaetes and bivalves. Intensive fishing has removed fragile or long-lived species, like reef-building tube worms and calcareous algae that formerly dominated areas of the European sea floor and provided microhabitats for many other species.

Many benthic invertebrates are exposed and damaged or killed by the passage of a trawl. These provide food for scavengers, both invertebrates and finfish, and a short term influx of scavengers into experimentally trawled areas has been observed off the coasts of Europe and Canada. One harvested finfish species on the sandy floor of the North Sea (sole) appears to have benefited over the long term from intensive trawling, probably because fishing disturbance has shifted the benthic community to small, opportunistic species appropriate for the sole's small mouth. Although research on trawling impacts in Europe was initiated as long ago as 1955, all studies began after much of the European sea floor had already been intensively trawled for many decades. Rogers calls for targeted sampling of benthic invertebrates and higher spatial resolution of data on fishing effort and fish populations to improve understanding of the effects of mobile bottom gear.

A number of scientists make the point that effects of fishing disturbance are likely to be more significant in areas that are not subject to high levels of natural disturbance. Organisms living in areas of high natural disturbance are adapted to disturbance by anatomy, behavior, or life history characteristics, but many organisms living in naturally undisturbed areas lack such adaptations and may take years, decades, or even centuries to recover from fishing disturbance. If fishing disturbance occurs more frequently than the recovery time, then susceptible species will be eliminated from the area of fishing and biodiversity will be lowered. This may be occurring with the long-lived deep sea corals for which abundance appears to be reduced (*see Butler*).

INFORMATION FROM FISHERMEN ON FISHING GEAR AND ITS IMPACTS

Fishermen have much to contribute to understanding the effects of fishing gear on the sea floor, but their views are rarely solicited. Fishing gear that contacts the sea floor may bring up diverse forms of marine life and pieces of bottom substrate. Because fishermen have opportunities to observe samples from the bottom every day they are fishing, the frequency with which they can examine bottom samples often far exceeds most sampling regimens that scientists can sustain. Furthermore, experienced fishermen may have decades of observations to bring to bear on this topic.

Many fishermen keep very detailed records of exactly where and when they fish and what they catch. Sophisticated electronic instruments on many fishing vessels allow for precise depth measurement and positioning, as well as improved visualization of fish schools and bottom textures, although fishermen often cannot identify substrate types. Although the goal of fishing is to provide income from the catch, rather than to test hypotheses, many fishermen seek to understand the very questions about the sea floor that motivate this book.

Twelve commercial fishermen have contributed papers to this volume. Their experience includes all five major bottom-tending gear types used in New England—bottom trawls, scallop dredges, lobster traps, sink gillnets, and bottom longlines. Fishermen provide descriptions of each gear type and its variations, how it is fished, how the gear and fishing has changed (or not) over time, and how they understand it to interact with their target species and with the sea floor. Some describe specific sea floor habitats that they seek out to catch their fish. As the fishermen in this volume describe the effects that they believe fishing gear to have on the sea floor, they argue a wide diversity of positions. Some report severe adverse impacts on fish habitat; others say there are no impacts; and a few maintain that the effects can be positive.

The greatest concern about fishing gear impacts is expressed by fishermen who report seeing significant losses of habitat good for fishing. Three distinct types of habitat are reported by New England fishermen to have disappeared: topographic features; benthic invertebrates, some of which previously formed large beds; and a hardened clay formation called pipe clay or clay pipes. Fishermen who report these losses attribute them to mobile gear disturbance.

Bennett reports that bottom peaks that formerly supported good cod fishing in two different locations have decreased in height or disappeared entirely after mobile bottom gear fished in their vicinity. Williamson mentions the disappearance of topographic features on which gillnetters formerly set their nets. It is not certain that these topographic changes are due to fishing gear rather than to natural disturbance, because storm waves and tidal currents are capable of major changes in bottom topography in shallower water. If fishing gear is indeed the cause, these reports represent reductions in bottom structure on a much larger scale (up to tens of meters) than observed to date in any of the scientific studies of fishing gear impacts.

A variety of benthic invertebrates that longliners have for decades associated with good fishing (beds of mussels, several species of ascidians) have been significantly reduced in abundance because of mobile gear disturbance. This is according to reports by Bennett and by Leach. As with the topographic changes mentioned above, it is not certain that mobile fishing gear is the cause. The claim is plausible, however, because reductions in similar benthic fauna have been documented in a number of scientific studies. Longliners reported reduced fishing success after these bottom changes occurred.

Pipe clay (also known as clay pipes) is another bottom habitat type that fishermen associate with good fishing and report to be much reduced in abundance because of mobile fishing gear (*see Williamson; Bennett*). This unusual bottom formation from Nantucket Shoals and the western Gulf of Maine was unknown to scientists until reported by fishermen, and it merits further study (*see Dorsey; Valentine*).

In other places, fishermen describe repeatedly trawled areas that remain productive in spite of intensive disturbance from trawling. Pendleton characterizes a muddy area outside of Casco Bay as being intensively trawled for decades and argues that trawling does not appear to have damaged the bottom or the fishing. Mirarchi reports that catches in heavily trawled areas on and near Stellwagen Bank declined after years of high fishing effort, but have started to rebound recently in the same areas after fishing pressure was reduced. He concludes that either trawling did not damage the area or the area has recovered from its damage over time.

Other fishermen maintain that disturbance from mobile gear can actually enhance a fishery. Kendall reports improved scallop recruitment on the southwest corner of Georges Bank soon after scalloping was resumed on a neglected scallop bed. Doughty states that stirring the bottom by mobile gear can help keep the bottom from going "sour" (becoming hypoxic or anoxic) and driving fish away. Porter mentions a bed of mahogany clams that he believes was improved by harvesting with a clam dredge.

All of these observations from fishermen deserve careful consideration. It is possible that all of them are valid and reflect differences in fishing gear impacts depending on substrate type and other variables. Considerable additional research must be conducted and more observations from fishermen collected before the relationship between fish productivity and sea floor habitats is clarified.

Some of the information from studies in Europe and Canada can be extrapolated to New England to improve understanding of gear impacts in this region, as long as differences in substrate types, gear, and bottom species are considered. Nevertheless, a regional program of additional research on the effects of fishing gear on the sea floor is clearly needed to resolve the many remaining uncertainties about those effects. This program should include a process for integrating fishermen's input into research to take advantage of their experience and observations. The provisions on essential fish habitat in the 1996 Magnuson-Stevens Fishery Conservation and Management Act (*see Kurland*) will help increase attention to sea floor attributes that support fish populations.

We believe that information from fishermen and scientists in this volume justifies protecting more areas of the ocean floor from fishing disturbance, both to maintain healthy fisheries and to protect marine biodiversity. We do not find in this material, however, a blanket condemnation of trawling and other mobile gear. As several contributors to this volume noted, bottom trawls can be designed to have reduced impact on the sea floor, and mobile gear probably has negligible or beneficial effects in some situations.

Mapping New England's bottom substrates according to vulnerability to fishing gear disturbance should be a high priority, a conclusion reached by the conference steering committee and by the people who attended the discussion session at the end of the conference. The other high-priority recommendation to emerge from the conference was for increased research to study the effects of fishing gear on the sea floor and to elucidate the relationship between sea floor habitats and fish productivity. The willingness of a wide diversity of people to engage in serious and productive discussions about the topic of this volume bodes well for New England's ability to address it in a responsible and fair manner.

REFERENCES OUTSIDE THIS VOLUME

Auster, P.J. and R.W. Langton. In press. Indirect effects of fishing. In L.R. Benaka, ed. *Fish Habitats: Essential Fish Habitat and Rehabilitation*. American Fisheries Society Symposium 22. Bethesda, MD.

National Research Council. 1994. *Improving the Management of U. S. Marine Fisheries*. National Academy Press. Washington, D.C.

The New England Sea Floor: Description and Natural Disturbance

Geological Overview of the Sea Floor of New England

Eleanor M. Dorsey

CONSERVATION LAW FOUNDATION, BOSTON, MASSACHUSETTS

The sea floor of New England presents a wide diversity of forms and substrates. There are shallow banks and deep basins, sheer cliffs and gentle slopes, long canyons and conical pinnacles, shifting dunes and stable pavements. Particles on the sea floor range in size from clay and silt through sand and gravel to rocks and boulders, and bedrock is exposed in places. The region has been dramatically altered by the effects of glaciation, which left New England with considerably more relief to its continental border than unglaciated areas to the south. This overview focuses on the areas within New England's political boundaries, with only limited attention to the Canadian portions of the Gulf of Maine. The sources used are listed in the bibliography.

The origin of the sea floor dates back to about 200 million years ago when the supercontinent called "Pangaea" began to split up. North America started to drift apart from Africa and Eurasia, and the rift between them gave birth to a new ocean, the Atlantic. All along the western edge of the new ocean, from Florida to Newfoundland, a wide apron of sediment slowly built up from material eroding off the ancient Appalachian Mountains. Over time, the deeper layers of this sediment solidified into sedimentary rock. Where this sediment apron is exposed to air on land, it is called the coastal plain, and where it lies submerged beneath sea water, it is called the continental shelf. The sediment apron still abuts the coastline everywhere except in the areas reached by glaciers during the ice ages of the past two million years.

These places underwent major transformations as a result of glaciation, both as the glaciers advanced and after they retreated.

TOPOGRAPHY

The glaciers scoured out and eroded away most continental shelf sediments in what is now the Gulf of Maine, leaving its basins deeper than surrounding areas. During the last glacial period, the ice stopped at the northern edge of Georges Bank and at the islands of Nantucket and Martha's Vineyard on Nantucket Shoals, depositing sand and gravel on the coastal plain at the ice edge. Glacial deposits and outwash formed Cape Cod. Thus the overall bathymetry of the New England sea floor (Figure 1) is profoundly influenced by the glaciers. Georges Bank and Nantucket Shoals sit higher—shallower—than the coastal plain to the southwest, which was not augmented by glacial deposition and outwash. They help define the Gulf of Maine as a basin.

On either side of Georges Bank run channels that separate it from Nantucket Shoals to the west (Great South Channel) and from Browns Bank to the northeast (Northeast Channel). The channels mark the locations of two rivers that drained the region when sea level was lower. Later, when glaciers filled the Gulf of Maine as far south as Georges Bank, the Northeast Channel provided a pathway for ice to reach the open ocean, while the shallower Great South Channel probably stopped the ice, receiving its deposits. Today, the Northeast Channel allows deep ocean water into the Gulf of Maine.

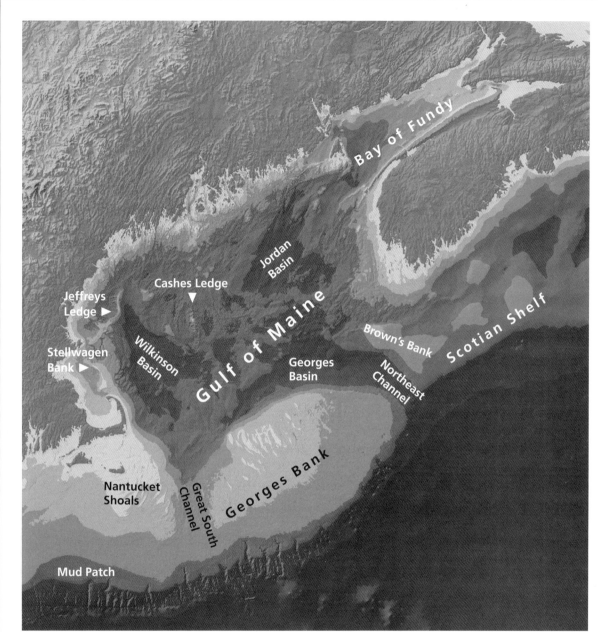

FIGURE 1. **Shaded relief map of the bathymetry of the sea floor of New England. The shallowest areas are pale gray, and deeper areas are progressively darker gray. Generated by Rich Signell and Ed Roworth, U.S. Geological Survey.**

The topography of Georges Bank and Nantucket Shoals is relatively smooth, except at shallower depths, where tidal currents form long ridges of sand. On the shallowest part of the bank, these sand ridges come within 4 meters (m) of the sea surface. Along its smooth northern edge, Georges Bank drops steeply into the Gulf of Maine. The southern flanks of Georges Bank and Nantucket Shoals slope gradually seaward to the edge of the continental shelf, where the sea bed descends more steeply from about 150 to 2,000 m forming the continental slope. From the base of the slope, the sea floor continues to fall more gently toward the deep ocean in an area known as the continental rise. The general shape of the continental shelf, slope, and rise on Georges Bank and southern New England is similar to what is found all along the Atlantic seaboard to the south.

More than 15 narrow canyons cut deeply into the steep seaward edge of Georges Bank and the continental shelf to its west. These canyons provide more diverse topography and substrates than the areas of smooth continental slope between canyons. South of Georges Bank, a number of conical sea mounts rise up from the deep in a chain that extends to the east and south.

The Gulf of Maine is topographically unlike any other part of the continental border along the U.S. east coast, with considerably rougher contours than the banks that define it to its south. It contains 21 distinct basins separated by ridges, low banks, or gentle swells. The basins are believed to sit in river valleys that drained the surrounding land during pre-glacial periods when the gulf was above sea level. The gulf's deepest point, over 350 m deep, is in Georges Basin just north of Georges Bank. High points within the gulf include irregular ridges, such as Cashes Ledge, which peaks at 9 m below the surface, as well as lower flat-topped banks and gentle swells. Some of these rises are remnants of the sedimentary shelf left after most of it was removed by the glaciers. Others are glacial moraines (accumulations of glacially moved sediment), and a few, like Cashes Ledge, are outcroppings of bedrock.

The landward edges of the gulf are highly variable. At the easternmost point of the Maine coast, cliffs plunge to the ocean and continue steeply down below the water. The bulk of the Maine coast is highly irregular, with many peninsulas and islands and pinnacles. Harder rock forms the headlands and islands, while the bays and low points mark locations of more easily eroded rock. The western edge of the gulf, south of Portland, becomes much smoother and the coastline becomes a series of gently curving embayments.

A noticeable topographic feature is Jeffreys Ledge, which forms a long, narrow, and gently sinuous rise extending east and north of Cape Ann. To its south the wider shoal of Stellwagen Bank separates a basin on its landward side from deeper water offshore, like a miniature version of Georges Bank. This basin is part of Massachusetts Bay, the largest bay in New England.

EFFECTS OF GLACIATION AND CHANGING SEA LEVEL

The line marking the furthest advance of the glaciers traverses New England, so its sea floor encompasses areas strongly modified by glaciation as well as areas largely unaffected by the ice sheets. Within the area overridden by glaciers, most loose materials on top of the bedrock—mud, sand, gravel, and rocks—were rearranged and deposited as unsorted and unstratified mixtures known as till. Much of the bedrock itself was scraped smooth. Some glacial deposits resulted in distinctive land forms like drumlins and boulder-strewn moraines, which can be recognized on the sea floor as well as on land. The enormous frictional forces of the glaciers ground many materials into very fine particles of clay known as rock flour, a substance that is unique to glaciated areas and very abundant in parts of New England, including the basins of the Gulf of Maine. Many sediments were again moved and redeposited by the voluminous runoff from melting glaciers.

Since the most recent glaciation, sea level has changed significantly in New England, producing major effects on the sea floor. Toward the end of the last ice age, about 20,000 years ago, worldwide sea level was lower than it is now because so much of the planet's water was bound up in glaciers. Depressed by the enormous weight of ice up to a mile thick, however, northern New England's land mass was so much lower than today that the ocean reached far inland when the glaciers first retreated. In contrast, Georges Bank was never burdened by heavy glaciers and was dry at this time. Sea level on the bank at its lowest point was about 120 meters lower than today, making the bank a large cape connected to southern New England. As the glaciers melted and removed their ice burden, northern New England rebounded more quickly than the oceans rose, so the level of the sea along the Maine coast fell to about 60 m lower than today before rising again to its current level.

As sea level rose, Georges Bank became an island, and the island shrank and eventually became a submerged bank about 6,000 years ago. Chunks of peat, teeth of mammoths, and tusks of walruses have been retrieved from Georges Bank and Nantucket Shoals, testaments to the progression from postglacial tundra to submerged bank. Sea level has continued to rise in the region much more slowly into recent times. New England's current rate of sea-level rise, 2–3 millimeters per year, is faster than at any time in the last 4,000 years, perhaps because of manmade global climate warming. This rise will present challenges to our civilization that is now heavily developed along the coast.

As sea level has moved down and then back up again along the New England coast, the location of the shoreline, where waves hit the sea floor with the greatest energy, moved with it. This has profoundly affected the shallower parts of the sea floor by eroding and redistributing sediments, including the enormous deposits of mud, sand, and gravel left in the wake of the glaciers. The constant reworking by wave action has winnowed out the finer sediments, which settled in adjacent deeper areas, in a process that is continuing today.

SEA FLOOR SEDIMENTS

New England's sea floor can be divided into three main regions according to the substrate type that predominates at the surface. One region is dominated by sand, one is dominated by mud (silt and clay), and one is highly heterogeneous, but dominated by bedrock. Significant areas of gravel occur in all three regions, but gravel does not predominate in a single coherent region.

Figure 2 is the only map of surface sediment types that encompasses all of New England. It predates the availability of acoustic tools like side scan sonar and is based on bathymetry and bottom sediment samples, the latter primarily taken in a grid with 10 kilometers (km) between sampling stations. This density of sampling is fairly good for the relatively uniform continental shelf that flanks most of the U.S. east coast, but it does not capture the heterogeneity of the sea floor in some places, such as near the coast, where variability increases. The summary below is informed by the detailed mapping efforts listed in the bibliography as well as by the information in Figure 2.

Where sand predominates—At the glacier's southern edge and southward, the sea floor is mostly sand. This region includes Georges Bank and the continental shelf to the west, as well as the sea floor around Cape Cod *(Figure 2)*. The sand is locally interrupted by other sediment types, like the gravel on the northern edge of Georges Bank and the very fine sediments in the Mud Patch in southern New England. The sand was eroded by glaciers from New England's uplands and from coastal plain deposits in the Gulf

of Maine. On the parts of Georges Bank and Nantucket Shoals shallower than 50 m, strong tidal currents and storm waves work medium-to-coarse sand into ridges 10 to 40 m high and up to 90 km long. On top of the ridges and running perpendicular to them are numerous smaller dunes. The dunes migrate at variable rates, up to 60 m in three months, and it is possible that the larger ridges migrate as well. On deeper parts of the bank, the sea floor is smoother and the grain size becomes finer. As depth increases off the edge of the continental shelf, fine sand grades to silt and clay.

Areas of glacially deposited gravel exist in the Great South Channel, on the northern edge of Georges Bank, and in the troughs between the sand ridges on Georges Bank and Nantucket Shoals, more areas than are indicated in Figure 2. There are several discrete boulder fields within the gravel on Georges Bank. Georges Bank no longer receives sediment from elsewhere, and finer sediments are continually being transported off the bank into deeper water after being resuspended by waves and currents, so the bank is slowly eroding. As it loses its finer grained sands, the bank's surface is becoming coarser and the extent of gravel sea floor is expanding.

Within this predominantly sandy region, the Mud Patch south of Nantucket Shoals is an interesting anomaly. The Mud Patch is an area of smooth topography where tidal currents slow significantly, allowing silts and clays to settle out. The mud is mixed in with sand, its deposition is recent and continuing, and it is occasionally resuspended by large storms. No other area on the outer continental shelf of the eastern U.S. contains significant proportions of silt and clay at the surface. To the west of the Mud Patch, the medium-to-coarse sand typical of the outer continental shelf resumes.

The canyons along the seaward edge of the continental shelf provide some additional heterogeneity in this most homogeneous of the three sea floor regions in New England. Probably formed by a complex history of erosion and excavation of material deposited on the surrounding slopes, the canyons contain gravelly sand and gravel on their rims and upper walls, semiconsolidated silt or mud on the lower walls, and sand on the floors. Occasional boulders, probably rafted there by ice, and exposed sedimentary rock on some walls adds to the diversity of substrates. A variety of organisms make burrows into the lower mud walls, which may contribute to slumping.

Where mud predominates—The second sea floor region in New England is a large area that comprises most of the Gulf of Maine and is predominantly mud (clay and silt), although significant expanses of other materials are present as well. The surface sediments of the gulf have been mapped in greater detail than shown in Figure 2 in two areas—over the gulf's eastern third and along the western edge in waters shallower than 100 m. Because large areas of the gulf have been sampled only at low densities, the gulf's sea floor may present more heterogeneity than described here.

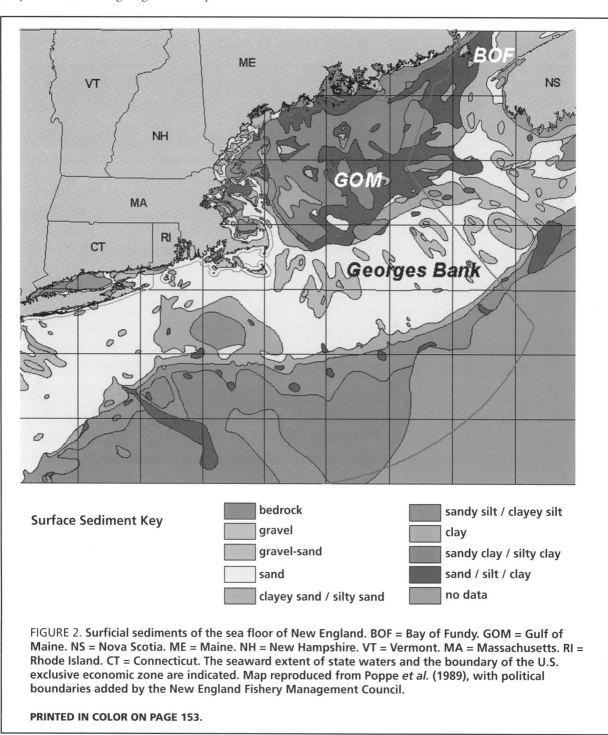

Surface Sediment Key

- bedrock
- gravel
- gravel-sand
- sand
- clayey sand / silty sand
- sandy silt / clayey silt
- clay
- sandy clay / silty clay
- sand / silt / clay
- no data

FIGURE 2. **Surficial sediments of the sea floor of New England. BOF = Bay of Fundy. GOM = Gulf of Maine. NS = Nova Scotia. ME = Maine. NH = New Hampshire. VT = Vermont. MA = Massachusetts. RI = Rhode Island. CT = Connecticut. The seaward extent of state waters and the boundary of the U.S. exclusive economic zone are indicated. Map reproduced from Poppe *et al.* (1989), with political boundaries added by the New England Fishery Management Council.**

PRINTED IN COLOR ON PAGE 153.

Very fine particles created and eroded by the glaciers have collected in thick deposits over much of the Gulf of Maine, particularly in its deep basins. These mud deposits blanket and obscure the irregularities of underlying bedrock, forming topographically smooth terrains. Where bottom currents are slow, modern mud from shallower areas is still being deposited on top of glacially derived mud, though at much slower rates. In addition to the deep basins in the Gulf, some shallower basins are covered with mud as well, such as the basins to the west of Stellwagen Bank and Jeffreys Ledge.

In the rises between the basins, other materials are usually at the surface. Unsorted glacial till cloaks some morainal areas, as on Sewell Ridge to the north of Georges Basin and on Truxton Swell to the south of Jordan Basin. Extensive areas of modified till—sand mixed with silt, clay, and gravel—cover the eastern edge of the Gulf where it climbs to the sand and gravel shoals of Browns Bank and the Scotian Shelf. Sand predominates on some high areas, such as Stellwagen Bank and Franklin Swell, and gravel, sometimes with boulders, predominates on others, such as Jeffreys Ledge, Platts Bank, and Fippennies Ledge. Bedrock forms the ridge of Cashes Ledge near the middle of the Gulf and becomes more common in the shallower parts of the western and northern Gulf of Maine, common enough that this area can be considered a distinct region.

Where bedrock predominates—Along the western edge of the Gulf of Maine north of Cape Cod is the third region of New England's sea floor, a narrow band in water less than about 60 m deep where the most abundant material is bedrock. This is the part of the gulf over which the shoreline passed as sea level changed after the glaciers melted. Here, glaciation and changing sea level have left the most heterogeneous sea floor along the U.S. Atlantic coast. Figure 2 captures some of the heterogeneity, but more detailed mapping has revealed considerably more complexity and more exposed bedrock (Kelley, this volume). In this region, well-sorted mud, sand, and gravel all occur, in addition to mixtures of sand and gravel and mixtures of gravel and shell, often interspersed with the rock in many small patches. Unmodified glacial till is rare.

The proportion of bedrock on the sea floor is greatest in far eastern Maine, along its cliffed shoreline with a high tidal range. Bedrock supports and surrounds Maine's many islands, and its rocky peninsulas continue underwater as rocky ridges. Numerous rocky pinnacles rise from the ocean floor. Gravel or gravel mixed with shell often abuts bedrock and fills crevices in it. Considerable areas of mud occur, often in the shelter of bays, islands, or submerged rises. Expanses of sand become more plentiful south of Portland, especially just offshore of sandy beaches, but bedrock continues underwater seaward of the rocky headlands.

The predominance of rock in this region is due to the proximity of bedrock to the surface. The bedrock formed millions of years ago under a variety of conditions. Volcanic, granitic, sedimentary, and metamorphic rock all occur in this region, their locations and formations shaped by collisions of continents, eruptions of the planet's molten interior, and eons of quiescent sedimentation. The softer of these diverse rocks eroded more quickly over time than their harder neighbors, with a resulting irregularity to the topography. Glacial scouring further eroded the rocks and deposited loose materials around and over them. Because the blanket of glacial deposits was thinner here than to the south, as the shoreline passed over this region of the sea floor, the glacial deposits were winnowed and sorted and most were removed, thus exposing the irregularities of the underlying bedrock. Those irregularities interrupt the movements of currents and waves and create highly complex patterns of sediment movement and deposition, thus resulting in the very heterogeneous sea floor that we see in this narrow band today.

THE SEA FLOOR YET TO BE DISCOVERED

Detailed studies of several parts of New England's sea floor are currently underway. Just as considerable research on Georges Bank was prompted in the 1970s and 1980s by interest in and controversy over extracting oil and gas from offshore, some of today's research is motivated by a desire to understand the relationship between bottom habitats and the region's troubled fisheries. Surprises may yet lie in store under the waves. It was only 10 years ago that unexpected fields of large pock marks were discovered from actively venting methane trapped in the muds of Penobscot Bay and elsewhere in Maine.

Another anomaly from the sea floor is just now coming to light. Fishermen report hardened clay formations called pipe clay or clay pipes from the western Gulf of Maine and from Nantucket Shoals (Williamson; Bennett; Valentine; all this volume). I have observed two distinct forms of pipe clay in pieces collected by fishermen. One form, reported to be more common in the Gulf of Maine, is a highly irregular shape with many small, rounded indentations (Williamson Figure 1, page 88). The other form is a smooth-sided hollow pipe with an inner diameter ranging from about two to five centimeters (cm) (Valentine Figure 1, page 20). These pipes may bifurcate, and lengths up to 1.3 m have been reported. The origin of the pipe clay is uncertain, its distribution has not been mapped, and it is unknown whether or not it is still being created. From fishermen's reports of good catches in its vicinity, pipe clay appears to be important groundfish habitat, and many different invertebrate species are attached to or associated with the fragments that fishermen collect.

The current interest in identifying and protecting essential fisheries habitat requires a better understanding of the sea floor in New England and in other regions.

ACKNOWLEDGMENTS

I would like to thank Page Valentine, Joseph Kelley, and Rebecca Dorsey for reviewing the manuscript for this paper.

EDITORS' NOTE:
This paper was not presented at the 1997 conference.

BIBLIOGRAPHY

Backus, R.H. 1987. Geology. Pp. 22-24 in R.H. Backus and D.W. Bourne, eds. *Georges Bank*. MIT Press, Cambridge, MA.

Bennett, F. **This volume.** Changes to the sea floor in the Chatham area.

Cooper, R.A., P. Valentine, J.R. Uzmann, and R.A. Slater. 1987. Submarine canyons. Pp. 52-63 in R.H. Backus and D.W. Bourne, eds. *Georges Bank*. MIT Press, Cambridge, MA.

Fader, G.B., L.H. King, and B. MacLean. 1977. *Surficial Geology of the Eastern Gulf of Maine and Bay of Fundy.* Mar. Sci. Pap. 19. (*Also* Geol. Surv. Can. Pap. 76-17) Fisheries and Environment Canada, Ottawa. 23 pp. + map (1:300,000).

Kelley, J.T., W.A. Barnhardt, D.F. Belknap, S.M. Dickson, and A.R. Kelley. 1998. *The Seafloor Revealed: The Geology of the Northwestern Gulf of Maine Inner Continental Shelf.* Maine Geological Survey Open File Report. Augusta, ME. In press.

Kelley, J.T. **This volume.** Mapping the surficial geology of the western Gulf of Maine.

Kelley, J.T., A.R. Kelley, and S. Apollonio. 1995. Landforms of the Gulf of Maine. Pp. 18-36 in P.W. Conkling, ed. *From Cape Cod to the Bay of Fundy. An Environmental Atlas of the Gulf of Maine.* MIT Press, Cambridge, MA.

Klitgord, K.D. and J.S. Schlee. 1987. Subsurface geology. Pp. 40-51 in R.H. Backus and D.W. Bourne, eds. *Georges Bank*. MIT Press, Cambridge, MA.

Poppe, L.J., J.S. Schlee, B. Butman, and C.M. Lane. 1989. Map showing distribution of surficial sediment, Gulf of Maine and Georges Bank. U.S. Geol. Surv. Misc. Invest. Ser., Map 1-1986-A.

Twichell, D.C., B. Butman, and R.S. Lewis. 1987. Shallow structure, surficial geology, and the processes currently shaping the bank. Pp. 31-37 in R.H. Backus and D.W. Bourne, eds. *Georges Bank*. MIT Press, Cambridge, MA.

Uchupi, E. and J.A. Austin, Jr. 1987. Morphology. Pp. 25-30 in R.H. Backus and D.W. Bourne, eds. *Georges Bank*. MIT Press, Cambridge, MA.

Valentine, P.C. **This volume.** Brief notes on habitat geology and clay pipe habitat on Stellwagen Bank.

Valentine, P.C. and R.G. Lough. 1991. *The sea floor environment and the fishery of eastern Georges Bank.* U.S. Geological Survey, Open-File Report 91-439. 25 pp.

Williamson, J. **This volume.** Gillnet fishing.

Mapping the Surficial Geology of the Western Gulf of Maine

Joseph T. Kelley

MAINE GEOLOGICAL SURVEY, ORONO, MAINE

The western edge of the Gulf of Maine has been the focal point for mapping by the Maine Geological Survey, the University of Maine, and the University of New Hampshire for the past 10 years. Initially, we approached the problem of mapping this highly heterogeneous sea floor by collecting several thousand bottom samples from the study area, the sea floor offshore Maine and New Hampshire out to 100 meters (m) depth. Bottom samples allow direct examination and analysis of sediments on the sea floor surface, but cover only a very small area per sample, a quarter of a square meter (m²). Recent advances in technology have put ncw tools at our disposal, which vastly increase our ability to image and understand the sea floor.

Side scanning sonar is the tool of choice today. A side scanning towfish towed behind a vessel images the sea floor on either side of the vessel to a distance ranging from 25 to 600 m, depending on speed and water depth. Differences in sea floor textures are recorded, surface features such as boulders and shipwrecks can be detected, and tracks from trawling and dredging are clearly visible. Rock, mud, gravel, and sand usually produce distinctive images from side scan sonar *(Figure 1)*. This is a very good and accurate way of looking at the sea floor surface.

In conjunction with side scanning sonar, we

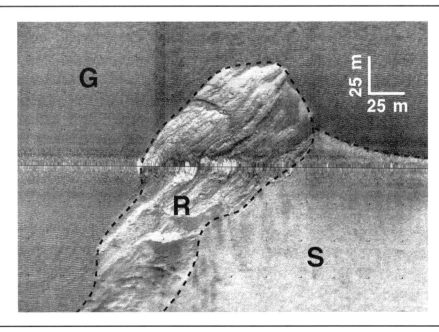

FIGURE 1. **Side scan sonar image of the sea floor off Cape Small, Maine. G is an area of gravel shaped into ripples about 20 cm high. R represents an area of exposed bedrock. S is an area of unrippled sand. The midline marks the ship's path. Modified from Barnhardt et al. 1998.**

have often used a seismic reflection profiler. With this device, sound waves are transmitted through the sea floor and reflect off layers of sand and mud, and ultimately, off the underlying bedrock. A variety of materials can be distinguished in seismic profiles, like bedrock, till, glacial-marine mud, modern mud, and sand *(Figure 2)*. Seismic reflection profiles allow a geologist to decipher the geological history of the sea bottom and interpret the surficial material imaged by side scan sonar. These two tools, when used in conjunction with one another, provide a very powerful description of the surface of the sea floor and the materials beneath.

We have also collected numerous sediment cores using drill pipes up to 6 m long to verify our geological understanding of the history of the region. In addition, we have made a number of submersible dives with support of the National Undersea Research Program to better understand the dynamics of the sea floor. Data from all these sources were combined with bathymetry in a geographic information system to produce an atlas of the sea floor offshore Maine and New Hampshire out to 100 m depth (Barnhardt *et al.* 1996a-g). This work was supported by NOAA's Regional Marine Research Program for the Gulf of Maine. The distribution of effort in the atlas is very uneven because it is a compilation of a series of graduate theses at the masters and Ph.D. levels.

In many parts of the study area, there are areas with small patches of gravel, small patches of bedrock, sandy mud, rippled gravel, and mud. There is no way to map a sea floor like that on a scale of one to one hundred thousand, which is the scale one has to deal with in the Gulf of Maine. To portray the unprecedented complexity of the sea floor in this region, we had to devise a new classification scheme for bottom types that includes composite map units *(Table 1)*. We mapped any area measuring 100 m x 100 m (10,000 m^2) of a single substrate—mud, gravel, rock or sand. In other areas, such as an area that is predominantly gravel with some mud outcrops or predominantly gravel with some rock, we mapped the sediment as composite units.

With side scan sonar we have directly imaged 12% of the sea floor from the shoreline to the 100-m isobath from Canada to Massachusetts. In imaged areas, we distinguish 16 map units in the atlas. The areas without side scan sonar have only four map units—rock, mud, gravel, and sand. This is how we handled the compromise between providing detailed

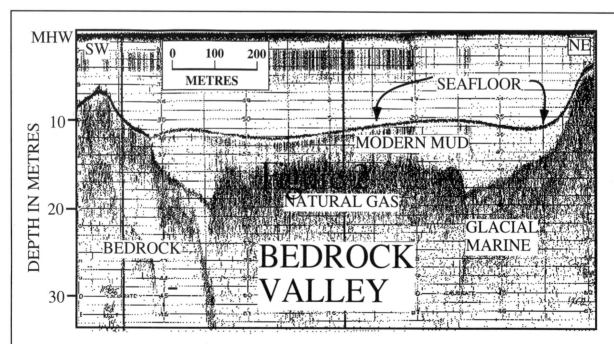

FIGURE 2. **Seismic reflection profile across Eggemoggin Reach, Maine. Beneath the sea floor are successively older layers of modern mud, glacial-marine mud, and bedrock. Natural gas obscures the signal in the center of the valley, which has been carved into bedrock by glaciers.**

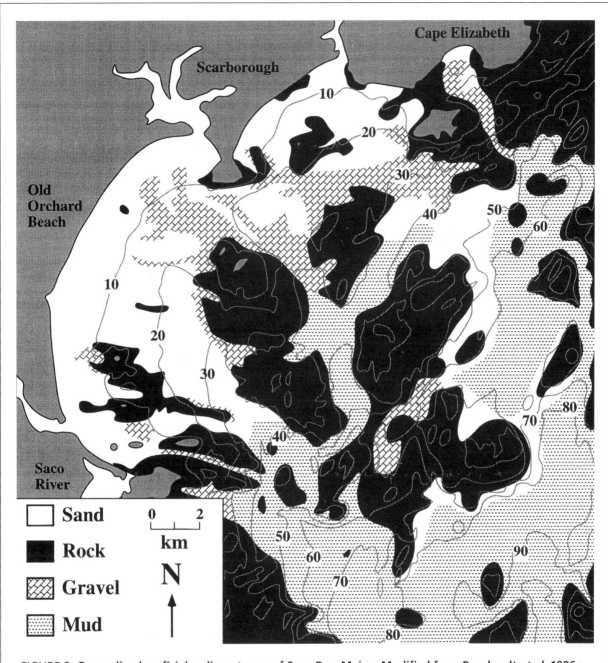

FIGURE 3. **Generalized surficial sediment map of Saco Bay, Maine. Modified from Barnhardt *et al*. 1996c.**

information where it exists and generalizing where data are scarce or absent. An example of the results from this mapping is presented in Figure 3.

PHYSIOGRAPHY OF THE WESTERN GULF OF MAINE

The topography and composition of many shallow areas in the western Gulf of Maine show clear similarities with the adjacent shoreline. Just offshore of

sandy beaches south of Cape Elizabeth are sandy ramps, which slope gently seaward to 30 or 40 m depth with contours that parallel the shore. Elongate bedrock peninsulas between Cape Elizabeth and Port Clyde continue offshore as bedrock extensions. Just offshore of muddy tidal flats in much of the midcoast region are shallow muddy basins that are protected from the open sea by mainland, islands, or shoals. The cliffs along the straight coastline in eastern

R	Rg	Gr	G
Rs	Rm	Gs	Gm
Sr	Sg	Mr	Mg
S	Sm	Ms	M

TABLE 1. **Classification scheme for surface sediments devised to handle the high heterogeneity of the sea floor on the inner continental shelf of Maine and New Hampshire. The dominant "end member" (Rock, Gravel, Sand, or Mud) is abbreviated with a capitalized first letter. A less abundant, subordinate sea floor type is represented with a lower case letter (r, g, s, or m). For example, a predominantly rocky sea bed with gravel infilling fractures is designated Rg.**

Maine to the Canadian border continue to plunge into deep water very close to shore. At their bottom are either extensive deep plains of mostly gravel or bedrock with rapid and extreme changes in bathymetry.

Bedrock zones occupy fully half of our study area and predominate in depths shallower than 60 m. This depth is the lowest point to which sea level fell since the last Ice Age, and the two passes of the shoreline over the sea floor to this depth removed most of the finer sediments. Bedrock surrounds many of the islands in the midcoast region of Maine and form shoals in places. Fractures in bedrock are filled with gravel or with gravel mixed with shells of dead organisms formerly attached to the rock surface. These sediment ponds in the rock are very hard to map because they are small, but they might be important habitat to marine life.

Below 60 m depth in much of the study area are valleys and basins where mud predominates, often bordering abruptly on rocky substrates. These areas are poorly studied, in part because of their remote location. Many of the basins extend without interruption into the deeper Gulf of Maine. Their bathymetry is more subdued than in shallower areas because glacial deposits have blanketed underlying topographic features. Currents and wave activity are too weak to erode muddy sediments, so modern mud accumulates in these deep settings and is only disturbed by fishing practices like bottom trawling. An exception to this description of deeper areas is found off eastern Maine, where a large hard-bottom plain occurs at 60 to 90 m. It is possible that strong tidal currents from the Bay of Fundy prevent mud from settling here, but few observational data exist from this area.

SURFACE SEDIMENTS IN THE WESTERN GULF OF MAINE

In spite of the highly heterogeneous nature of surface sediments in this region, some generalizations are possible. Rocky sea beds are the most abundant surface materials at all depths less than 60 m and in all parts of the study area except extreme eastern Maine. Rocky areas become less common with increasing depth, but some rock outcrops poke through the mud mantling the deeper sea floor. We inferred rocky bottoms in areas where little data exist but the sea floor topography is very irregular. Gravel, often mixed with shell, is common adjacent to bedrock outcrops and in fractures in the rock. Large expanses of gravel are not common, but do occur off the Kennebec River mouth, near reworked glacial moraines, and in areas where the sea bed has been scoured. Gravel often has a rippled surface and is most abundant at depths of 20 to 40 m, except in eastern Maine where a gravel-covered plain exists to depths of at least 100 m. Sandy areas are relatively rare along the inner shelf of the western Gulf of Maine. The sandiest region is in depths less than 40 m off New Hampshire and southern Maine, offshore of sandy beaches. Sand is found mixed in with gravel in a complex mosaic off the Kennebec River mouth in a drowned delta area. Sand is mixed with mud in Saco Bay and possibly at the seaward margin of the nearshore sandy ramps.

After rocky areas, muddy regions are the most abundant areas on the inner continental shelf. Mud is common both in shallow water and in deep water and dominates surfaces in deep water except off southern Maine. Mud accumulates where there is a supply of fine-grained sediment and quiet conditions that favor the slow settling of small particles. Mud is usually associated with a smooth sea floor with few features. Trawl marks left by fishing boats are very common in all sedimentary environments along the inner shelf, but are most noticeable over muddy sea beds. Some deposits of mud contain natural gas (methane), and the gas has erupted from the sea bed in some locations, like Penobscot and Passamaquoddy Bays, leaving thousands of pockmarks on the sea floor, some as big as a football stadium. Some gas-escape pockmark fields may overlie lakes and bogs drowned by rising sea level, and often the holes are arranged in lines.

If one looks at the overall distribution of surface materials in the Gulf of Maine, there is an organization to it. Rocky areas are more common in shallow water, becoming less common in deeper water. Sand and mud have been removed from the shallow areas by repeated sea level changes across the near shore region. Mud becomes predominant in deeper water. It was washed away from the shallow regions during the last movement of the ocean across them and concentrated out in the deeper regions of the gulf. Sand and gravel are relatively minor components of the Gulf of Maine, in marked contrast with the southern part of New England, where sand predominates on Georges Bank and on the continental shelf to its south.

REFERENCES

Barnhardt, W.A., J.T. Kelley, D.F. Belknap, S.M. Dickson, and A.R Kelley. 1996a. Surficial geology of the inner continental shelf of the northwestern Gulf of Maine: Piscataqua River to Biddeford Pool. *Maine Geological Survey Geologic Map 96-6,* 1:100,000. Augusta, ME.

Barnhardt, W.A., J.T. Kelley, D.F. Belknap, S.M. Dickson, and A.R Kelley. 1996b. Surficial geology of the inner continental shelf of the northwestern Gulf of Maine: Ogunquit to the Kennebec River. *Maine Geological Survey Geologic Map 96-7,* 1:100,000. Augusta, ME.

Barnhardt, W.A., J.T. Kelley, D.F. Belknap, S.M. Dickson, and A.R Kelley. 1996c. Surficial geology of the inner continental shelf of the northwestern Gulf of Maine: Cape Elizabeth to Pemaquid Point. *Maine Geological Survey Geologic Map 96-8,* 1:100,000. Augusta, ME.

Barnhardt, W.A., J.T. Kelley, D.F. Belknap, S.M. Dickson, and A.R Kelley. 1996d. Surficial geology of the inner continental shelf of the northwestern Gulf of Maine: Boothbay Harbor to North Haven. *Maine Geological Survey Geologic Map 96-9,* 1:100,000. Augusta, ME.

Barnhardt, W.A., J.T. Kelley, D.F. Belknap, S.M. Dickson, and A.R Kelley. 1996e. Surficial geology of the inner continental shelf of the northwestern Gulf of Maine: Rockland to Bar Harbor. *Maine Geological Survey Geologic Map 96-10,* 1:100,000. Augusta, ME.

Barnhardt, W.A., J.T. Kelley, D.F. Belknap, S.M. Dickson, and A.R Kelley. 1996f. Surficial geology of the inner continental shelf of the northwestern Gulf of Maine: Mt. Desert Island to Jonesport. *Maine Geological Survey Geologic Map 96-11,* 1:100,000. Augusta, ME.

Barnhardt, W.A., J.T. Kelley, D.F. Belknap, S.M. Dickson, and A.R Kelley. 1996g. Surficial geology of the inner continental shelf of the northwestern Gulf of Maine: Petit Manan Point to West Quoddy Head. *Maine Geological Survey Geologic Map 96-12,* 1:100,000. Augusta, ME.

Barnhardt, W.A., J.T. Kelley, S.M. Dickson, and D.F. Belknap. 1998. Mapping the Gulf of Maine with side scan sonar: a new bottom-type classification for complex seafloors. *J. Coast. Res.* 14:646-659.

Kelley, J.T., W.A. Barnhardt, D.F. Belknap, S.M. Dickson, and A.R. Kelley. 1998a. Physiography of the inner continental shelf of the northwestern Gulf of Maine. *Maine Geological Survey Geologic Map,* 1:300,000. Augusta, ME. In press.

Kelley, J.T., W.A. Barnhardt, D.F. Belknap, S.M. Dickson, and A.R. Kelley. 1998b. The Seafloor Revealed: The Geology of the Northwestern Gulf of Maine Inner Continental Shelf. *Maine Geological Survey Open File Report.* Augusta, ME. In press.

Benthic Fauna
of Soft Substrates in
the Gulf of Maine

Les Watling

UNIVERSITY OF MAINE, WALPOLE, MAINE

To understand soft bottom communities in the Gulf of Maine, one has to start by thinking about them at the right scale. Most of the animals that live in soft bottoms live, literally, in the upper most couple of centimeters (cm). There are a few deeper species, as well, but they are not as abundant. Over the past 20 years or so, we have begun to take a worm's eye view of the mud. I will explain what that means and then review the typical larger organisms that live in mud. In order to understand what happens to these muddy-bottom communities when they are physically disturbed, we must understand how their inhabitants are distributed and how they live. Figure 1 presents a map of the Gulf of Maine with the placenames mentioned below.

Mud is made up of a large number of very small mineral grains and some amorphous organic matrix. These are visible in a magnified view of mud from the Gulf of Maine, collected in Jordan Basin at 250 meters (m) depth *(Figure 2)*. To get this view of the structure of the mud, I took a subsample of mud collected with a box core (a device for quantitative sampling in soft sediments), embedded the subsample in plastic, and then sectioned it as if it were a rock. This exemplifies what a worm is confronted with on an average day as it makes its way through the mud. Most of the worms and brittle stars that live in Jordan Basin are eating this mud, ingesting the sediment grains and the organic matter and using the organic component as food.

A geochemical perspective is useful to understand mud. A microelectrode can be very carefully lowered through the sediment/water interface to measure oxygen concentrations at various distances from the surface. Oxygen measurements on subtidal marine mud in many places around the world yield very similar results. A typical oxygen profile *(Figure 3)* shows why muddy bottom is not a very hospitable environment for most organisms, even though a lot of organisms live in it. The oxygen completely disappears a few millimeters (mm) into the sediment. By half a cm into the sediment there is almost always no oxygen at all. However, there are a lot of organisms that live far deeper than a half cm, and virtually all of them that are larger than bacteria require oxygen. In order to live in the mud, they must maintain some kind of connection to the overlying water where oxygen is present, usually by using a burrow or tube opening. Almost all organisms living in mud depend upon this lifeline—a burrow or tube opening—to the oxygenated water.

Many organisms living in mud deal with obtaining food and oxygen by building tubes that extend above the surface. An example is the ampeliscid amphipod, which makes a tube 6–7 cm long with about 1 cm protruding above the sediment surface. Most ampeliscids live in nearshore bays, and they can be

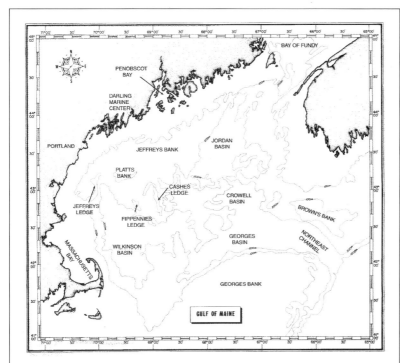

FIGURE 1. **Map of the Gulf of Maine, showing placenames mentioned in text.**

billion) per gram of sediment, which is a cubic millimeter (mm³) or two. This means that there are at least a billion bacteria in every few mm³ of sediment. These bacteria are all respiring, thus taking up oxygen, so oxygen quickly gets depleted in the mud. Larger organisms cannot compete with bacteria for oxygen, so the only way they can get the oxygen they need is by maintaining a burrow or a tube. Some larger organisms take advantage of the bacteria by feeding on them.

As Joe Kelley describes in the previous paper, the floor of the Gulf of Maine is very heterogeneous with respect to sediment composition. That bottom heterogeneity is reflected in the organisms that live at the sea floor, with very different communities on rock, gravel, sand, and mud. On the muddy bottoms, which predominate in much of the Gulf of Maine, especially at depths below 30 m, the density of animals varies by a factor of more than twenty within the Gulf *(Figure 4)*. This determination is made from box core samples from which only the macrofauna—invertebrates larger than a half mm or so—are retained and counted. Nearer to shore,

so abundant that they completely carpet large areas of the bottom.

Oxygen is low in muddy bottoms partly because of very high concentrations of bacteria in the organic matrix surrounding the sediment grains. Throughout the Gulf of Maine, bacterial abundance in the bottom ranges from 10^8 to 10^9 (a hundred million to a

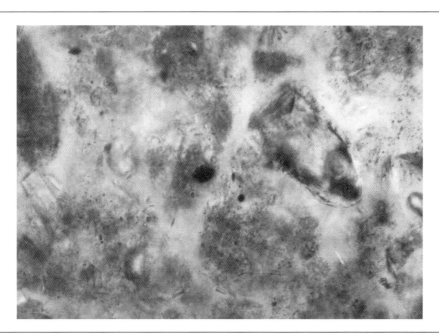

FIGURE 2. **Section of mud from Jordan Basin at 250 m depth. This picture is 200 micrometers wide, so five pictures across equals a mm. A bullet-shaped tintinnid ciliate (a single-celled organism) that fell from the plankton and was buried in the bottom is visible to right of center. Photograph by Les Watling.**

PRINTED IN COLOR ON PAGE 154.

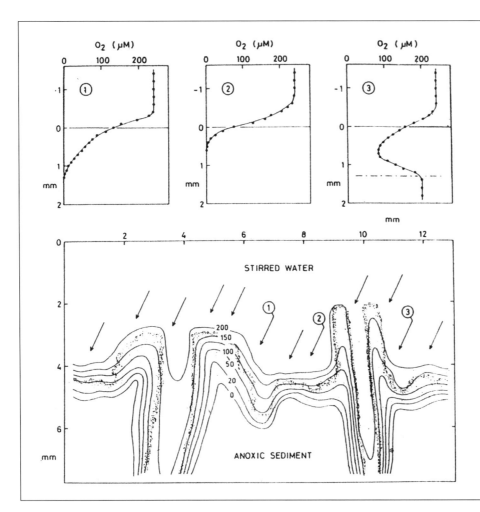

FIGURE 3.
Oxygen profile through muddy sediment with two polychaete tubes from Limfjorden, Norway. The isopleths of oxygen in the vertical profile were constructed from 12 microprofiles, of which three are shown. Numbers on the isopleths indicate μmol O_2 per liter. This profile is typical for subtidal marine mud. Source: Jørgensen and Revsbech 1985.

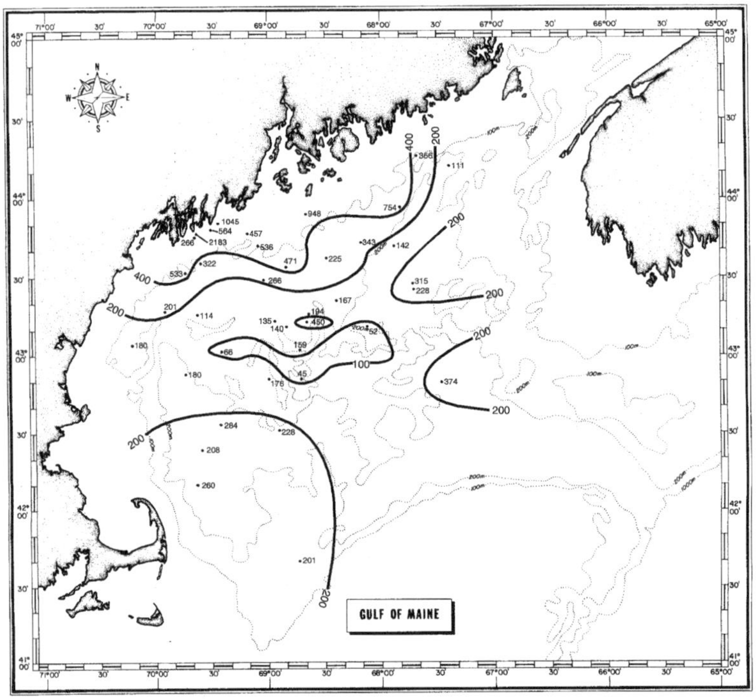

FIGURE 4. **Density of macro invertebrates in the sea floor of the Gulf of Maine. Data are from box cores taken during the summers of 1982–84. Numbers by each station are total number of individuals per 0.1 m² averaged from two box cores per station.**

especially off the midcoast region of Maine, the density of animals is extremely high, generally greater than 400 animals in a tenth of a m^2 and often as high as 1,000 animals, which translates to 4,000 to 10,000 animals per m^2. The higher figure is not very common. There is a general pattern of high abundance near shore, where the quantity and quality of food reaching the bottom is high, and lowest densities in the middle of the Gulf of Maine.

It is interesting to look at the same data on animal densities in another way, plotted against depth. Abundance generally declines with depth until just after 200 m, after which it rises again (*Figure 5*). This pattern is probably explained by food availability at the bottom. Deeper water offers more opportunity for settling food particles to be eaten by animals in the water column before they reach the bottom, so deeper bottoms in general get less food. In addition, depths approaching 200 m in the Gulf of Maine happen to be near the center of the Gulf. A counter-clockwise gyre that flows around the whole Gulf impedes food transport to the middle of the gyre, further reducing the rate of food delivery to the sea floor in the middle. Depths greater than 200 m are at the outer edge of the Gulf gyre and contain higher densities of benthic animals, probably because higher food availability at the gyre's periphery more than compensates for the greater loss of settling food in deeper water.

A number of benthic assemblages can be described in the Gulf of Maine. These are mapped in Figure 6, and some of the major animals are described in the accompanying caption and below. The assemblages are characterized by different groups of major species, and they seem to reflect both the sediment type and water mass distributions. The bottom water in the Gulf of Maine is warm and salty as it enters at the Northeast Channel and moves through to the sills near the center of the Gulf. The water gradually cools and becomes less saline as it moves through the basins and mixes upward in the region of the Bay of Fundy. The water entering through the Northeast Channel is generally about 10° C year round, but as low as 8° C in some years. Most of the Gulf of Maine sea floor is covered with waters that are from 7° to 4° C, depending on the depth and location. Close to shore, however, temperature varies considerably on a seasonal basis, from

0° to more than 20° C in shallow nearshore areas.

In the waters of the easternmost part of the gulf, there is a community made up of species that are most abundant in much deeper water, at 1,000 to 1,500 m depth. This upper bathyal community (*assemblage 7, Figure 6*) extends into the Gulf of Maine only in the vicinity of the Northeast Channel. An intermediate community (*assemblage 6*) occupies the bottom through Georges Basin and Lindenkohl Basin to the region of the sills where colder water mixes with the warm bottom water. Much of the Gulf of Maine is covered by a cold water bottom community (*assemblages 4 and 5*), which includes some true boreal or subarctic species.

The northern pink shrimp (*Pandalus borealis*) and the tube-dwelling anemone of the cerianthid family (*Cerianthis borealis*) are examples of species with distributions far to the north for which the Gulf of Maine is the southern limit. They occur in assemblages 4 and 5 and are illustrated in Figure 7, a photograph taken off the edge of Jordan Basin in about 200 m of water. The burrows and tubes throughout this photograph are typical of muddy bottoms. Hard bottom ecologists sometimes call this kind of scene a featureless bottom. To a muddy bottom ecologist, however, there is a lot of structure present. Much of it is under the surface and not visible. My colleagues and I think that the closely spaced holes are openings of one gallery of a mud-burrowing shrimp, but we have not been able to sample to see what species it is. When we look at the bottom with a submersible or bottom camera, we get a chance to see a lot of interesting things, but we do not, unfortunately, get a chance to sample much of it.

Cerianthid anemones (*Figure 8*) generally occur only in places where there is some gravel underlying a muddy surface. If the gravel is deep below the surface and the bottom is nothing but mud for a meter or so, then sea pens (*Pennatula aculeata*) will predominate. But where the gravel rises up closer to the surface underneath the mud veneer, cerianthids occur and build their tubes through the mud into the gravel. The surface looks equally muddy and soft in both types of areas, but the presence of either cerianthids or sea pens indicates the depth to gravel.

In a 1995 project funded by the National Undersea Research Center, I investigated the biology

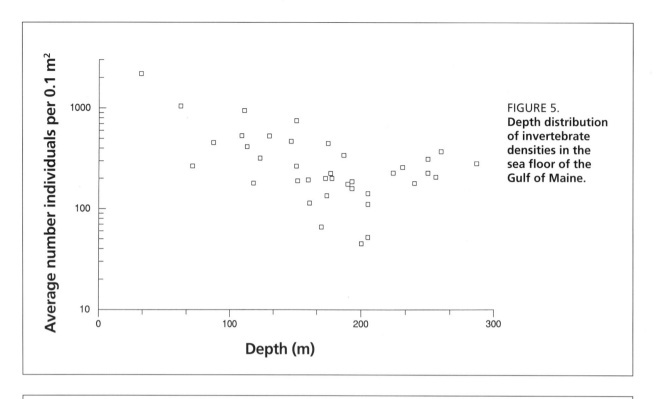

FIGURE 5.
Depth distribution of invertebrate densities in the sea floor of the Gulf of Maine.

Benthic Assemblages in Figure 6

Assemblage 1. Comprises all sandy offshore banks, most prominently Jeffreys Ledge, Fippennies Ledge, and Platts Bank; depth on top of banks about 70 m; substrate usually coarse sand with some gravel; fauna characteristically sand dwellers with an abundant interstitial component.

Assemblage 2. Comprises the rocky offshore ledges, such as Cashes Ledge, Sigsbee Ridge, and Three Dory Ridge; substrate either rock ridge outcrop or very large boulders, often with a covering of very fine sediment; fauna predominantly sponges, tunicates, bryozoans, hydroids, and other hard bottom dwellers; overlying water usually cold Gulf of Maine Intermediate Water.

Assemblage 3. Probably extends all along the coast of the Gulf of Maine in water depths less than 60 m; bottom waters warm in summer and cold in winter; fauna rich and diverse, primarily polychaetes and crustaceans; probably consists of several (sub-) assemblages due to heterogeneity of substrate and water conditions near shore and at mouths of bays.

Assemblage 4. Extends over the soft bottom at depths of 60 to 140 m, well within the cold Gulf of Maine Intermediate Water; bottom sediments primarily fine muds; fauna dominated by polychaetes, shrimp, and cerianthid anemones.

Assemblage 5. A mixed assemblage comprising elements from the cold water fauna as well as a few deeper water species with broader temperature tolerances; overlying water often a mixture of Intermediate Water and Bottom Water, but generally colder than 7° C most of the year; fauna sparse, diversity low, dominated by a few polychaetes, with brittle stars, sea pens, shrimp, and cerianthids also present.

Assemblage 6. Comprises the fauna of the deep basins; bottom sediments generally very fine muds, but may have a gravel component in the offshore morainal regions; overlying water usually 7 to 8° C, with little variation; fauna shows some bathyal affinities but densities are not high, dominated by brittle stars and sea pens, and sporadically by a tube-making amphipod.

Assemblage 7. The true upper slope fauna that extends into the Northeast Channel; water temperatures are always above 8° C and salinities are at least 35‰; sediments may be either fine muds or a mixture of mud and gravel.

Source: Watling *et al*. 1988

of cerianthids and the distribution of other animals around them. The tubes constructed by the cerianthids are quite large, 7–8 cm in diameter and at least as long as 75 cm, though it is difficult to pull one out intact. Most of the tubes I collected were over 50 cm in length, while the anemones themselves grow up to 25 cm long. They feed mostly on suspended particles, but we have seen them capture large invertebrates as well. The cerianthid tubes are important because the older ones have an entire community of invertebrates

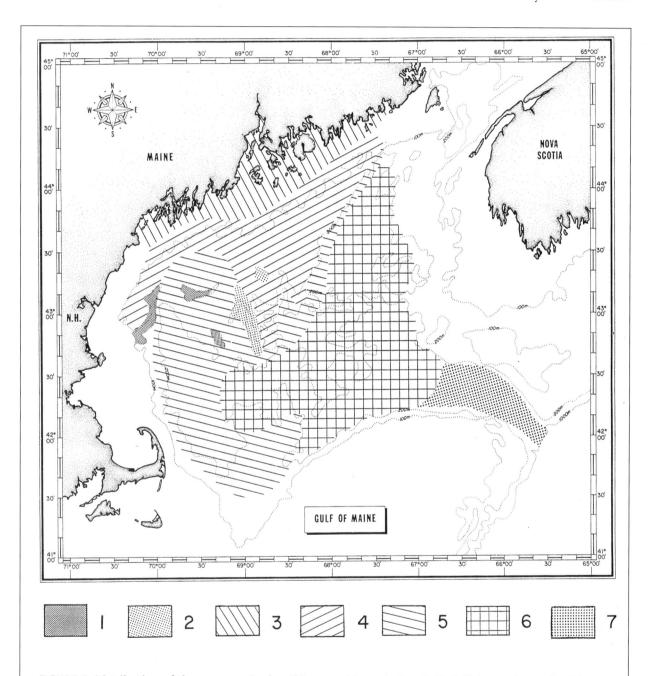

FIGURE 6. **Distribution of the seven major benthic assemblages in the Gulf of Maine as determined from both soft bottom quantitative sampling and qualitative hard bottom sampling. The assemblages can be characterized as follows (see box, page 24, for more detail): 1. Sandy offshore banks; 2, rocky offshore ledges; 3, shallow (< 50 m) temperate bottoms with mixed substrate; 4, boreal muddy bottom, overlain by Maine Intermediate Water, 50–160 m (approx.); 5, cold deep water, species with broad tolerances, muddy bottom; 6, deep basin warm water, muddy bottom; 7, upper slope water, mixed sediment. Source: Watling *et al*. 1988.**

FIGURE 7.
A muddy bottom at about 200 m depth near Jordan Basin. Two fish species (snake blenny, *Lumpenus lumpretaeformis*, and silver hake, *Merluccius bilinearis*), a shrimp (*Pandalus borealis*), and a cerianthid anemone (*Cerianthis borealis*) are visible, along with numerous burrows. Photograph by Les Watling.

FIGURE 8.
Cerianthid anemones from Jeffreys Bank. At the base of the leftmost cerianthid tube is aset of presumed mud shrimp burrows. Photograph by Les Watling.

living on them, characterized primarily by small worms, but also by a lot of other animals. There are 25 or 30 species that live on these anemone tubes.

The anemones can pull back into their tubes very quickly when disturbed, which may offer some protection from fishing gear. However, they are very long-lived animals with life spans that probably exceed 50 years. They appear to reproduce only very slowly, because young animals are a very small proportion of all groupings I have seen. The young are almost always next to an adult, which suggests that they settle preferentially near them. Thus several life history characteristics could be expected to hamper the reestablishment of these anemones if they were removed by fishing. A dragger fisherman from Maine once told me that when he found a lot of anemones in a haul, he would never find them in that place again.

FIGURE 9.
A 1985 photograph from the southwest corner of Jeffreys Bank showing two sea pens, a cerianthid anemone, and a witch flounder (*Glyptocephalus cynoglossus*). The tentacle crown of the anemone is about 15 cm across. Photograph by Les Watling.

PRINTED IN COLOR ON PAGE 154.

FIGURE 10.
Aggregations of amphipod tubes from Jordan Basin. These are only seen in undisturbed areas. Photograph by Les Watling.

Like cerianthids, sea pens occur in both assemblages 4 and 5 in the Gulf of Maine. An example of an area dominated by sea pens is the southwest corner of Jeffreys Bank (*Figure 9*). The area is a popular spot for commercial trawling for hake and other groundfish. In 1993, I participated in a project to look at the biology and the distribution of sea pens. They are feather-shaped relatives of anemones, are usually pink, and grow up to 15 cm long. About two-thirds of their length extends above the sediment surface. Each sea pen is made up of many individuals living in a colony and feeding on suspended fine particles. Like cerianthids, sea pens probably live for several decades and probably reproduce very slowly because small sea pens are rare. Unlike cerianthids, small sea pens can be anywhere and are not restricted to the proximity of an adult. Sea pens cannot contract into the mud except very slowly. I have seen sea pens lying on their side out of the sediment in a trawl track that was less than a day old, but I do not know whether or not they can reposition themselves.

There are places, such as in Crowell Basin, where mud is mixed with clean gravelly sand, providing quite a complex habitat. This bottom is most likely created from a moraine left by the retreating glaciers and is not covered with new sediment because of relatively strong currents in the area. There is an interesting mix of rocks and small stones, sand grains, and a little bit of mud, depending on where you are. A very large diversity of invertebrates lives on this kind of bottom, including hard corals, soft corals, sponges, brachiopods, and a variety of other smaller animals, all part of assemblage 6.

In muddy basins that have not been disturbed for a long time, such as in Jordan Basin, certain small structures are typically present on the mud surface. These are tubes of amphipods (*Erichthonius* spp.), small crustaceans about 7 mm in length, another part of assemblage 6 *(Figure 10)*. These amphipods tend to live very socially, so we call the tubes "amphipod condo units." Each little branch of this structure has an individual in it. When the tubes get smashed, especially when the animals are older, it is difficult for them to remake the tubes. In most of the places that I have looked where the muddy bottom is completely undisturbed, this amphipod is quite predictably

present, but in places where disturbance is moderately frequent, this amphipod does not exist.

Brittle stars, mostly of the species *Ophiura sarsi*, seem to dominate muddy bottoms in the deeper basins of the gulf in both disturbed and undisturbed areas. They are important components of assemblages 5 and 6. They are deposit feeders that eat the organic material in mud once it has reached the ocean floor, and they appear be the major organism responsible for cycling the incoming chemical energy in these soft bottom areas. Brittle stars may live for about a decade, and the age composition on the bottom is very different in disturbed and undisturbed areas. Adults are restricted to places undisturbed by trawling, probably because their very stiff arms readily entangle them in trawl mesh. In areas with a lot of trawling, like Wilkinson Basin, there are almost no adults, but lots of juveniles, which have much more flexible arms and probably slip easily out of a trawl net.

An example of the deep sea species that intrude into the Gulf of Maine in the Northeast Channel is shown in Figure 11. The white vertical tubes are single-celled animals, foraminiferans, that are 5 cm long. About half of that length is buried in the sediment. They belong to the genus *Bathysiphon*, which is very common in much deeper waters at 2000 m. This is the shallowest depth record of this genus

FIGURE 11.
Foraminiferans (white tubes) in the Northeast Channel at 300 m, the shallowest depth record in the world for the genus *Bathysiphon*. The above-sediment portion of the tubes is 2.5 to 3 cm long. Photograph by Les Watling.

anywhere in the world. They come into the Gulf of Maine with the deep water that upwells into the Northeast Channel from beyond the continental shelf. At this particular site, there are about 200 species of invertebrates living within the mud, all of which are small, like most deep sea invertebrates.

To conclude, the muddy bottoms in the Gulf of Maine harbor about a thousand species of macro invertebrates, according to the current estimate. The number of the smaller animals is unknown. Even though the Gulf of Maine is a relatively young system (it has had seawater in it for only about 13,000 years since the last glacier), it has a very large diversity of species. Most are North Atlantic cold water species that came with the colder water as the Gulf of Maine filled up, but there are also some species that are new to science and may have evolved relatively recently. Most of the invertebrates in the Gulf of Maine—a very large number—are of no commercial value. Some of them may help support species of interest to fisheries by providing food and shelter, but all of them represent their part of the record of the evolution of life on this planet and should be valued for that reason.

REFERENCES

Babb, I. and M. De Luca (eds). 1988. *Benthic Productivity and Marine Resources of the Gulf of Maine*. National Undersea Research Program Res. Report 88-3. U.S. Dept. of Commerce.

Jørgensen, B.B. 1996. Material flux in the sediment. Pp. 116-135 in B.B. Jørgensen and K. Richardson, eds. *Eutrophication in Coastal Marine Systems*. Coastal and Estuarine Studies Vol. 52. American Geophysical Union, Washington, D.C.

Jørgensen, B.B. and N.P. Revsbech. 1985. Diffusive boundary layers and the oxygen uptake of sediments and detritus. *Limnol. Oceanogr.* 30:111-122.

Langton, R.W., E. Langton, R. Theroux, and J.R. Uzmann. 1988. Distribution, abundance and behavior of sea pens, *Pennatula* sp. in the Gulf of Maine. Pp. 121-130 in I. Babb and M. DeLuca, eds. *Benthic Productivity and Marine Resources of the Gulf of Maine*. National Undersea Research Program Res. Report 88-3. U.S. Dept. of Commerce.

Mountain, D.G., R.W. Langton and L. Watling. 1994. Oceanographic processes and benthic substrates: influences on demersal habitats and benthic communities. Pp. 20-25 in R.W. Langton, J.G. Pearce and J.A. Gibson, eds. *Selected living resources, habitat conditions, and human perturbations of the Gulf of Maine*. NOAA Tech. Mem. NMFS-NE-106.

Wallace, G.T. and E.F. Braasch, eds. 1997. Proceedings of the Gulf of Maine Ecosystem Dynamics Scientific Symposium and Workshop. Regional Association for Research on the Gulf of Maine Report 97-1.

Watling, L. 1991. The sedimentary milieu and its consequences for resident organisms. *Amer. Zool.* 31:789-796.

Watling, L, J. Dearborn, and Linda McCann. 1988. General distribution patterns of macrobenthic assemblages in the Gulf of Maine. Pp.109-119 in I. Babb and M. DeLuca, eds. *Benthic Productivity and Marine Resources of the Gulf of Maine*. National Undersea Research Program Res. Report 88-3. U.S. Dept. of Commerce.

Natural Disturbance and Colonization on Subtidal Hard Substrates in the Gulf of Maine

Jon D. Witman

Brown University, Providence, Rhode Island

Introduction

The objective of this paper is to provide a brief overview of the natural disturbance regime in subtidal hard substrate habitats of the Gulf of Maine, as background for considering effects of anthropogenic disturbance on these communities. Patterns of benthic invertebrate and algal community structure in these habitats have been described by Sears and Cooper (1978), Hulbert *et al.* (1982), Witman and Cooper (1983), Witman (1985, 1987, 1996), Sebens 1985, Sebens *et al.* (1988), Witman and Sebens (1988, 1990), Watling *et al.* (1988), Ojeda and Dearborn (1989), Vadas and Steneck (1989), and Leichter and Witman (1997). The descriptions will not be repeated here.

Disturbance is defined as a physical or biological process that creates a space suitable for colonization (Grime 1977). Physical disturbances impacting marine communities include storms, hurricanes, landslides, ice scour, low salinity excursions, and unusually large temperature changes (Dayton 1971, Paine and Levin 1981, Wethey 1985, Connell and Keough 1985, Witman 1987, Minchinton *et al.* 1997, Witman and Grange 1998). Biological disturbances generally refer to the direct or indirect effects of predators or herbivores that remove organisms they consume or dislodge organisms while moving across the substratum (e.g., "bulldozing," Dayton 1971). In order to understand how disturbance changes an ecological community, it is important to characterize various aspects of the disturbance regime such as the areal extent, intensity, and frequency of the disturbance (Pickett and White 1985). For example, an intense disturbance such as a once-in-a-century storm may create large clearings (patches) that will provide a unique opportunity for colonization, possibly causing large-scale changes in patterns of abundance and distribution of species on the sea floor. A disturbance that is frequent or timed during a specific season would provide a more predictable source of space for colonization, space that could be occupied only by species that produce larvae or asexual propagules in the season of disturbance. In most marine habitats subjected to wave action, the disturbance regime varies greatly with depth. Consequently, I have structured this paper to consider how disturbance and colonization vary from shallow to deep habitats.

Physical Disturbance

The predominant form of physical disturbance in the Gulf of Maine subtidal is wave-induced water motion. Sponges, sea urchins, sea stars, the mussels *Mytilus edulis* and *Modiolus modiolus*, the stalked ascidian *Boltenia ovifera*, and most species of kelp living at shallow depths are commonly dislodged from hard substrates when hydrodynamic forces exceed the attachment strength of individual organisms during

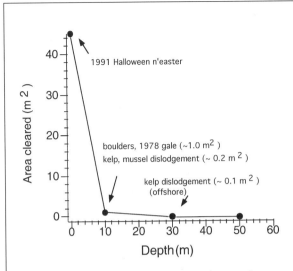

FIGURE 1. **Variation with depth in the maximum size of patches (clearings) created by physical disturbance at wave-exposed rocky sites in the Gulf of Maine. See text for a description of location and duration of observations. No patches were observed due to physical disturbance at the 50 m site.**

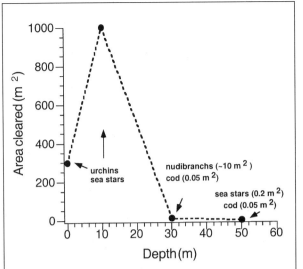

FIGURE 2. **Variation with depth in the maximum size of patches created by biological disturbance at wave-exposed rocky sites in the Gulf of Maine. See text for a description of location and duration of observations. Note that the scale of the y axis here is larger than in Figure 1.**

periods of high water velocity. As a consequence of the near-exponential decrease in wave-induced water velocity with depth (Riedl 1971), physical disturbance is uncommon at depths of 30 m and greater. Depth variation in physical disturbance is reflected in a striking decrease in the maximum area cleared with depth *(Figure 1)*. There is roughly a fortyfold decrease in the size of patches created between the low intertidal at 0 m and the shallow subtidal at 10 m depth. The February 1978 "Groundhog Day Gale" and the October 1991 Halloween northeaster ("The perfect storm" of Unger 1997) were the most severe physical disturbances I have observed over the past 20 years. The Halloween northeaster created multiple clearings up to 44.0 m² area in the low intertidal zone at East Point, Nahant, Massachusetts (J. Witman unpublished data). Areas previously covered by blue mussels (*Mytilus edulis*) and rockweed (*Fucus* sp.) were scoured down to bare rock. These are among the largest patches ever recorded in the intertidal zone (Paine and Levin 1981) and are undoubtedly a rare event since the National Weather Service classified this as the most severe storm of the past century. It appeared that the largest clearing was created by the scouring action of cobbles and boulders that abraded the shore during the exceptional 13-m-high waves

breaking against the coast (J. Witman, unpublished observations).

In addition to this spatial pattern of physical disturbance, there is some temporal predictability in the frequency of physical disturbance in the Gulf of Maine since northeaster storms tend to be more common from October to March (National Weather Service, Portland, Maine). However, in a three year study of the effect of storm dislodgment on shallow (<10 m) subtidal communities off southern Maine and New Hampshire, Witman (1987) found that severe episodes of mussel and kelp dislodgment occurred during all seasons.

Physical disturbance is chronic in the shallow subtidal, creating a high frequency of small to medium patches usually less than 1.0 m². A study of physical disturbance effects on subtidal communities at Murray Rock, a shallow ledge about 5 km off Kittery, Maine, identified two major types of disturbance-generated patches: mussel dislodgment patches and kelp holdfast patches (Witman 1987). The mussel patches were created when horse mussels, *Modiolus modiolus*, were overgrown by kelp and torn loose from the substratum during storms, leaving patches ranging from 0.025 m² to 0.45 m². Clearings created when *Laminaria digitata* or *Laminaria saccharina* kelp plants failed at the holdfast tended to be smaller than mussel dislodgment patches, with an average size of .09 m² (*Figure 1*, Witman 1987). The colonization of both types of patches was fairly predictable: kelp settled in the patches and dominated space within a few months after they were created. Horse mussels were not able to recover from storm disturbance by colonizing via larval recruitment in over 10 years of observation (Witman 1987, unpublished observations).

Patches up to 1.0 m² were observed at 8 to 10 m depth off Star Island at the Isles of Shoals when boulders were overturned during the February 1978 "Groundhog Day Gale" (J. Witman and L. Harris, Univ. of New Hampshire, unpublished observations). This probably represents the maximum size of clearings created by physical disturbance in the shallow subtidal zone.

In contrast to the shallow zone, depths of 30 m or greater rarely experience natural physical disturbance sufficient to dislodge organisms from rock surfaces. Communities at 30 m depth have been monitored for a decade at four sites in the Gulf of Maine—

Ammen Rock Pinnacle on Cashes Ledge, Columbia Ledge off Mt. Desert Rock, Gull Rock off Monhegan Island, and Star Island at the Isles of Shoals. The only patches created by storms during this time were a few kelp holdfast patches (< .01 m²) at Ammen Rock Pinnacle (Witman 1996, unpublished data) and several patches created by dislodgment of encrusting bryozoans, *Parasmittina jeffreysi* (Genovese 1996). At 50 m depth, observations are limited to a single site, a rock wall on Ammen Rock Pinnacle. During five years of photographic monitoring (1987 to 1991), no patches created by natural physical disturbance opened up in the community at this site (J. Witman and K. Sebens, Univ. of Maryland, unpublished observations).

BIOLOGICAL DISTURBANCE

Like physical disturbance, biological disturbance is a frequent feature of shallow rocky subtidal ecosystems in the Gulf of Maine. There are pronounced differences, however, in the size of patches created by the two forms of disturbance, as well as in the pattern of patch size change with depth *(Figures 1 and 2)*. In the intertidal and shallow subtidal, biological distur-

FIGURE 3. **Rock wall at 30 m depth at Ammen Rock Pinnacle, Cashes Ledge. A. (left) Wide angle photograph of a dense aggregation of the sea anemone *Metridium senile* that originally covered most of the top of the ledge. B. (right) Close-up photograph of a nearby spot in June 1987 showing patches created by nudibranch (*Aeolidia papillosa*) predation on the sea anemones. One nudibranch is visible at left, and the sea anemones are contracted in this photograph. Anemones previously occupied the areas covered with white spiraled masses of nudibranch eggs. Bar below photograph indicates 5 cm. Photographs by Jon Witman.**

PRINTED IN COLOR ON PAGE 155.

bance by sea urchin and sea star predation opens up much larger areas for colonization than physical disturbance. This is in contrast with terrestrial habitats, where physical disturbance creates larger clearings than biological disturbance (Pickett and White 1985).

Sea stars (*Asterias vulgaris* and *A. forbesi*) remove large areas (e.g., several hundred m²) of blue mussel beds at the intertidal-subtidal fringe (Menge 1979, Hulbert 1980, J. Witman unpublished observations). They are restricted from clearing even larger areas in the shallow zone by wave-induced water motion, which can restrict the abundance of these predators at shallow exposed sites (J. Witman and C. Siddon unpublished data). As a consequence of this hydrodynamic constraint on sea urchin and sea star foraging in the shallowest zone, the largest areas cleared by biological disturbance occur deeper in the subtidal zone, around 4 to 12 m depth *(Figure 2)*. For example, a dense band or "front" of green sea urchins, *Strongylocentrotus droebachiensis*, consumed a kelp bed measuring over 1000 m² at 8 m depth over four months in 1982 at Star Island, Isles of Shoals (Witman 1987). This large patch remained an urchin barrens or coralline algal flats for several years, then was recolonized by kelp (J. Witman unpublished observations, Harris *et al.* 1998). Since sea urchins are most common at shallow-to-intermediate depths (i.e., 4 to 12 m), the size of patches cleared by biological disturbance in the Gulf of Maine decreases below this depth range *(Figure 2)*.

Predation by nudibranchs can also open large clearings. Twice in the past decade, large patches on the order of 5 to 10 m² were cleared at 28 to 35 m depth at two sites on Cashes Ledge in aggregations of the sea anemone, *Metridium senile*, by nudibranchs, *Aeolidia papillosa*, preying on the sea anemones (Witman 1996, *Figure 3*). These two disturbance events caused a major long term shift in the distribution and abundance of benthic invertebrates on large spatial scales at the peaks of Ammen Rock Pinnacle and North Ammen Rock Pinnacle on Cashes Ledge. The patches were colonized by bryozoans (primarily *Crisia* sp.) within a year, and the bryozoan-dominated state of these benthic communities has persisted since 1991 (J. Witman unpublished observations).

Cod predation is another agent of patch creation in offshore, hard substrate habitats of the Gulf of Maine (Witman and Cooper 1983). Cod feeding on the network of polychaete and amphipod tubes covering rock surfaces at 30 m depth on Jeffreys Ledge created up to a 5.0 percent increase in patch space over a one-year period (Witman and Cooper 1983). The size of individual cod feeding patches was small, seldom exceeding 0.05 m².

Since offshore rocky ledges at 30 to 45 m depth at some sites in the Gulf of Maine are dominated by sponges (Witman and Sebens 1990, *Figure 4*), spongivorous predators have the potential to be important agents of space creation in the deep subtidal zone. The blood star *Henricia sanguinolenta* is a spongivore (Sheild and Witman 1993) that occurs in feeding aggregations on the sponges *Mycale lingua* and *Halichondria panicea* at 30 m depth on Cashes Ledge (Shellenbarger 1994). The blood star occasionally consumes an entire sponge, resulting in patches up to 0.2 m² (J. Witman unpublished observations). We have observed the polychaete *Euphrosine borealis* feeding on the sponges *Iophon* sp. and *Halichondria panicea* at 30 to 50 m depth at Ammen Rock Pinnacle, but the role of this predator as a source of patch creation is presently unknown.

NATURAL MORTALITY

Although not a type of disturbance, the natural mortality of sessile invertebrates often opens up space for colonization in deep rocky subtidal habitats of the central Gulf of Maine. Several species of sponges have a well-known tendency to become necrotic and slough off rock surfaces (Bergquist 1978, Ayling 1981) releasing a space on the rock surface as large as the sponge. In the Gulf of Maine, populations of the orange mounding sponge, *Myxilla fimbriata*, experience a high degree of turnover due to natural mortality. For example, approximately 25 percent of 200 monitored *Myxilla* sponges turned black, died and fell off rock walls at 30 m depth at Ammen Rock Pinnacle between 1986 and 1988 (J. Witman unpublished data, *Figure 4*). The average size of these mortality-generated patches ranged from 10 to 50 cm² (0.005 m²). Along with nudibranch predation, sponge mortality is an important process influencing ecological succession in deep rocky habitats by increasing the number of small clearings available for colonization.

Natural clearings or patches rarely occur on hard

substrates as deep as 50 m *(Figure 1)*. In a five-year monitoring period (1986 to 1991) we observed only two "natural mortality" patches open up on a section of rock ledge measuring approximately 10 m² at 50 m depth on Ammen Rock Pinnacle (J. Witman and K. Sebens unpublished observations). One was caused by the mortality of a sea anemone, *Urticina crassicornis,* and the other resulted from the death of a large sponge, *Mycale lingua.*

COLONIZATION

Patches cleared by disturbances may be colonized by the growth of species from the perimeter of the space or colonized from the overlying water column by larvae or asexual propagules (buds, fragments). We initiated a manipulative experiment at 30 m depth at Ammen Rock Pinnacle in 1986 to examine the sequence of colonization by invertebrate species and to test Connell and Keough's (1985) hypothesis that small clearings in subtidal communities would be colonized primarily from vegetative (asexual) growth of species surrounding the patch. Sponge patches were mimicked by removing 15 *Myxilla fimbriata* sponges from rock walls (treatments). "Natural" patches in the same size range (20 to 40 cm²) served as the controls, and colonization of both treatment and control patches was followed by close up photography four times over a 15-month interval. The results indicated that the early colonists were two bryozoans, *Crisia eburnea* and *Idmidronea atlantica*, and the serpulid polychaete *Spirorbis spirorbis (Figure 5A)*. Ascidians, (*Aplidium pallidum* and *Ascidia callosa*) were later arrivals, occupying on average only 5 percent cover after 15 months *(Figure 5B)*. In over two years of observation, none of the patches was colonized by the sponges that are the major component of the community at Ammen Rock Pinnacle (J. Witman and K. Sebens unpublished data). In contrast to Connell and Keough's (1985) predictions, all of the patches were colonized by planktonic recruitment. A related study of colonization on artificial hard substrata at 30 to 80 m depth at Ammen Rock Pinnacle found that bryozoans and serpulid polychaetes were the spatial dominants after one year (Sebens *et al.* 1988). There was a clear trend of increasing bare (noncolonized) space with depth below 30 m, indicating that colonization proceeds more

FIGURE 4. **Area of rocky bottom at Ammen Rock Pinnacle (33 m depth) dominated by sponges. The encrusting sponge is *Hymedesmia* sp. and the mounding sponge is *Myxilla fimbriata*. Natural mortality of *Myxilla* is an important source of space creation in rocky subtidal communities in the Gulf of Maine. Note the sponge at upper left that is black and necrotic. The next photograph in the time series indicated that it fell off the wall, creating a patch the same size as the sponge. Two other *Myxilla* mortality patches are visible just left of center and at lower right in this photograph. Bar below photograph indicates 5 cm. Photograph by Jon Witman.**

PRINTED IN COLOR ON PAGE 156.

slowly in deeper (50 to 80 m) than shallower (30 m) subtidal habitats (Sebens *et al.* 1988).

IMPLICATIONS FOR UNDERSTANDING ANTHROPOGENIC DISTURBANCE

There are several summary points about natural disturbance and recovery that have obvious implications for predicting the ecological consequences of anthropogenic disturbance in the rocky subtidal zone of the Gulf of Maine. Benthic communities at shallow depths (< 10 m) are subjected to a high frequency of physical and biological disturbance. The potential for relatively rapid recovery of disturbance-generated clearings in the shallow subtidal is high for some types of assemblages, such as kelp beds, but low for others, like beds of horse mussels, which have not recovered from physical disturbance in over a decade

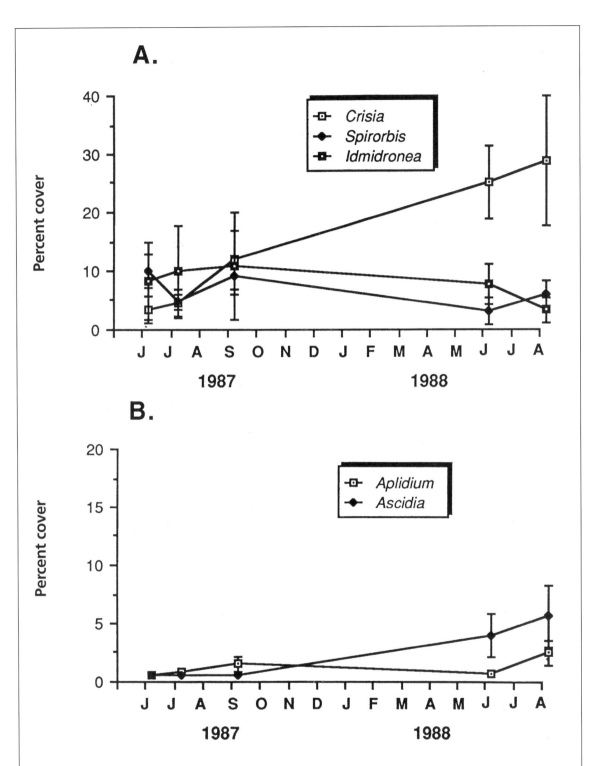

FIGURE 5. Colonization of small patches (~ 25 cm²) created by experimental removal of the sponge, *Myxilla fimbriata,* in rocky subtidal habitats at 30 m depth at Ammen Rock Pinnacle. Data represent the mean percent cover of species in 15 patches ± one standard error during the 15 months of observation. All of the patches in Figures 3A and 3B were colonized by larval recruitment. A. Percent cover occupied by two species of bryozoans (*Crisia eburnea* and *Idmidronea atlantica*) and one species of polychaete (*Spirorbis spirorbis*). Note that most of the patch space is occupied by the bryozoans after 15 months. B. Percent cover occupied by the solitary ascidian *Ascidia callosa* and the colonial ascidian *Aplidium pallidum*. Ascidians occupied only 6 percent of the patch space after 15 months of colonization.

of observation. Patches generated by disturbance or natural mortality at 30 m depth are initially colonized by larval recruitment and dominated by bryozoans, which may persist for more than seven years without any return to the natural community dominated by sponges, sea anemones, and ascidians. Large clearings are rarely created naturally in deep (30 m and greater) rocky habitats of the Gulf of Maine. Due to low rates of colonization at depths greater than 30 m, clearings created on deep, hard substrates will take many years to recover whether they are created by natural or by anthropogenic disturbance, such as from fishing gear.

ACKNOWLEDGMENTS
Sustained research on the ecology of subtidal communities in the Gulf of Maine would not have been possible without support from the Biological Oceanography Program of the National Science Foundation ,and from NOAA's National Undersea Research Center at Avery Point, Connecticut. I am also grateful for the insight provided by my collaborators on early offshore cruises, R. Cooper, K. Sebens, M. Patterson, R. Steneck, R. Vadas and D. Townsend. Thanks to a great group of graduate students and post-docs including S. Genovese, J. Leichter, G. Shellenbarger, T. Loher and C. Shield for their help in the field and for their own research investigations.

REFERENCES

Ayling, A. M. 1981. The role of biological disturbance in temperate subtidal encrusting communities. *Ecology* 62: 830-847.

Bergquist, P.R. 1978. *Sponges*. University of California Press, Berkeley, CA.

Connell, J. H. and M.J. Keough 1985. Disturbance and patch dynamics of subtidal marine animals on hard substrata. Pp. 125-151 in S.T.A. Pickett and P.S. White, eds. *The ecology of natural disturbance and patch dynamics*. Academic Press, Orlando, FL.

Dayton, P.K. 1971. Competition, disturbance and community organization: the provision and subsequent utilization of space in a rocky intertidal community. *Ecol. Monog.* 41:351-389.

Grime, J.P. 1977. Evidence for the existence of three primary strategies in plants and its relevance to ecological and evolutionary theory. *American Naturalist*. 111:1169-1194.

Genovese, S. J. 1996. Regional and temporal variation in the ecology of an encrusting bryozoan in the Gulf of Maine. Ph.D. Thesis, Northeastern University, Boston, MA.

Harris, L.G. M. Tyrell, C.M. Chester. In press. Changing ecological patterns for two *Asterias* species in the south-western Gulf of Maine over a twenty year period. Proceedings 9th Echinoderm Conference.

Hulbert, A.W. 1980. The functional role of *Asterias vulgaris* in three subtidal communities. Ph.D. Thesis, University of New Hampshire, Durham, NH.

Hulbert, A.W., K.J. Pecci, J.D. Witman, L.G. Harris, J.R. Sears and R.A. Cooper. 1982. *Ecosystem definition and community structure of the macrobenthos of the NEMP monitoring station at Pigeon Hill in the Gulf of Maine*. NOAA Technical Memorandum NMFS-F/NEC-14. 143 pp.

Leichter, J.J and J.D. Witman. 1997. Water flow over subtidal rock walls: relation to distributions and growth rates of sessile suspension feeders in the Gulf of Maine. *J. Exp. Mar. Biol. Ecol.* 209:293-307.

Menge, B.A. 1979. Coexistence between the sea stars *Asterias vulgaris* and *A. forbesi* in a heterogeneous environment; a non-equilibrium explanation. *Oecologia* 41:245-272.

Minchinton, T.E., R.E. Scheibling and H.L. Hunt 1997. Recovery of an intertidal assemblage following a rare occurrence of scouring by sea ice in Nova Scotia, Canada. *Botanica Marina* 40:139-148.

Ojeda, F.P. and J.H. Dearborn 1989. Community structure of macroinvertebrates inhabiting the rocky subtidal zone of the Gulf of Maine: seasonal and bathymetric distribution. *Mar. Ecol. Prog. Ser.* 57:147-157.

Paine, R.T. and S.A. Levin. 1981. Intertidal landscapes: disturbance and the dynamics of pattern. *Ecol. Monog.* 51:145-178.

Pickett, S.T.A. and P.S. White. 1985. *The ecology of natural disturbance and patch dynamics*. Academic Press, Inc. Orlando, FL.

Riedl, R. 1971. Water movement: animals. Pp. 1123-1149 in O. Kinne, ed. *Marine Ecology*, Vol. 1. Wiley-Interscience, London.

Sears, J.R. and R.A. Cooper. 1978. Descriptive ecology of offshore, deep water benthic algae in the temperate Western North Atlantic. *Mar. Biol.* 44: 309-314.

Sebens, K.P. 1985. The ecology of the rocky subtidal zone. *Am. Sci.* 73: 548-557.

Sebens, K.P., J.D. Witman, R. Allmon, E.J. Maney. 1988. Early community development experiments in rocky subtidal habitats (Gulf of Maine, 30-80 m). Pp. 45-66 in I. Babb and M. De Luca eds. *Benthic Productivity and Marine Resources of the Gulf of Maine.* National Undersea Research Program Research Report 88-3.

Sheild, C.J. and J. D.Witman. 1993. The impact of *Henricia sanguinolenta* predation on the finger sponges, *Isodictya* spp. *J. Exp. Mar. Biol. Ecol.* 166:107-133.

Shellenbarger, G. G. 1994. Defenses of Gulf of Maine sponges: implications for predation and population structure. Masters Thesis, Northeastern University, Boston, MA.

Unger, S. 1997. *The Perfect Storm.* W.W. Norton & Co. New York.

Vadas, R.L and R.S. Steneck. 1989. Zonation of deep water benthic algae in the Gulf of Maine. *J. Phycol.* 24: 338-346

Watling, L., J. Dearborn and L. McCann. 1988. General distribution patterns of macrobenthic assemblages in the Gulf of Maine. Pp. 109-119 in I. Babb and M. De Luca, eds. *Benthic Productivity and Marine Resources of the Gulf of Maine.* National Undersea Research Program Research Report 88-3.

Wethey, D.S. 1985. Catastrophe, extinction, and species diversity: a rocky intertidal example. *Ecology* 66:445-456.

Witman, J.D. 1985. Refuges, biological disturbance and rocky subtidal community structure in New England. *Ecol. Monog.* 55:421-445.

Witman, J.D. 1987. Subtidal coexistence: storms, grazing, mutualism and the zonation of kelps and mussels. *Ecol. Monog.* 57:167-187.

Witman, J.D. 1996. Dynamics of Gulf of Maine benthic communities. Pp. 51-69 in D. Dow and E. Braasch, eds. *The Health of the Gulf of Maine Marine Ecosytem: Cumulative impacts of multiple stressors.* RARGOM Report 96-1. Hanover, N.H.

Witman, J.D. and R.A. Cooper. 1983. Disturbance and contrasting patterns of population structure in the brachiopod *Terebratulina septentrionalis* from two subtidal habitats. *J. Exp. Mar. Biol. Ecol.* 73:57-79.

Witman, J. D. and K.R. Grange. 1998. Links between rain, salinity and predation in a rocky subtidal community. *Ecology.* In press.

Witman, J. D. and K.P. Sebens. 1988. Benthic community structure at a subtidal rock pinnacle in the central Gulf of Maine. Pp. 67-104 in I. Babb and M. De Luca, eds. *Benthic Productivity and Marine Resources of the Gulf of Maine.* National Undersea Research Program Research Report 88-3.

Witman, J. D. and K.P. Sebens. 1990. Distribution and ecology of sponges at a subtidal rock ledge in the central Gulf of Maine. Pp. 391-396 in K.Rutzler, ed. *New Perspectives in Sponge Biology.* Smithsonian Institution Press, Washington, D.C.

Bottom Habitat Requirements of Groundfish

Richard Langton

MAINE DEPARTMENT OF MARINE RESOURCES, WEST BOOTHBAY HARBOR, MAINE

I will address the habitat requirements for commercially important groundfish species and will start by posing the question, what is habitat? A map of northern Georges Bank, for example *(Figure 1),* shows that it is made up of a series of different types of sediment. The important thing is not the sediment, however, it is the relationship that the animals have with the sediment. Figure 1 shows the relationship between the different life stages of Atlantic cod, *Gadus morhua,* and the parts of the bank. The life stages of cod, a pelagic spawning fish, begin with eggs and larvae up in the water column. The larval fish settle onto the entire surface of Georges Bank, but because of predation they are very quickly restricted to an area of gravel pavement on the northern edge (Lough *et al.* 1989; Langton *et al.* 1996). When they grow larger, they spread out. Adults are widely distributed over the entirety of Georges Bank and move off the bank as well. Each life stage of fish can be considered as a different species because each stage has different requirements and, in particular, each stage relates to the environment on an entirely different scale.

I want to focus on the word *scale.* Fisheries management often deals with a very large scale. The National Marine Fisheries Service (NMFS), for example, uses a stratified random sampling design in its bottom trawl survey that covers the northwest Atlantic Ocean from Cape Hatteras to the Canadian border. NMFS looks at the northwest Atlantic as a series of discrete strata that are set up to represent the different depth zones in the region and are assumed

to be internally homogeneous in terms of fish abundance. Those zones are very large-scale features. Sampling at this scale gives an idea of what the population of fish is doing over an entire area such as the Gulf of Maine. It does not provide much insight into how a fish considers the Gulf of Maine, and that is what I want to do. I want to contrast the large-scale features that are considered for management purposes with the small-scale features that a fish might respond to when it makes its decision on whether to go left or right around a boulder. The large-scale strata used in the bottom trawl survey reflect community structure and aggregations of fish, which are useful for management purposes. But an individual fish might consider the environment quite differently.

It is clear that our perceptions of the sea floor depend on the scale used in sampling. In many places in the Gulf of Maine, every time the intensity of sampling the sea floor is increased, the number of recognized patches of different sediment types increases (Kelley, this volume; Langton *et al.* 1995). Zeroing in on a smaller area significantly improves the characterization of the area, and few areas have been characterized on a scale that adequately describes the features that fish and other benthic animals associate with.

To summarize the concept of scale, consider the nested diagram in Figure 2. This diagram shows that on a large scale, the scale of the NMFS bottom trawl surveys, temperature and depth are the controlling features. On the next smaller scale there is the sedimentary structure. Within this sedimentary structure,

GEORGES BANK COD

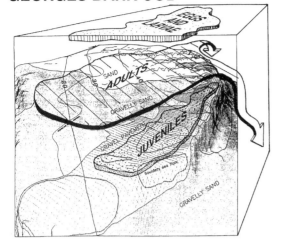

FIGURE 1. **Sediment and contour map of eastern Georges Bank, from a perspective looking southwest from Northeast Channel, overlaid with the distribution of the different life stages of Atlantic cod. Perspective view map from Valentine and Lough (1991).**

there are structures such as sand wave fields or fairly large geological features. To start thinking about animals, even smaller scales must be used, scales of tens of square meters or less. Thus within a field of sand waves there are sand wave crests and sand wave troughs. Those are the features that fish actually orient to, and in a trough there might be a series of amphipod tubes with amphipod distribution relating to the actual particle size of the sand.

I have been involved in several studies conducted by the Department of Marine Resources that attempt to elucidate the habitat associations for groundfish in my favorite part of the ocean, the Gulf of Maine. One of the areas that we have focused on is Sheepscot Bay in the midcoast region of Maine. We selected Sheepscot Bay because it is historically known as a spawning area for cod and it is also a nursery for young cod.

One part of the study was a groundfish tagging program in the Sheepscot Bay area from 1978 to 1983 to determine the movements of cod. Out of 4191 cod tagged, we had 255 tag returns from known locations by March 1985. Almost half of the returns came from within the tagging site, and many others came from the adjacent coastal area (Perkins *et al.* 1997). Although some fish moved out of the area,

the important conclusion is that these fish are not randomly or regularly distributed throughout the Gulf of Maine. They have a pattern of behavior that is repetitive and predictable and largely constrained to a limited area. These results parallel the observation of cod highways off Newfoundland by Rose (1993), but they contrast noticeably with the assumption made in NMFS stock assessments that the Gulf of Maine has a single stock of cod. Our tag returns from one location in the Gulf of Maine show a pattern of movement that suggests, instead of random distribution around the Gulf, a distinct coastal population of cod.

One of the reasons cod come into the Sheepscot Bay is because it is a spawning location. There has been a recent effort in Maine to identify historic spawning grounds based on interviews with older fishermen (Ames 1997). That effort has shown that people have known for years about cod coming into Sheepscot Bay. This raises questions of why Sheepscot Bay is important to cod and why fish keep coming back.

We addressed these questions by trawling at several stations in Sheepscot Bay and studying the fish community at each station. Geologically, Sheepscot Bay is a drowned river valley with a mud bottom and a sandy delta that both date to the last Ice Age. Three stations spaced three to four nautical miles apart were repeatedly sampled. Stations A and C

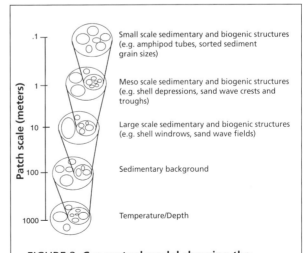

FIGURE 2. **Conceptual model showing the interdependency between scales and physical and biological structures. After Kotlair and Wiens (1990).**

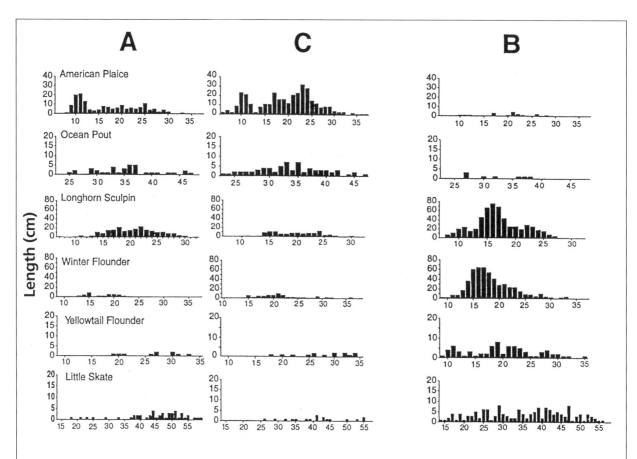

FIGURE 3. Length frequency plots of the six dominant fish species occurring in Sheepscot Bay at three otter trawl stations, A, B, and C. Note the similarity in species composition for the stations A and C and their contrast with station B. Reprinted with permission from Langton *et al.* (1995).

are in mud, while station B is in gravel. In spite of the proximity of the stations, they contain two dramatically different fish communities *(Figure 3;* Langton *et al.* 1995). The six dominant species in the fish community show distinct patterns of distribution that reflects patchiness on a very small scale. The fish that tend to make up the A and C station grouping (the American plaice community) hardly occur at all at station B, while the longhorn sculpin community occurs infrequently at stations A and C, but much more frequently at station B. (For scientific names of the fish species, see caption for *Figure 4.*)

How can we explain these differences over such a small scale? Stations A and C share not only the same depth zone but also the same substrate type—mud. Station B is in shallower water and has a mixed sand and gravel substrate. Therefore both depth and sediment type may explain the distribution of these fish. We took the study one step further and looked for

reasons why the fish occur on each sediment type. Instead of taking grab samples to collect benthic invertebrates at each station, we used fish to collect the samples, which is cheaper and more selective. Fish stomach contents give a pretty good idea of what a fish is eating. A particular amphipod occurred much more frequently in the stomachs of fish caught predominantly at station B (longhorn sculpin, winter flounder, yellowtail flounder, and little skate) than in the stomachs of fish caught predominantly at stations A and C (American plaice and ocean pout) *(Figure 4).* The fish are not just zeroing in on depth, they are not just zeroing in on sediment types, but they are zeroing in on lunch!

Next we looked at the amphipod and asked why it is there. The amphipod, *Unciola inermis,* is a tube dweller and is there because the area has the right size gravel to build its tube. Furthermore, at station B, there is a gradation from sand to gravely sand. We took samples, using a mechanical grab sampler, and we compared the number of amphipods with sediment type over a series of months. We found that this little amphipod occurred much more often in the gravel component of that station (Langton unpublished data).

What we have discovered when looking at the appropriate scale, i.e., a fish eye view of the world, is that the fish are occurring at station B because of prey that is dependent upon the substrate type for its existence. Thus ratcheting the scale down from the population level to the level of the individual fish starts to explain the fish's relationships with habitat. They are very complex, but they are also very interesting. Throughout the Gulf of Maine there are similar habitats to Sheepscot Bay.

Not only is there a habitat requirement that is dependent on depth and temperature in Sheepscot

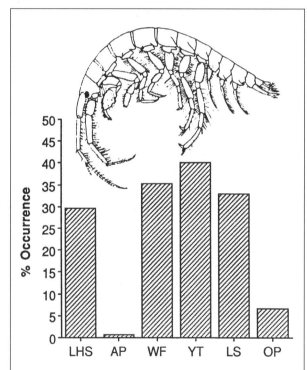

FIGURE 4. Occurrence of the amphipod, *Unciola inermis,* in the stomachs of the six dominant fish species in Sheepscot Bay. LHS = longhorn sculpin (*Myoxocephalus octodecimspinosus*); AP = American plaice (*Hippoglossoides platessoides*); WF = winter flounder (*Pleuronectes americanus*); YT = yellowtail flounder (*Pleuronectes ferruginea*); LS = little skate (*Raja erinacea*); OP = ocean pout (*Macrozoarces americanus*).

Bay, but there may be a relationship that depends on time. I have looked at the occurrence, or the catch rate, of winter flounder and longhorn sculpin together with the occurrence of the amphipod over slightly more than a year. As the amphipod population builds up over the year, there is also an increase in the occurrence of these two fish species. The fish move out before a crash occurs in the amphipod population, but as the amphipods build up again the next year, the fish start to reappear (Langton unpublished data). Perhaps there is a time component that we might want to consider when we consider habitat. I mention that, simply because spawning closures are often proposed for managing groundfish, and perhaps we need to think about more than just the spawning fish.

I will conclude with a few comments about where we have been with habitat and where we might go in the future. I think that all of us, scientists in particular, must sit back and look at what we already knew 100 years ago. An example of that understanding is a map drawn in 1887 charting North American fishing grounds and then revised in 1929 by Walter Rich specifically for the Gulf of Maine *(Figure 5)*. There are locations where fish aggregated in the past and continue to aggregate now. These are areas where fishermen are fishing (or at least were). This offers the scientific community the opportunity to ask the same questions I have addressed in the Sheepscot area, why is the Kettle Bottom, for example, a productive area? What is going on out there that makes this an area fishermen continue to fish year after year?

Once we have decided that an area is very important for the sustenance of a particular species, what should we do with this kind of habitat? One suggestion is to set aside these areas as reserves. The rationale for reserves is to protect the benthic community, which in turn nourishes the fish population. The overflow from the reserve provides fish to catch outside of the protected area.

Another possibility is to take an area such as Sheepscot Bay, that we know has been very productive for cod in the past, and put buckets of fish back into the ocean. The Department is currently asking whether or not we can reestablish populations of fish that have a pattern of reoccurrence in Sheepscot. We have recently released a small number of hatchery-

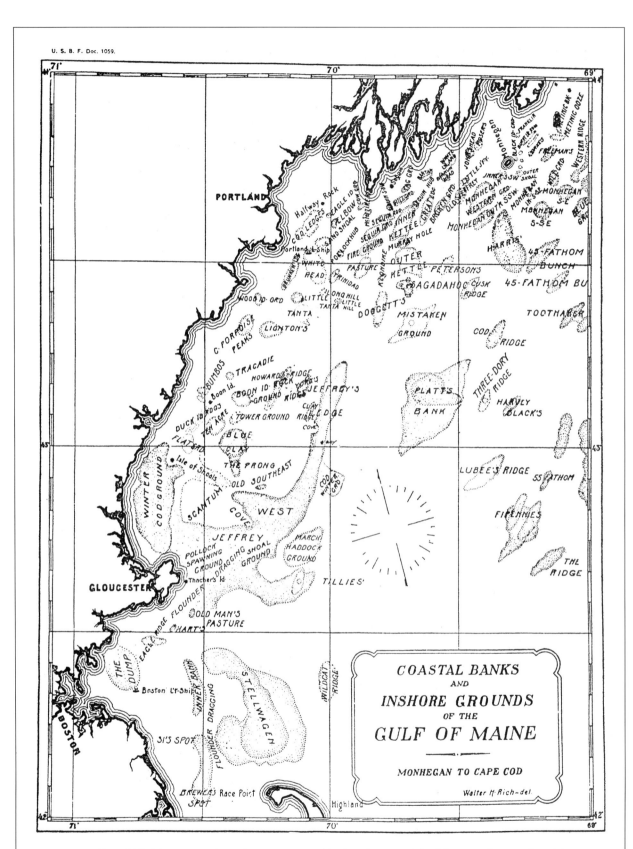

FIGURE 5. **Historic fishing grounds in the western Gulf of Maine. Modified from Collins and Rathbun (1887) by Rich (1929).**

raised juvenile cod into the Sheepscot, and we are offering an exorbitant reward of $50 for the first one that somebody catches and returns to us. I do not expect to be paying out $50, but I would be more than happy to if we could demonstrate that this is a feasible approach for use in the future, to help restore fisheries.

When we think about fishing and about habitat, it is necessary to realize that the kind of gear being used today to catch the majority of fish is not habitat selective. The bottom trawl is a very good integrator of habitats. We should appreciate the scale at which any fishing gear works, relate that to the way that the animal thinks and hopefully come up with an appreciation of the ecology of the area. If we want sustainable fisheries, we should realize that we are constrained by the ecology of the area, not by our ingenuity in catching fish. We are very effective at developing harvesting technology, but now we must begin to understand habitat relationships with the same ingenuity that we have used in the past to catch fish. We still have the opportunity to do this. We do not yet apply an agricultural mentality to ocean productivity, as is done in some other parts of the world. There is a lot of natural habitat left in New England, and if we start to understand the complexities of it, I believe that we will start to have sustainable fisheries into the future.

REFERENCES

Ames, E.P. 1997. *Cod and haddock spawning grounds in the Gulf of Maine, from Grand Manan Channel to Ipswich Bay*. Island Institute, Rockland, ME. 33 pp.

Collins, J.W. and R. Rathbun. 1887. *The Fisheries and Fishing Industries of the United States*. Pp. 5-80. (R. Rathbun, ed.) U.S. Government Printing Office, Washington, D.C.

Kelley, J.T. **This volume.** Mapping the surficial geology of the western Gulf of Maine.

Kotlair, N.B and J.A. Wiens. 1990. Multiple scales of patchiness and patch structure: a hierarchical framework for the study of heterogeneity. *Oikos* 59:253-260.

Lough, R., P.C. Valentine, D.C. Potter, P.J. Auditore, G.R. Bolz, J.D. Neilson and R.I. Perry. 1989. Ecology and distribution of juvenile cod and haddock in relation to sediment type and bottom current on eastern Georges Bank. *Mar. Ecol. Prog. Ser.*56:1-12.

Langton, R.W., P.J. Auster and D.C. Schneider. 1995. A spatial and temporal perspective on research and management of groundfish in the northwest Atlantic. *Rev. Fish. Sci.* 3:201-229.

Langton, R.W., R. S. Steneck, V. Gotceitas, F. Juanes and P. Lawton. 1996. The interface between fisheries research and habitat management. *N. Am. J. Fish. Manage.* 16:1-7.

Perkins, H.C., S.B. Chenoweth and R.W. Langton.1997. The Gulf of Maine Atlantic cod complex, patterns of distribution and movement of the Sheepscot Bay substock. *Bull. Natl. Res. Inst. Aquacult.*, Suppl. 3:101-107.

Rich, W.H. 1929. *Fishing Grounds of the Gulf of Maine*. U.S. Commissioner of Fisheries. Washington, D.C.

Rose, G.A. 1993. Cod spawning on a migration highway in the northwest Atlantic. *Nature* 366:458-461.

Valentine, P.C. and R.G. Lough. 1991. *The sea floor environment and the fishery of eastern Georges Bank*. U.S. Geological Survey, Open-File Report 91-439. 25 pp.

Scientific Studies of Fishing Gear Effects on the Sea Floor

Bottom Tending Gear Used in New England

Ronald Smolowitz

COONAMESSET FARM, EAST FALMOUTH, MASSACHUSETTS

I will address how we create wealth from the marine environment by harvesting the larger animals that live amongst the rocks and mud and eat the little critters. Basic wealth is created by only a few industries—farming, fishing, forestry, mining, and idea creation. All other human endeavors are built upon this wealth. Our task is not only to create wealth from our New England marine ecosystem in a sustainable manner, but also to enhance the production of this wealth. As a starting point, we need to know how we currently harvest this wild crop and what sustainability issues are associated with the harvesting tools. Key among these issues are bycatch and habitat impact, which are in fact closely related. I will briefly describe the principal bottom tending gear used in the region and indicate the points of impact with the bottom.

Bycatch is a combination of the target and nontarget species. In many cases, the nontarget benthic organisms are discarded. In the past these organisms were referred to as trash by scientists and fishermen alike. I remember filling out trash logs on the data sheets on fisheries research cruises. It is interesting how our view of the world changes. I suggest that as our knowledge of ecosystems matures, some of today's bycatch will become classified as weeds, to be controlled, and some will become prized targets.

In many cases, bycatch is defined by regulations. Certain fisheries are only allowed to catch a particular species. One important point is that bycatch is not always bad and that making gear selective for species or species complexes is not always good. Figure 1 illustrates the complexity of a typical local ecosystem and presents a real case scenario from Nantucket waters. There is a fishery for tautog, a hook and line fishery. The tautog are known to feed on the green crab, which are known to feed on the small bay scallop larvae. A few years ago fishermen overfished the tautog, and there was a population explosion of the green crab. The green crab then fed on the incoming scallop spat, and the scallop fishery collapsed. In this case, a very selective fishery for the tautog had negative ecological consequences on another fishery. It might have been better in the long run to have a less selective fishery with some bycatch mortality of the crabs in balance with the tautog harvest. This may have resulted in better production and a more balanced ecosystem. When we think about habitat, we need to be aware that the issues are broad and complex, and that the solutions are not as simple as they may appear.

Figure 2 is an artist's rendition of the New Bedford style scallop dredge, with the top removed to better illustrate the gear. Although removing the dredge top is not a management proposal for scallop fishing, large mesh twine tops are being explored as a means of reducing finfish bycatch in the scallop fishery. Scallop dredges are commonly defined by the width of their frame. Most of the vessels tow two 15-foot dredges or two 13-foot dredges. The front of the steel frame is called the bale and usually rides off the sea floor, except in hard rocky bottoms where it might hit. The bottom of the aft part of the frame is called the cutting bar. It rides about four inches off

46 Effects of Fishing Gear on the Sea Floor of New England the bottom. In a flat area, it remains off the bottom, but in areas with sand waves, for example, the cutting bar hits the tops of the sand waves and tends to knock them out.

The sweep chain is attached to each end of the dredge frame at a reinforced bottom pad called the shoe, which is basically a short dredge runner. The chain sweeps back in an arc to which the bottom of the ring bag is attached. There is a club stick at the very end of the ring bag that is responsible for maintaining the bag's shape, especially during handling on deck. The ring bag drags on the bottom. A scallop fishing vessel working an area repeatedly for a long time will tend to flatten out the sand waves.

For hard bottom scalloping, in addition to tickler chains that run from side to side between the frame and the ring bag, there are also chains that run from front to back, known as rock chains *(Figure 2)*. On rocky bottom, fishermen put a lot of rock chains in to prevent boulders from getting into the ring bag.

Underwater video of dredges being towed at speeds of five knots show that the chains do not dig into the bottom. They skip over the surface and hit it periodically. The chains tend to pop up organisms like starfish that are on the bottom. Some digging into the sand must take place, because at times burrowing clams end up in the dredges.

In the past (mostly before 1975), scallop dredges were relatively light gear limited in width and structural strength. The vessels were smaller than at present, so they were limited in the seasons they could fish. They had lower horsepower, so they could not tow the gear over many types of hard bottom and substrate. There has been an expansion in dredge size and weight and strength, and the horsepower of scallop vessels has increased. This enables the vessels to tow faster and to get into types of bottom that they were not able to tow in formerly.

Current issues related to scallop dredging include bycatch of monkfish, flounders, lobsters, and benthic

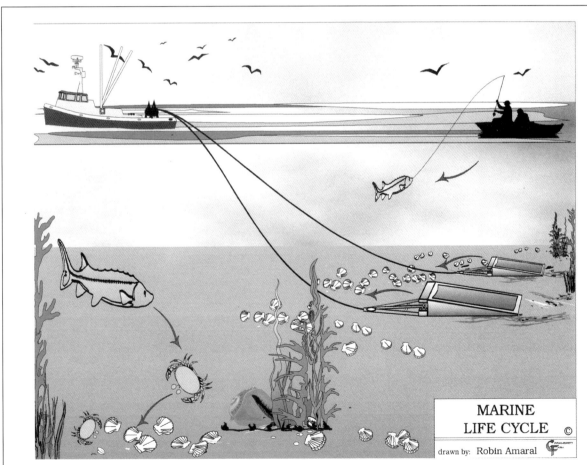

FIGURE 1. **A typical New England marine ecosystem. Drawing by Robin Amaral.**

organisms. Selectivity of the dredge is now controlled by the size of the rings. Current regulations require rings of 3.5" diameter. With larger rings, fewer bottom organisms come up in the dredge bag. However, this does not mean that they are not disturbed by the gear. Another key issue related to the gear is the impact scallop gear may have on the bottom. There is an indication that working the bottom with scallop gear resuspends sediment. Sediment impacts might cause some damage and mortality to small scallops. Fishermen have also noticed that working the bottom may increase the production of scallops from year to year. This might be the result of spreading out the scallops and/or somehow controlling predators.

The next type of gear I will review is the bottom trawl *(Figure 3)*. Trawl doors, which function to keep the net open laterally, tend to leave a groove on the bottom, depending on the hardness of the substrate. They could dig in as much as 10–15 cm. There are many different types of ground gear that can be used on the sweep of bottom trawls, from simple drop chains to sweeps made of six-inch roller cookies to large bobbins to rollers. The overall impact to bottom habitat of each type of rig is not necessarily obvious at first glance. For example, fishing hard bottom gear with large rollers allows many bottom organisms to escape unharmed under the net. There are spaces between the rollers on the sweep that allow small fish and organisms to escape. On the other hand, this rig allows the net to be towed over substrate that would normally support many organisms that grow vertically and would otherwise remain unaffected by mobile gear.

The doors and other parts of trawl gear have been designed to generate mud clouds, because mud clouds tend to herd fish into the path of a trawl and keep them in that path. As mentioned above with scallop gear, there are concerns now about the impact

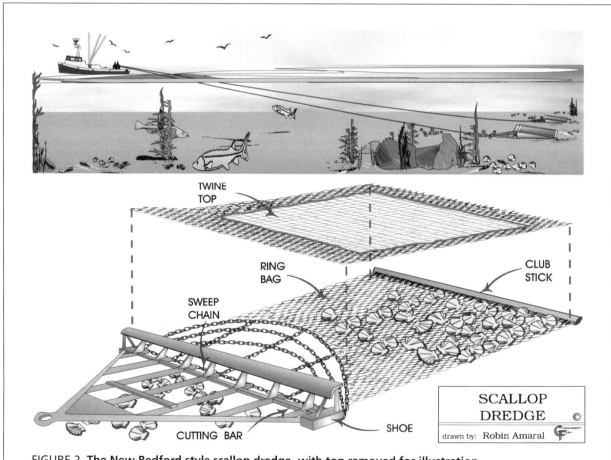

FIGURE 2. **The New Bedford style scallop dredge, with top removed for illustration. Drawing by Robin Amaral.**

PRINTED IN COLOR ON PAGE 156.

of sediment resuspension. In addition, trawl gear used to be smaller and towed at lower speeds. In New England, the primary target was haddock, which meant towing over a particular type of bottom and leaving other bottom types unfished. By using larger trawls, higher speeds, and mixed-species targets, fishermen are now trawling the whole ocean in a general sense. Habitat that once remained untouched by mobile gear in the past now is being fished. Bycatch problems with trawls are often generated by the management regime, with species by species management, and the gear clearly tends to resuspend sediment. From a management perspective, concerns about trawls relate to the fishing power of the gear, species selectivity, size selectivity, and bottom disturbance. In my opinion, it would be good to develop low impact bottom trawls and to define critical habitat in which it might not be appropriate to use mobile gear.

Bottom set gillnets used in New England are diagrammed in Figure 4. An individual gill net is usually 300 feet long. Usually 10 to 20 nets are tied together in a string, and a fishing vessel might fish 5 to 20 strings. Groundfish gillnets are currently limited to 80 or 160 nets per vessel, depending on target species. In temperate regions like New England, few questions have been raised about habitat impacts of gillnets, *per se*. There is concern about ghost fishing after nets are lost and what impact that has on organisms on the bottom. In more tropical regions, there is concern about damage to coral when hauling and setting strings of gillnets.

Gillnets in the past were made of inefficient twine materials—twine made of natural fibers such as cotton. In many cases fishermen had to fish the gear only at night to make it efficient, and the vessels were not able to handle all the gear that was needed. Gillnetters used to need three sets of gear. A vessel had to have one set fishing, one set in transport, and one set

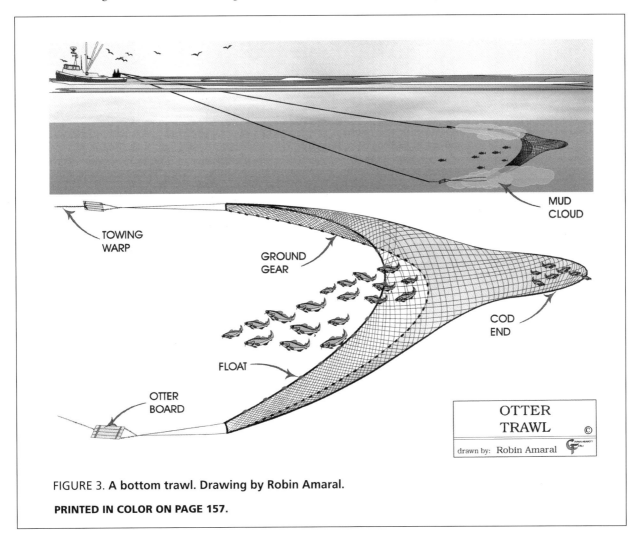

FIGURE 3. **A bottom trawl. Drawing by Robin Amaral.**

PRINTED IN COLOR ON PAGE 157.

on the beach, drying. Now we have very efficient materials—monofilament and multifilament synthetic mesh, as well as high net numbers. The main issues surrounding gillnets have to do with marine mammal entanglement and fishing power. Gillnets have many positive attributes because they are able to target fish by size and to be selective for certain species. In general, the gear is considered habitat friendly compared to towed gear. In my opinion, the key issue with gillnets is fishing power, or the number of nets that an individual vessel is allowed to fish. Marine mammal entanglement concerns are also related to net numbers. Reducing net numbers will also address another concern—inappropriate fishing strategies, whereby gillnetters leave nets out to occupy bottom and prevent other users from fishing on that bottom.

Figure 5 illustrates the design of lobster traps. The entrance head usually allows lobsters very easy access into the front part of the trap, or the kitchen. From the kitchen there is a long sloping head to the second part of the trap, the parlor. In the parlor there is an escape vent to allow small organisms, such as small lobsters and crabs, to escape from the trap. Lobster traps can be fished singly or strung together in trawls. Single traps are often used in rough, hard bottom areas where trawl strings tend to foul on bottom structure. They are fished in trawls on flatter types of bottom. The process of hauling a trawl drags the traps over the bottom. The amount of bottom that is affected by a single string of traps during the setting and hauling process is not significant. However, if one multiplies that effect by the three million traps being hauled several times a week, a significant cumulative effect is possible.

During colonial days, lobsters were so abundant that they were harvested with hoop nets and spears. Eventually, lobstermen started using single parlor traps in the inshore waters. As lobsters became more scarce and longer sets further offshore were needed, the two-compartment trap was developed. This trap

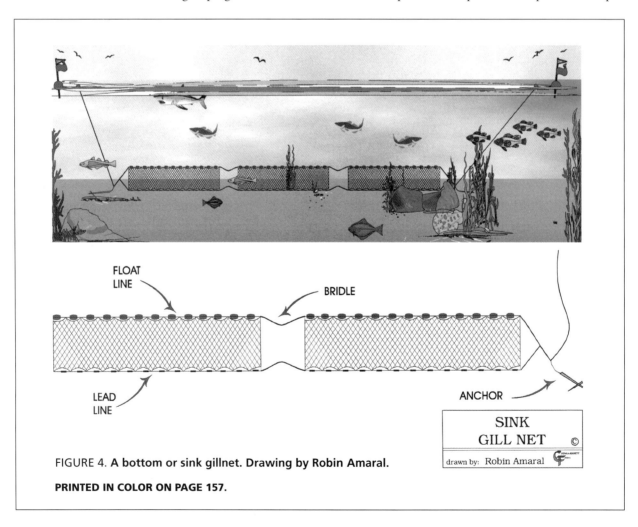

FIGURE 4. **A bottom or sink gillnet. Drawing by Robin Amaral.**

PRINTED IN COLOR ON PAGE 157.

FLOAT LINE

BRIDLE

LEAD LINE

ANCHOR

SINK GILL NET ©

drawn by: Robin Amaral

design could contain more lobsters for a longer time. In most cases, the bycatch from lobster traps is released in good condition, so bycatch is not a major issue. The escape vents offer pretty good size selectivity. An important concern with lobster traps, currently, is whale entanglement in the buoy and string lines.

Figure 6 illustrates bottom longline hook gear. One of the interesting things about hook gear is how much its fishing effort has decreased. At the turn of the century, a fishing schooner might have quite a few dories on board which could be handling 16,000 hooks and hauling them twice a day. Thus it fished 32,000 hooks daily. Today, hooks are used mostly on small coastal vessels that set around 500 hooks per day. A few vessels in New England gear up with 10,000 to 15,000 hooks. In other places in the world, 40,000 hooks automatically hauled and set daily is not out of the question. The new circle hooks are a little bit more efficient than the old "J" hooks. In general, I don't think there is any direct impact on habitat

by hook gear, though there may be some indirect effects on the habitat from the selectivity of the gear.

In conclusion, the definition of overfishing is a key concern from a habitat standpoint, in my opinion. Overfishing is currently defined in the Federal Register as the rate of fishing mortality that jeopardizes the long term capacity of the stock to produce the largest average annual catch on a sustained basis. Overfishing must be defined in measurable parameters, according to national standard one of the Magnuson-Stevens Fishery Conservation and Management Act. Measurable parameters include fishing effort, catch and catch rates, and abundance estimates. Numbers are an excellent aid to reasoning, but it is an increasingly common error to use only the numbers available and to fail to quantify the rest of the situation. An important part of the rest of the situation is fish habitat. Because impacts to habitat can not be quantified, they tend to be ignored.

Scientists have not been able to quantify sub-

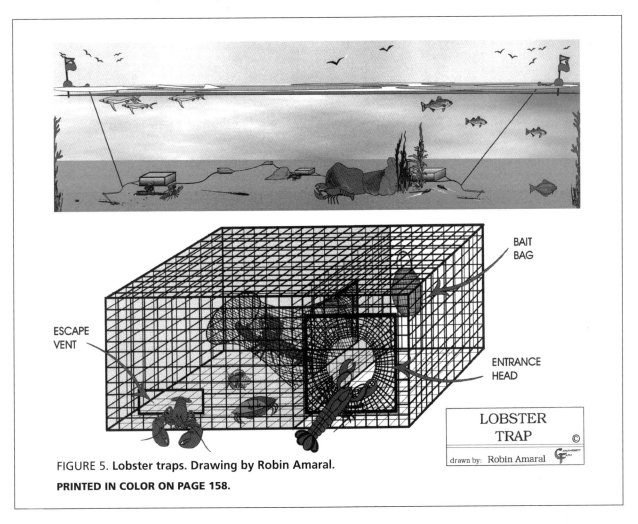

FIGURE 5. Lobster traps. Drawing by Robin Amaral.
PRINTED IN COLOR ON PAGE 158.

strate alterations, sediment resuspension, destruction of benthos, and alteration of behavior. Fishery managers tend to forget that they are dealing with living organisms. In my opinion, the habitat impacts of fishing may insidiously keep ecosystem production depressed by an undetectable amount by chronic sublethal effects on reproduction and feeding. These effects are indetectable because they are masked by the overall fishing effort. I would propose to replace the rate of fishing mortality definition with cumulative fishing impact, and to describe and quantify, where possible, all gear impact on ecosystem productivity.

Finally, discussions about habitat in a management context usually focus on closed areas. It is interesting that the term *closed areas* is used instead of *managed areas*. *Closed area* is automatically a pejorative term for commercial fishermen. The biggest problem at present with closed areas is that they cannot be enforced effectively. They are also difficult to reopen mainly because the reasons they were closed in the first place do not vanish. For example, if these areas were closed in order to protect habitat, any gain would then be lost as soon as the area was reopened. There are also questions about how to allow access into a newly opened closed area. One proposed solution is to allow only fixed gear in areas that might be critical habitat. One advantage to this approach is that it could be self-enforced by the passive gear users. The benefits inside these areas could be harvested to create basic wealth, which might provide incentives to move the industry toward habitat-friendly gear types. Another possible solution involves farming strategies. Fisheries depend on natural sets of animals, with no control over where they set. It might be beneficial to set commercially important animals in the types of habitat that are most appropriate for towed gear.

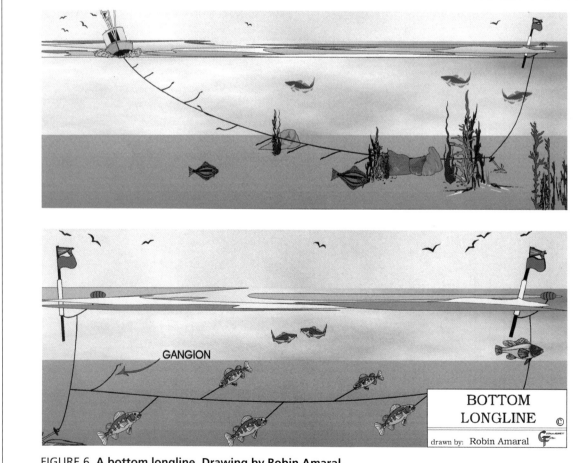

FIGURE 6. **A bottom longline. Drawing by Robin Amaral.**

PRINTED IN COLOR ON PAGE 158.

Studies in New England of Fishing Gear Impacts on the Sea Floor

Jeremy Collie

UNIVERSITY OF RHODE ISLAND, NARRAGANSETT, RHODE ISLAND

The previous papers on geology, benthic ecology, and fishing gear provide a good introduction to this summary of the main published studies from New England on fishing gear impacts. Concerns about the denudation of the bottom by otter trawlers were voiced in the early development of the otter trawl fishery. Alexander *et al.* (1914) reported that "Otter trawls do not seriously disturb the bottom over which they are fished nor materially denude it of organisms which directly or indirectly serve as food for commercial fishes." This conclusion may no longer hold because of two principal changes since 1914. First, the 1914 studies were based solely on material collected by the trawl (the so-called *trash*), because at that time they couldn't directly observe what was happening on the sea floor. Now we can take photographs, videotapes, sonar images, and various samples of the bottom. Second, there were only eight steam trawlers then, and the trawls they used were much smaller than gear used now. Now there are hundreds of trawls, and although the impact of a single trawl may be limited, the cumulative impact can be substantial.

One indication of the cumulative impact of fishing in New England is provided by calculating the area swept by otter trawls and scallop dredges in the Gulf of Maine and on Georges Bank. Auster *et al.* (1996) combined fishing effort data compiled by the National Marine Fisheries Service from 1976 to 1991 with estimates of average speed, duration, and width, of tows. Most of the effort was by otter trawls, and the effort by scallop dredges was relatively small *(Figure 1)*. However, the impact of scallop dredges should not be overlooked because the dredges have more area in contact with the bottom than trawls, and can have localized impacts on the bottom. Auster *et al.* (1996) compared the total area swept by these two gear types with the areas of the Gulf of Maine and of Georges Bank. In the Gulf of Maine the area swept each year was approximately equal to the area of the Gulf itself. On Georges Bank the area swept would have covered the bank three times in the more recent years *(Figure 1)*. Of course, the distribution of the fishing effort is not uniform: some areas are not fished at all and some are fished many times per year. Clearly, the cumulative amount of fishing is large in relation to the area that is fished. Since 1994, large area closures and fishing effort reductions have changed the level and distribution of fishing impacts.

The locations of gear impact studies that have been conducted in the region are shown in Figure 2. These studies can be characterized as either spatial comparisons of disturbed and undisturbed sites (such as on Swans Island and Georges Bank) or before and after disturbance studies (such as what was observed at Jeffreys Bank). Studies have been made on Stellwagen Bank, but are not reviewed here.

SWANS ISLAND

One of the problems facing scientists who wish to study the impacts of fishing gear in this region is the difficulty in finding areas unaffected by fishing, to use as control sites. Swans Island, off the coast of

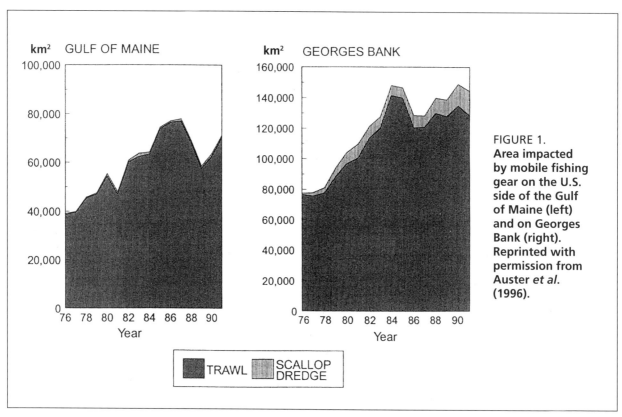

FIGURE 1. **Area impacted by mobile fishing gear on the U.S. side of the Gulf of Maine (left) and on Georges Bank (right). Reprinted with permission from Auster _et al._ (1996).**

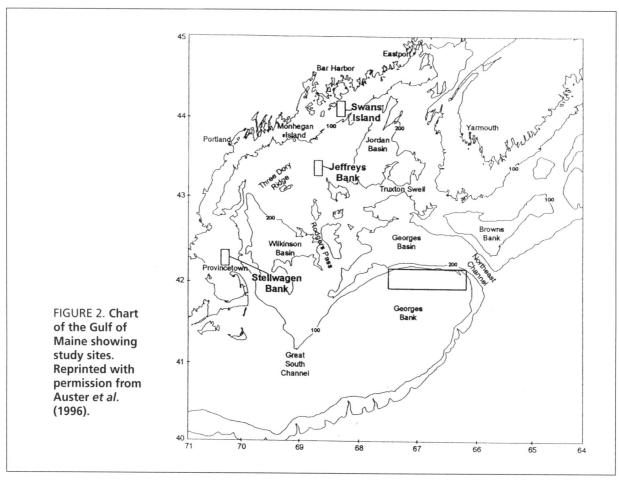

FIGURE 2. **Chart of the Gulf of Maine showing study sites. Reprinted with permission from Auster _et al._ (1996).**

Maine, offers one such control site because a conservation area adjacent to the island was closed to mobile fishing gear in 1983 *(Figure 2)*. Habitat complexity within the conservation area has been compared to habitat complexity just outside this area, using video transects made with a remotely operated vehicle in July 1993 (Auster *et al*. 1996). Two main bottom types were studied, a cobble-shell bottom and a sand-shell bottom, in water 30 to 40 meters (m) deep. Habitat complexity was provided either by erect epifaunal animals (animals that live on or near the sediment surface, such as sponges, bryozoans, hydroids, and sea cucumbers) or by depressions made in the sediment by mobile animals (such as scallops, lobsters, crabs and white hake). Habitat types were quantified by superimposing random dots on video frames and counting the proportion of dots that fell on each habitat type. From this, a cover index was determined and compared between inside and outside the conservation area.

On the cobble-shell bottom, there were more emergent epifauna and more sea cucumbers (holothurians) living inside the conservation area than outside, and on the sand-shell bottom, there were more biogenic depressions and more sea cucumbers inside the conservation area than outside *(Figure 3)*. The differences between inside and outside the conservation area were highly significant statistically. These differences were attributed to removal by mobile fishing gear of epifauna and of species that create depressions.

JEFFREYS BANK
Jeffreys Bank is a mud-draped, gravel area dotted with boulders in the Gulf of Maine *(Figure 2)*.

A 1987 survey with a submersible found many large erect sponges and numerous other invertebrates living on the boulders at a depth of 94 m (Auster *et al*. 1996). A return visit in 1993 found that most of this fauna—the sponges and the associated species —was severely reduced. Video transects were made, and the percent cover of sponges was measured from sequential frames along the transects. It is clear that in 1987 sponges were observed at a much higher frequency than in 1993 *(Figure 4)*. In 1987 some frames had 30 percent cover of sponges, while in 1993 no frames had more than 7 percent cover of sponges. There were indications that boulders had been moved in the second survey, and the changes seen were attributed to trawling. It was presumed that until recently the boulders discouraged trawling in this area, but fishermen have developed methods of trawling in this difficult habitat. Attributing the effects to trawling is somewhat circumstantial, but the researchers actually observed trawling taking place on their second visit. Since no natural forces are known to be capable of rolling boulders at this depth, it seems very likely that trawling was the cause of the severe reduction in sponges and other invertebrates.

GEORGES BANK
Beginning in 1994, I have conducted studies with several colleagues on the northern edge of Georges Bank, focusing on a gravel pavement area *(Figure 2)*. This important habitat is a scallop ground, a nursery area for cod and haddock, and also an area where herring spawn on the gravel pavement. Figure 5 shows the distribution of scallop fishing in this area in 1993 on the U.S. side of the Hague line. The high-

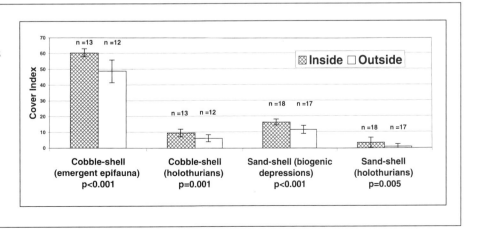

FIGURE 3. **Cover index of various habitat types inside and outside of Swans Island Conservation Area on cobble-shell bottom and sand-shell bottom. Fishing with mobile gear is allowed only outside the conservation area. Data from Auster** *et al.* **(1996).**

est scalloping effort was concentrated on the gravel habitat on the northern part of Georges Bank and also in the western part of Georges Bank in Great South Channel. The degree of disturbance to benthic habitats was documented with side scan sonar surveys conducted in 1994. Some places in the study area appear undisturbed by fishing because of the presence of relic boulders, which discourage bottom fishing.

In response to the collapse of groundfish stocks on Georges Bank, the New England Fishery Management Council instituted two large closures on Georges Bank in December 1994, known as Area I and Area II (indicated by broken lines in *Figure 5*). These closures were intended to directly reduce fishing mortality, and they have done that already. They have the added benefit of protecting the benthic habitat.

Before the closures were instituted, we made two cruises to northern Georges Bank, in April and November 1994, to sample gravel pavement habitats at six study sites *(Figure 5)*. The purpose of the study was to characterize these sites and assess the impact of bottom fishing. Both bottom trawls and scallop dredges are used in this area. The study concentrates on scallop dredging because the area is a very important scallop ground. The study sites are located at two depths, at 80–90 m in the Canadian zone and at 40–50 m in the U.S. zone. We chose varying depths and contrasting degrees of disturbance, as measured by side scan sonar surveys.

We classified the six sites by disturbance level, either disturbed or undisturbed, and by depth, either deep or shallow *(Table 1)*, and we planned the data collection to be amenable to analysis of variance. At each station we made photographic transects and collected bottom samples of the benthic megafauna (bottom-dwelling animals larger than 5 millimeters) with short tows of a 1 m Naturalists' dredge. It is important to collect animals and bring them on board to identify and weigh them and to help identify animals seen in bottom photographs.

We used five ecological indices to summarize the occurrence of benthic animals at the different sites. Three of these indices—abundance, biomass, and species diversity—are presented here; more detailed results were published by Collie *et al.* (1997). We compared the means of these indices between sites

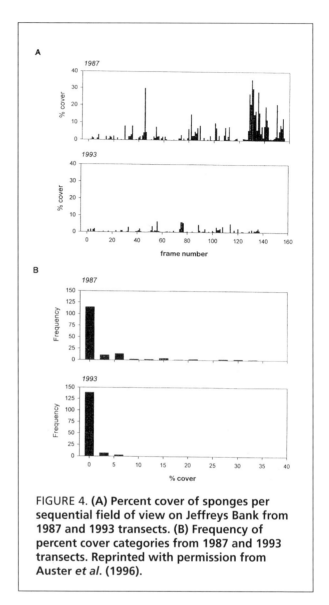

FIGURE 4. **(A) Percent cover of sponges per sequential field of view on Jeffreys Bank from 1987 and 1993 transects. (B) Frequency of percent cover categories from 1987 and 1993 transects. Reprinted with permission from Auster *et al.* (1996).**

with a three-way analysis of variance. There was a cruise factor, a depth factor and a dredge factor. Numerical abundance was higher at the deep sites than at the shallow sites, but abundance also was significantly higher at the undredged sites than at the dredged sites at both depths *(Figure 6)*. The same pattern was evident for the biomass of animals: biomass was higher at the deep sites than at the shallow sites, and biomass was also higher at the undredged sites compared to the dredged sites *(Figure 7)*. The results for abundance and biomass were consistent over both cruises in 1994. Species diversity measures the number of species as well as the equitability of distribution of individuals among species. Species diversity was significantly higher at the deep sites than at the shallow sites, and species diversity also was higher at undredged sites than at dredged sites *(Figure 8)*. This pattern was not completely consistent on the second cruise, when we found a decrease in diversity at the undredged sites and an increase at one of the dredged sites.

We also performed multivariate analysis of these data sets. The output is presented by Collie *et al.* (1997) and summarized here. The deep undredged sites are characterized by higher numbers of fragile animals, such as shrimps, brittle stars, anemones, sponges, and juvenile fish. In contrast, the disturbed sites are characterized by hard-shelled mollusks, which are probably more resistant to disturbance, and by scavengers, such as sea stars and hermit crabs. The most apparent difference between disturbed and undisturbed sites, however, is the lack of emergent colonial animals at the disturbed sites. These are animals that we cannot count from the dredge samples because they come up in bits and pieces. They can be seen in photographs, however, and their percent cover can be estimated.

In November of 1994, we were fortunate to have Page Valentine's camera to take still photographs of the sea bottom. The camera was mounted about 65 cm off the bottom, so the area of the photographs is about a third of a m². At deep undisturbed site 20, the gravel is covered with plant-like animals (hydroids and bryozoans) with colonies of the tube worm, *Filograna implexa (Figure 9a)*. The calcareous tubes of *F. implexa* are thin and very fragile, like shredded wheat. It is pretty clear when you see an area covered with them that it has not been disturbed, because a single pass of towed gear would crush them. In contrast, in a disturbed area the gravel is almost completely bare, and there are fewer free-living

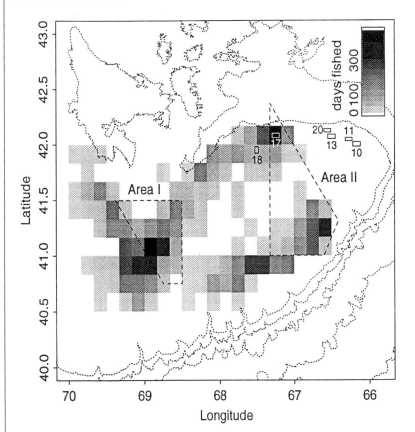

FIGURE 5. **Spatial distribution of sea scallop dredging effort (days fished) in 1993. Also shown are the two areas closed to fishing starting in December 1994 and location of sample sites. The scallop effort data were provided courtesy of Dr. Lai, Northeast Fisheries Science Center. Reprinted with permission from Collie et al. (1997).**

TABLE 1.
Summary of Naturalists' dredge samples collected on two cruises to northern Georges Bank. The site locations are indicated in Figure 5. Printed with permission from Collie et al. (1997).

Site	Depth (m)	# of replicates 4/94	# of replicates 11/94	Disturbance level
10	Deep (88)	6	6	Undisturbed[a]
11	Deep (86)	0	3	Undisturbed
13	Deep (81)	7	6	Disturbed
17	Shallow (47)	4	3	Disturbed
18	Shallow (44)	3	6	Undisturbed[b]
20	Deep (85)	0	6	Undisturbed

a. Light dredging disturbance was observed in November 1994.

b. This site may have been previously disturbed.

animals except for burrowing anemones *(Figure 9b)*.

The differences between Figures 9a and 9b are visually very apparent. To quantify the differences, we superimposed a grid on each photograph to aid enumeration. We estimated the percent cover of attached epifauna in each sector of the grid, then summed over the grids to obtain the total for each photograph. The mean percent cover of the worm *F. implexa* was higher at the deep sites than at the shallow sites, and also higher at the undredged sites compared with the dredged sites (Collie *et al.* 1996). Similarly, the mean percent cover of plant-like animals (bryozoans and hydroids) was higher at the undredged sites than at the dredged sites.

To summarize our work on Georges Bank, gravel habitats are sensitive to disturbance by mobile bottom fishing gear. The most conspicuous effect of disturbance is the removal of the three dimensional cover provided by colonial epifaunal animals. Undisturbed sites have higher abundance, biomass, and species diversity. The undredged areas are characterized by fragile species such as sponges, nudibranchs,

worms, and small fish. The dredged sites are characterized by scavengers, such as hermit crabs and sea stars. These conclusions apply equally to other hard bottom gravel habitats in the region.

A potential criticism of these spatial comparisons is that we have no direct control over the levels of fishing disturbance. It is possible that the disturbed sites have always been as bare of epifauna as we see now and that fishing was not responsible for the reduced abundance of epifauna. A more direct experimental approach that controlled fishing effort would clearly be desirable. Such an experiment was unintentionally provided by the groundfish closures that began in December 1994. It happened that one of the areas we had studied earlier that year was inside the northern part of closed area II *(Figure 5)*. Previous to the closure, it was one of the most heavily dredged sites on northern Georges Bank. The closure, which applied to all groundfish gear as well as to scallop dredges, provides an almost unique opportunity to follow the recolonization of a disturbed area over time.

FIGURE 6.
Numerical abundance of benthic megafauna from northeastern Georges Bank. Box-Cox transformation (λ=0.125) was applied to density per m³. Symbols represent mean and 95 percent confidence intervals. Site identifiers: D, Deep; S, Shallow; u, undisturbed; d, disturbed. Reprinted with permission from Collie *et al.* (1997).

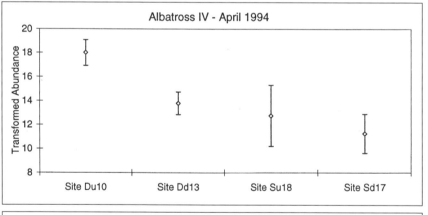

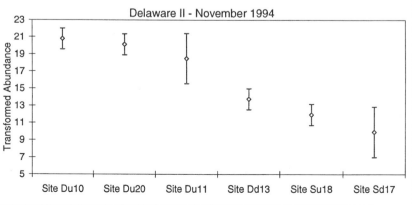

We resampled these areas in the summers of 1995, 1996, and 1997 to monitor for potential recovery. We are surprised by a rapid initial recovery of disturbed site 17, starting six months after the closure and continuing until present. In contrast to the bare gravel seen in November 1994, a photograph taken in 1997 shows some colonization by epifauna and a greater diversity of animals *(Figure 10)*. Compared with Figure 9b, there were more sponges and bryozoans and more free-living species such as the crabs, scallops, and sea urchins seen in Figure 10. So now, instead of only making comparisons between areas, we are able to follow the sites over time.

We have made preliminary comparisons of ecological indices at two sites. Site 17, which is inside closed area II, was previously disturbed. Site 18 is near site 17 and at the same depth, but outside the closure. We think that site 18 was not heavily fished prior to the closure, but has seen an increase in fishing since then, because effort has been displaced from inside closed area II to around its sides. After the closure, we would expect to see benthic epifauna increase in site 17 relative to site 18. In fact we have already seen significant increases in epifaunal abundance, biomass, and species diversity relative to site 18 (J. Collie unpublished data). We are continuing to follow this site, and based on our preliminary observations, we expect to see a continued divergence in these ecological indices between the two sites.

CONCLUSIONS

Studies conducted to date indicate significant impacts of bottom fishing gear on benthic habitats in New England, particularly habitats with three-dimensional structure. Hard bottoms (e.g., boulders on Jeffreys Bank and the gravel pavement on northern Georges Bank) support complex epifaunal communities that are removed by bottom fishing. In contrast, mobile sand habitats that cover a large area of Georges Bank and parts of Stellwagen Bank are less vulnerable to gear impacts because the sediments are periodically resuspended by severe storms. A logical next step is to categorize habitats according to their vulnerability to disturbance.

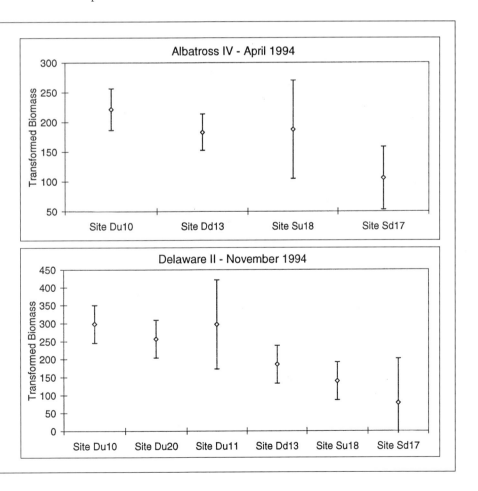

FIGURE 7. **Biomass of benthic megafauna from northeastern Georges Bank. Box-Cox transformation ($\lambda=0.5$) was applied to g per m³. Symbols represent mean and 95 percent confidence intervals. Site identifiers as in Figure 6. Reprinted with permission from Collie *et al.* (1997).**

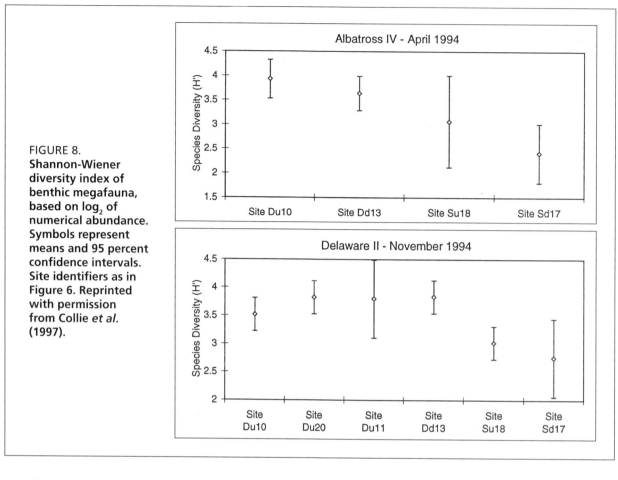

FIGURE 8. Shannon-Wiener diversity index of benthic megafauna, based on log$_2$ of numerical abundance. Symbols represent means and 95 percent confidence intervals. Site identifiers as in Figure 6. Reprinted with permission from Collie *et al.* (1997).

The ecological consequences of fishing gear disturbance are reductions in habitat complexity and in biodiversity. Juvenile stages of commercially important fishes depend on these complex habitats for protection from predators and for food from prey that live on the epifaunal species (Collie *et al.* 1997). Another important research priority for defining Essential Fish Habitat is to establish the relationships between habitat condition and fish productivity.

The management implications of these gear impact studies were anticipated with remarkable prescience by Alexander *et al.* (1914) in their report on the otter trawl fishery. In their words, "Our present information indicates that it is not fishing with the otter trawl but overfishing which is to be guarded against." One might counter this statement by noting that some modern trawls (e.g., rock-hopper and street-sweeper gear) are more injurious than trawls used in 1914. However, to a large extent it is the cumulative impact of bottom fishing, rather than the characteristics of particular gear, that affects benthic communities. To this end, the effort reduction and area closures

implemented under Amendment 7 to the Northeast Multispecies Fishery Management Plan should reduce the impacts of bottom fishing.

Alexander *et al.* (1914) also recommended that "the restriction of the use of the otter trawl to certain definite banks and grounds appears the most reasonable, just, and feasible method of regulation which has presented itself to us." Recent gear impact studies have identified habitats that are more vulnerable to bottom fishing disturbance. The Essential Fish Habitat amendments to fishery management plans are expected to identify habitats that warrant extra protection. Restricting the use of otter trawls and other bottom fishing gear involves allocating harvest among gear sectors, and in making these allocation decisions, it is easy to lose sight of the underlying conservation issues. Perhaps this explains why the recommendation made by Alexander *et al.* (1914) 84 years ago is not in force today. However, given the new mandate in the Magnuson-Stevens Act to identify and protect essential fish habitat, it is time to reconsider marine protected areas as management tools.

FIGURE 9. Photographs of the gravel habitat on northern Georges Bank. A. (above) Gravel pavement in an undredged area, site 20. Abundant hydroids and tubes of the worm *Filograna implexa* are attached to the gravel. Visible in the center of the photograph are a horse mussel, northern red anemone, and toad crab. B. (below) Gravel pavement in a dredged area, west of site 17, outside closed area II. There are few attached organisms on the gravel, and few animals apart from burrowing anemones and a juvenile scallop. Photographs by Page Valentine and Dann Blackwood, U.S. Geological Survey.

PRINTED IN COLOR ON PAGE 159.

REFERENCES

Alexander, A. B. 1914. Otter-trawl fishery. Pp. 1-97 in *Report of the U.S. Commissioner of Fisheries*, Appendix VI.

Auster, P. J., R. J. Malatesta, R. W. Langton, L. Watling, P. C. Valentine, C. L. S. Donaldson, E. W. Langton, A.N. Shepard, and I. G. Babb. 1996. The impacts of mobile fishing gear on sea floor habitats in the Gulf of Maine (Northwest Atlantic): Implications for conservation of fish populations. *Rev. Fish. Sci.,* 4:185-202.

Collie, J. S., G. A. Escanero, L. Hunke, and P. C. Valentine. 1996. Scallop dredging on Georges Bank: photographic evaluation of effects on benthic epifauna. *ICES C.M. 1996*/Mini:9.

Collie, J. S., G. A. Escanero, and P. C. Valentine. 1997. Effects of bottom fishing on the benthic megafauna of Georges Bank. *Mar. Ecol. Prog. Ser.* 155:159-172.

Figure 10. **Photograph of the gravel habitat on northern Georges Bank at site 17, taken in July 1997, 2.5 years after the area was closed to bottom fishing. Photograph by Page Valentine and Dann Blackwood, U.S. Geological Survey. Sponges, bryozoans, crabs, scallops, and sea urchins show evidence of partial recovery at this site.**

PRINTED IN COLOR ON PAGE 160.

Studies in Eastern Canada on the Impact of Mobile Fishing Gear on Benthic Habitat and Communities

Donald C. Gordon Jr., Peter Schwinghamer, Terrence W. Rowell, Jens Prena, Kent Gilkinson, W. Peter Vass and David L. McKeown

DEPARTMENT OF FISHERIES AND OCEANS, CANADA

ABSTRACT

Since 1990, the Department of Fisheries and Oceans has been conducting an experimental program on the impacts of mobile fishing gear on benthic ecosystems in Atlantic Canada. Much of the initial effort went into developing the imaging and sampling technology needed to conduct controlled disturbance experiments on continental shelf benthic ecosystems. The major accomplishment to date has been a three-year experiment (1993–1995) on the effects of otter trawling on a sandy bottom ecosystem of the Grand Banks of Newfoundland (120–146 m depth). Each year, three 13-km corridors were trawled 12 times with an Engel 145 otter trawl equipped with rock-hopper footgear, which created a disturbance zone on the order of 120 to 250 m wide. Side scan sonar, RoxAnn™, DRUMS™ and video imagery observations clearly indicated that the experimental trawling changed physical habitat structure, but sediment grain size was not affected. The biomass of epibenthic organisms in the trawl bycatch decreased significantly with repeated trawling, and an influx of scavenging snow crabs was observed after six trawl sets (approximately 10–12 h). Total biomass of invertebrates, as sampled by an epibenthic sled, was on average 25 percent lower in trawled corridors than in adjacent, untrawled reference corridors, and this difference was statistically significant. The biomass of snow crabs, sand dollars, soft corals, and brittle stars was significantly lower in trawled corridors. In addition, sand dollars, sea urchins, and brittle stars showed significant levels of physical damage. No significant effects of trawling were apparent in the four dominant mollusc species collected by the epibenthic sled. An extensive series of grab samples was also collected, and data are currently being analyzed. Two new mobile gear experiments are being planned for the Scotian Shelf. The first will be another otter trawling experiment on a gravel bottom area on Western Bank. The second will be a hydraulic clam dredging experiment on Banquereau Bank.

INTRODUCTION

Since 1990, a Department of Fisheries and Oceans (DFO) research program has been investigating the impacts of mobile fishing gear on benthic marine ecosystems in Atlantic Canada (Messieh *et al.* 1991). Specific objectives have included the following: 1) obtaining quantitative information on the impacts of mobile fishing gear on benthic habitat (both physical structure and biological communities), 2) obtaining quantitative information on the recovery rate of benthic habitat after disturbance by mobile fishing gear, and 3) developing new instrumentation for viewing and sampling marine benthic habitat in order to quantify its productive capacity. This program has involved a large number of DFO scientists and engineers and has benefited from support provided by the Geological Survey of Canada (Atlantic), various contractors, and numerous European colleagues. Research to date has concentrated on investigating the impacts of otter trawls, but future plans call for studies with hydraulic clam dredges and scallop rakes. The initial experiments were conducted in the intertidal region of the Bay of Fundy (Brylinsky *et al.* 1994), while more recent efforts have concentrated on offshore fishing banks. This paper briefly summarizes some of the instrumentation that has been developed, describes a three-year otter trawling experiment that has been conducted on the Grand Banks of Newfoundland, presents plans for further experiments, and identifies some important information gaps on this issue.

INSTRUMENTATION

Four different kinds of instrumentation for sampling and/or imaging benthic habitat and communities have been improved and/or developed. They are described in detail by Rowell *et al.* (1997).

BRUTIV (Benthic Referenced Underwater Towed Instrumented Vehicle—Substantial improvements have been made to an earlier model of BRUTIV including the purchase of a new winch and cable and improved video camera. BRUTIV is now operational and can be towed at a speed of several knots just a few meters off the sea bed to obtain color video imagery of benthic habitat and large epibenthic organisms (such as sand dollars, crabs, scallops) over several kilometers of sea floor.

Epibenthic Sled—An epibenthic sled is a device for sampling organisms living on or near the sediment surface. It is pulled over the sea floor for a short distance (i.e., 50 m), and a cutting blade in front directs sediment and benthic animals into a steel collection box with 1 cm holes. Substantial improvements have been made to the Aquareve III epibenthic sled to make it more quantitative. These improvements include stability wings, wider skis, narrower mouth (0.34 m), positively closing door and improved video system to monitor performance. Procedures were

developed for safely handling the sled at sea and hitting a small target area on the sea bed from a moving ship.

Videograb— A completely new video-equipped 0.5 m² grab with hydraulically operated jaws has been designed and built to collect sediment and associated organisms specifically for this project. To accommodate the 800-m cable, it was necessary to design and construct a new winch, which has its own self-contained power supply. The new system has remote controls that allow a scientist in the ship's laboratory to take over operation of the grab winch once the bottom comes into view. The position and operation of the grab is monitored by video, and, with practice, it can be landed in microhabitats of choice on the sea floor. If there are problems with closure, the grab can be raised off the bottom, opened hydraulically, and landed again in a different area. Procedures have been developed for safely handling the grab at sea.

DRUMS (Dynamically Responding Underwater Matrix Sonar)—The DRUMS™ acoustic imaging system has been developed specifically for this project under contract by Guigné International, Ltd. It utilizes new technology in broad frequency spectrum, narrow beam acoustics to provide high resolution measurement of sediment habitat structure. It is currently mounted on the videograb, but plans are underway to deploy it as a stand-alone instrument. Further details on DRUMS and its application are given in Schwinghamer *et al.* (1996).

Use of the above instrumentation in mobile gear impact experiments requires the ability to position it accurately on the sea bed. This was done using dGPS (differential Global Positioning System) for accurate positioning of the research vessel (to within 3 to 4 m), an ORE Trackpoint acoustic positioning system for recording the position of sampling equipment relative to the ship (to within 4 to 20 m, depending upon distance from the ship), and the AGC navigation system for the display and logging of navigation data. Details of this equipment are provided by McKeown and Gordon (1997).

The development and application of this instrumentation could not have been carried out without the collaboration of the Ocean Science Division (Bedford Institute of Oceanography (BIO)), the Engineering and Technical Services Division (BIO), the Geological Survey of Canada Atlantic (BIO), Guigné International, Ltd., and other contractors. This instrumentation has generated considerable interest in the international scientific community, and many inquiries have been received concerning its availability for other applications. This instrumentation will be valuable for investigating a wide spectrum of benthic habitat issues.

GRAND BANKS OTTER TRAWLING EXPERIMENT

A three-year otter trawling impact experiment was conducted at a site in 120 to 146 m of water on the Grand Banks of Newfoundland between 1993 and 1995 *(Figure 1)*. Reasons for selecting this site are provided by Prena *et al.* (1996). A 10 × 10 nautical mile experimental box was established and has been closed to all fishing activity indefinitely. This site had not been fished intensively for over ten years. The sea bed is a homogeneous, well-sorted, fine sand sediment. The benthic community is species rich (~238 macrofaunal species), high in biomass (~1 kg wet wt per m²) and relatively homogeneous.

Experimental design is described in detail by Rowell *et al.* (1997). Within the experimental box, three 13 km long corridors *(Figure 1)* were trawled 12 times each year with an Engel 145 otter trawl (equipped with rockhopper foot gear) by the CSS *Wilfred Templeman*. This gear is standard for both commercial fishing and, until 1995, DFO research surveys in the Newfoundland Region. Parallel reference corridors were established 300 m to one side. In 1995, a RoxAnn™ (Marine Micro Systems, Ltd., Aberdeen, Scotland) acoustic bottom classification system was used to determine whether the trawling produced a noticeable change in bottom acoustic characteristics. The trawl catch (both fish and invertebrates) of each set was sorted by species and weighed in the shipboard laboratory.

The CSS *Parizeau* was used to collect information on benthic habitat and communities before and after each trawling event in the experimental corridors as well as in the parallel reference corridors. An additional cruise was run in September 1993 to collect data two months after the initial trawling event. Sampling consisted of side scan sonar surveys, BRUTIV video surveys, epibenthic sled, and video-grab (equipped with DRUMS). Invertebrates were sorted by species and damage categories, counted and weighed.

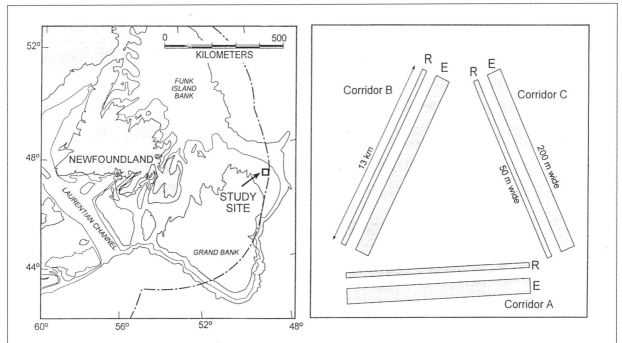

FIGURE 1. **Location of the study site on the Grand Banks of Newfoundland, and orientation of the three experiment (E) and reference (R) corridors.**

The impacts of trawling on physical habitat were clearly demonstrated. Trawl marks were readily apparent in the side scan sonar surveys immediately after trawling and in some instances were still faintly visible after one year. RoxAnn data indicated an increase in the E2 signal (proxy for sediment disturbance) with consecutive trawl sets. DRUMS data demonstrated that trawling reduced the complexity of small scale internal sediment structure down to a depth of 4.5 cm. Video footage from BRUTIV indicated that the properties of surface sediment are more uniform in trawled corridors compared to reference corridors. High resolution video observations made with the videograb indicated that trawling reduces biogenic sediment structures and the abundance of flocculated organic matter. There was no significant effect of trawling on sediment grain size, but natural inter-annual variations were detected.

The biomass of epibenthic organisms caught in the otter trawl (< 20 kg wet weight per 13 km set) decreased significantly with repeated trawling, especially in the first six sets. An influx of scavenging snow crabs (*Chionoecetes opilio*) was observed during the later trawl sets (approximately 10–12 h after trawling began). The catch of the three dominant invertebrate species in the trawl bycatch (snow crab, the sea urchin *Strongylocentrotus pallidus,* and the basket star *Gorgonocephalus arcticus*) declined steadily over the three years. The fish catch was very low (< 25 kg wet weight per 13 km set) and also declined steadily over the three years.

The dominant organisms caught in the epibenthic sled were sand dollars (*Echinarachnius parma*), sea urchins, brittle stars (*Ophiura sarsi*), snow crabs, soft corals (*Gersemia* sp.), and four species of molluscs (*Astarte borealis, Clinocardium ciliatum, Cyclocardia novangliae* and *Margarites sordidus*). The total biomass of organisms sampled by the epibenthic sled was on average 25% lower in the trawled corridors compared to reference corridors. However, unlike the trawl catch, the sled catch did not decrease significantly from 1993 to 1995. The biomass of sand dollars, brittle stars, snow crabs, and soft corals was significantly lower in the trawled corridors. Some of the sand dollars, sea urchins, and brittle stars were physically damaged by trawling. There were also indications of size-specific impacts, especially on sand

dollars which were significantly smaller in trawled corridors. There was no apparent significant effect of trawling on the four dominant mollusc species.

Under contract to DFO, C-CORE (Centre for Cold Ocean Research Engineering at Memorial University) has conducted a series of laboratory experiments to study the physical interaction of an otter trawl door with a simulated Grand Banks sandy sea bed containing bivalve molluscs planted at different depths. It was observed that considerable displacement of molluscs occurred along with sand in the fluidized zone in front of the moving door, which resulted in a low incidence of damage (Gilkinson *et al.* 1997). These experimental observations support the field observations of little damage to molluscs.

The extensive database of epibenthic and infaunal invertebrates collected with the video grab (200 samples) is currently being analyzed.

FUTURE PLANS

The experience gained by DFO scientists in conducting this program to date will be applied to future experiments on different kinds of sea beds and with different kinds of fishing gear in Atlantic Canada. In 1996, a cruise explored potential study sites for future experiments on the Scotian Shelf. Surveys were conducted at various sites on Emerald Bank, Western Bank, Sable Island Bank, and Banquereau using the same instrumentation as in the Grand Banks experiment. On the basis of this experience and input from managers and industry, it is proposed to conduct two new mobile gear impact experiments. The first, which began in October 1997, will investigate the effects of an otter trawl on an area of gravel bottom on Western Bank that is within the 4TVW Haddock Nursery Area, which has been closed to mobile groundfish gear since 1987 to protect immature haddock from capture in trawls.

The second experiment, scheduled to begin in 1998, will investigate the effects of a hydraulic clam dredge on the sandy bottom of Banquereau in collaboration with the fishing industry.

INFORMATION GAPS

There are several information gaps that have to be filled before the effects of mobile gear on the sustainability of marine habitat and fisheries can be fully understood. Because the effects vary depending upon the type of gear, the kind of habitat and the species present, it is necessary to conduct additional well-designed experiments with other kinds of gear and on other kinds of bottom. International scientific collaboration in sharing equipment, experience, and data is important. Once the effects of different kinds of mobile gear on benthic habitat and communities are better understood, it will be important to determine if these effects have important consequences for commercial fisheries. For example, will changes in physical habitat structure change the vulnerability of small fish to predation? Will commercial species of fish find better feeding conditions because trawls may make benthic prey more available, or poorer feeding conditions because trawls may reduce populations of benthic prey? As they become available, the results of this research will be incorporated into the fisheries management process to ensure that the best decisions are made to protect the long term sustainability of fisheries resources and the habitat supporting them.

REFERENCES

Brylinsky, M., J. Gibson and D.C. Gordon Jr. 1994. Impacts of flounder trawls on the intertidal habitat and community of the Minas Basin, Bay of Fundy. *Can. J. Fish. Aquat. Sci.* 51:650-661.

Gilkinson, K., M. Paulin, S. Hurley, and P. Schwinghamer. 1997. Impacts of trawl door scouring on infaunal bivalves: results of a physical trawl door model/dense sand interactions. *J. Exp. Mar. Biol. Ecol.* 224:291-312.

McKeown, D.L. and D.C. Gordon Jr. 1997. Grand Banks otter trawling impact experiment: II. Navigation procedures and results. *Can. Tech. Rep. Fish. Aquat. Sci.* 2159:xi + 79 pp.

Messieh, S. N., T.W. Rowell, D.L. Peer, and P.J. Cranford. 1991. The effects of trawling, dredging and ocean dumping on the eastern Canadian continental shelf sea bed. *Cont. Shelf Res.* 11:1237-1263.

Prena, J., T.W. Rowell, P. Schwinghamer, K. Gilkinson and D.C. Gordon Jr. 1996. Grand Banks otter trawling experiment: I. Site selection process, with a description of macrofaunal communities. *Can. Tech. Rep. Fish. Aquat. Sci.* 2094:viii + 38 pp.

Rowell, T.W., P. Schwinghamer, M. Chin-Yee, K. Gilkinson, D.C. Gordon Jr., E. Hartgers, M. Hawryluk, D.L. McKeown, J. Prena, D.P. Reimer, G. Sonnichsen, G. Steeves, W.P. Vass, R. Vine and P. Woo. 1997. Grand Banks otter trawling impact experiment: III. Sampling equipment, experimental design, and methodology. *Can. Tech. Rep. Fish. Aquat. Sci.* 2190:viii + 36 pp.

Schwinghamer, P., J.Y. Guigné, and W.C. Siu. 1996. Quantifying the impact of trawling on benthic habitat structure using high resolution acoustics and chaos theory. *Can. J. Fish. Aquat. Sci.* 53:288-296.

Ecosystem Effects of Demersal Fishing: A European Perspective

Stuart I. Rogers

THE CENTRE FOR ENVIRONMENT, FISHERIES AND AQUACULTURE SCIENCE, LOWESTOFT LABORATORY, LOWESTOFT, UNITED KINGDOM.

Michel J. Kaiser

THE CENTRE FOR ENVIRONMENT, FISHERIES AND AQUACULTURE SCIENCE, CONWY LABORATORY, CONWY, UNITED KINGDOM.

Simon Jennings

SCHOOL OF BIOLOGICAL SCIENCES, UNIVERSITY OF EAST ANGLIA, NORWICH, UNITED KINGDOM.

ABSTRACT

This paper reviews the most recent developments in European research on the ecosystem effects of demersal trawling. We provide a summary of the most prevalent demersal gear types in the waters of northwestern Europe, and show how the perceived effects of these gears on the sea bed has stimulated interest in the potential for damage to benthic communities. There has been a rapid increase in experimental work on the short term effects of trawling on nontarget communities since the 1970s. Some of the more recent studies are described and related to the main focus of interest, the North Sea marine ecosystem. New techniques for describing the structure and diversity of marine assemblages focus on the impact of fishing on the size structure of populations, and identify fish species which may be most vulnerable through unfavorable life history characteristics. The utility of these measures is described.

INTRODUCTION

Fishing in European waters has had a long history, with much of the activity before 1900 centered on the southern North Sea and in the coastal waters of the industrialized nations of northwest Europe (Wood 1956; *Figure 1*). Important technical developments occurred at the end of the nineteenth century, including the development of steam trawlers and the otter trawl (1870–1890). These improvements in fishing technology have continued to the present day, resulting in greatly increased levels of fishing intensity (Wood 1956). For demersal fisheries, an important development was the modern heavy beam trawl in the 1960s, which led directly to a targeted flatfish fishery for sole (*Solea solea*) initially in the shallow and predominantly sandy coastal waters of the eastern North Sea, but later throughout most of the southern North Sea (Millner and Whiting 1996). The earliest studies into the direct effects of trawling on the sea bed were conducted in the North Sea, and these provided basic information such as the depth to which trawls penetrated the substrate, and the number and identity of nontarget benthic biota removed from the sea bed. The majority of early published work in Europe on the effects of demersal gears examined the effects of beam trawl disturbance on the benthic infauna and scavenger populations (*Table 1*). While developing these fields of research, subsequent studies

TABLE 1
The major studies undertaken or currently in progress in northern Europe that examine the effects of physical disturbance of benthic communities by mobile demersal fishing gear.

	Gear Studied	Area	Main Objectives	Date
1950–1970	Otter trawl	North Sea	Benthic bycatch	1955
1970–1980	Beam trawl	North Sea	Benthic bycatch	1971
	Beam trawl	North Sea	Penetration of gear into sediment	1972
1980–1990	Scallop dredge	Irish Sea	Physical damage to epifauna	1985
	Hydraulic dredge	North Sea	Changes in infauna	1990
	Beam trawl	North Sea	Changes in benthic communities	1990
1990–1997	Beam trawl	North Sea	Changes in benthic communities	1991
	Otter trawl	North Sea	Damage to infauna caused by different parts of the gear	1991
	Beam trawl	North Sea	Catch composition, survival of bycatch and macroinfauna	1992
	Scallop dredge	Scottish sea loch	Changes in epifauna and infauna	1992
	Demersal trawls	North Sea	Use of wrecks as control areas	1993
	Beam trawl	Irish Sea	Scavenger aggregation in trawled areas	1994
	Beam trawls	North & Irish Sea	Effects of beam trawling on the sea bed	1994
	Beam trawls	North Sea	Incidence of damage in bivalve shells	1994
	Scallop dredge	Irish Sea	Changes in epibenthic communities	1994
	Beam trawl	Irish Sea	Survival of benthic bycatch	1995
	Scallop dredge	Clyde Sea	Effects of dredging on maerl beds	1995
	Scallop dredge	Irish Sea	Benthic bycatches and survival	1996
	Beam trawl	Irish Sea	Changes in macroinfauna, scavenger aggregation in trawled areas, incidence of damaged mobile epifauna	1996
	Beam trawl	North Sea	Micro-distribution of fishing effort	1996
	Beam trawl	Irish Sea	Intra- and interspecific competition between scavengers in different habitats	1996
	Various	Irish Sea	Comparison of disturbance effects by different years	1997
	Beam trawl	Irish Sea	Changes in epifaunal communities and scavenger populations	1997
	Beam trawl	North Sea	Historical changes in epifauna	1997
	Various	North & Irish Sea	Effects of bottom trawling on the sea bed	1997
In progress	Various	UK waters	Bivalves and echinoderms as indicators of fishing disturbance	
	Otter trawls	NW Mediterranean	Effects of trawling on infauna and sediment	
	Otter trawls	North Sea	Long term effects of trawling estimated from flatfish stomach contents data	
	Scallop dredge	Irish Sea	Long term effects of different intensities of dredging effort and seasonal variation	
	Beam trawl	UK Waters	Time-series changes in fish populations	

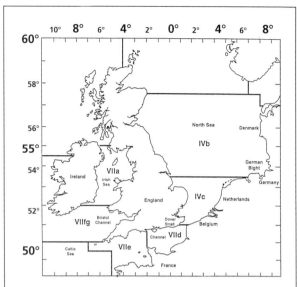

FIGURE 1. **Map of the continental shelf seas of the eastern North Atlantic, showing some place names of interest. The Roman numerals refer to fisheries stock assessment divisions used by the International Council for the Exploration of the Seas (ICES). Reprinted with permission from Rogers *et al.* 1998a.**

have also concentrated on the wider implications of demersal trawling, such as the physical disturbance to the sea bed, the discarding of fish and benthos, and the damage to organisms in the path of the gear, which make food available to other members of the ecosystem (Hall *et al.* 1993; Jennings and Kaiser 1998). The rapid increase in the amount of published work in the 1990s was partly a consequence of an international recognition of the importance of the field, and the increased cooperation between the research institutes of European Union member countries. Despite clear, and in many cases quantifiable, effects, it has still been difficult to separate the effects of commercial fisheries from natural fluctuations in reproductive success and predator-prey interactions.

Recent international cooperation through the International Council for the Exploration of the Sea (ICES) has enabled estimates of total international catch-at-age to be produced for most of the major stocks, and the time-series of fishing mortalities derived from these data have proved valuable in assessing the effect of fishing on stock size. In addition to the removal of the target species from the community, fishing has other effects on the ecosystem, yet fisheries management tools are generally not yet able to

address these wider issues. A recent feature of assessments and resulting management advice has been the inclusion of such factors as, for example, predator-prey interactions in stock assessments and forecasts, using multispecies virtual population analysis (MSVPA) (Gislason and Helgason 1985; Rice and Gislason 1996). This is a step towards a more integrated approach to population and ecosystem management.

THE DIRECT EFFECTS OF FISHING

Many different types of demersal fishing gear are used in European waters of which scallop dredges, otter trawls and beam trawls disturb the largest areas of sea bed annually (ICES 1995). This section describes how these gears are designed to catch their target species, and explains the direct consequences of these features for the target and the nontarget demersal communities.

Gear design—The boards of otter trawls can weigh several tons in air and are considered to be the most destructive part of this gear (Jones 1992). Although the boards are fitted with metal shoes up to 30 cm wide in areas of soft sediment, Krost *et al.* (1990) estimated that otter boards penetrated soft mud to a depth of 15 cm in the Baltic Sea. Some otter trawls are modified to increase catch rates or range of use by the addition of tickler chains between the otter boards, large rubber discs (> 50 cm diameter), and metal bobbins weighing over 10 kg (rockhopper gear). These modifications increase the potential of the gear to impact the nontarget demersal population (Harden-Jones and Scholes 1974).

Beam trawls comprise a rigid beam to hold the net open, which itself is held off the sea bed by two beam shoes. Gear modifications have included increasing the beam width (to 12 m) and the addition of more tickler chains to disturb fish within the sediment, and the use of chain mats and flip-up ropes to allow access to rocky areas. Consequently, beam trawls have increased in weight from a mean of 3.5 metric tons (mt) in the 1960s (Cole 1971) up to 10 mt in the early 1980s (Beek *et al.* 1990). Beam trawlers in European waters target benthic species that are normally buried in or rest on surface sediments, such as the flatfishes, sole and plaice, *Pleuronectes platessa*, and shrimp, *Crangon crangon*. Varying numbers of tickler chains are fitted to the gear depending on the sediment characteristics of the fishing grounds; between 17 and 25 are used on some of the largest trawls (Polet *et al.* 1994). Increased weight of beams and towing power of modern trawlers has allowed these gears to be pulled at speeds of up to 8 knots.

There are two main types of dredge currently in operation—mechanical dredges, which dig target species out of the sediment, and hydraulic dredges, which remove target species along with the sediment and nontarget species. Some of the largest commercial hydraulic dredges are used in the Dutch Wadden Sea to harvest lugworms, *Arenicola marina*. The dredge head can leave furrows in the sediment 1 m wide and 40 cm deep (Beukema 1995). Similar devices are used to harvest cockles, *Cerastoderma edule* and, on a smaller scale, Manila clams, *Tapes philippinarum*, at mid to high tide on sandflats in northern Europe (Hall and Harding 1997; Kaiser *et al.* 1996). Suction dredges are also used on a much smaller scale by divers to remove razor clams, *Ensis siliqua*. Although the area disturbed is relatively small, pits are often excavated to depths of 60 cm (Hall *et al.* 1990).

Mechanical dredges are distinct from trawls because they dig into the substrate to remove infaunal bivalves and reach greater depths than those achieved by beam trawls. Most dredge designs incorporate long (< 30 cm) digging tooth bars, and as dredges tend to be used over rough grounds, steel ring bellies are usually fitted to the net bag. Large scallop boats can fish a total of between 36 to 40 dredges attached to beams, and the total width and weight of a set of scallop gear is comparable to that of a large beam trawl. Dredges are rarely towed at speeds in excess of 2.5 knots because the gear is less efficient at higher speeds (Caddy 1973; Dare *et al.* 1993). Consequently they disturb smaller areas of sea bed per 100 h fishing than beam trawls (ICES 1995; Jennings and Kaiser 1998).

The direct effects of these gears on infauna—Bycatches of nontarget infaunal species indicate the extent to which benthic communities are perturbed by a particular gear. For example, the occurrence of the infaunal bivalve, *Arctica islandica*, and the heart urchin, *Echinocardium cordatum*, in a 12 m beam trawl catch indicated that the tickler chains had penetrated hard sandy substrata to a depth of at least 6 cm (Bergman and Hup 1992). While it has been relatively simple to detect significant changes in the abundance of large macroinfauna as a result of fishing disturbance, smaller invertebrates (< 10 mm) show conflicting responses. Bergman and Hup (1992) found both decreases and increases in the abundance of small invertebrates after fishing an area of the sea bed with a beam trawl. Kaiser and Spencer (1996) studied the effects of beam trawl disturbance at a site 27 to 40 m deep in the Irish Sea. Their experimental area encompassed two distinct habitats—(1) stable sediments composed of coarse sand, gravel, and shell debris, which supported a rich epifaunal filter-feeding community of soft corals and hydroids, and (2) mobile sediments characterized by ribbons of megaripples with few sessile epifaunal species. Despite a robust experimental design with paired treatment and control areas, the effects of beam trawl disturbance were undetectable in the mobile sediments. This is not surprising given the levels of natural disturbance experienced by fauna living in megaripple habitats (Shepherd 1983). In addition, animals living in the troughs of megaripples are less likely to be disturbed as the fishing gear rides over the crest of each sand wave. Conversely, in stable sediments the effects of fishing are more noticeable. Kaiser and Spencer (1996) found that the number of species and individuals in the stable sediment community was reduced by a half and a third respectively. Their analysis also revealed that less common species were most severely depleted by beam trawling.

It is likely that the effects of physical disturbance will be short-lived in communities adapted to frequent natural perturbations, in contrast to those communities found in habitats exposed to fewer disturbances. In addition, in naturally disturbed areas the role of trawl impact in structuring the community will be correspondingly smaller. An extreme example of this situation is Hall and Harding's (1997) study of the effects of mechanical and suction dredging and the scale of disturbance on intertidal benthic communities in the Solway Firth, Scotland. The immediate effects of cockle harvesting produced a drastic reduction in the abundance of individuals; however, the community in disturbed areas was comparable to that in similar undisturbed areas after only eight weeks. This rapid recolonization was attributed to the immigration of adult fauna (Hall and Harding 1997).

While the changes associated with disturbance are relatively short-lived for the majority of small species, longer-lived organisms recolonize more slowly. For example, Beukema (1995) reported that the biomass of gaper clams, *Mya arenaria*, took two years to recover after commercial lugworm dredging in areas of the Dutch Wadden Sea, whereas small polychaetes and bivalves had recolonized the dredged areas within 12 months.

In soft mud communities, a large proportion of the macrofauna live in burrows up to 2 m deep (Atkinson and Nash 1990). Consequently, few of these deep burrowers, such as thalassinid shrimps, are likely to be killed by passing trawls; however, diel variation in behavior may periodically increase the vulnerability of such species to fishing activities. These animals, along with other bioturbators, have an important role in maintaining the structure and oxygenation of muddy sediment habitats (Fenchel 1996; Rowden and Jones 1993). Any adverse effects of fishing on these organisms may lead to substantial changes in habitat complexity and community structure.

The direct effects of these gears on epifauna—The regular passage of trawl gears through areas of fragile or long-lived epibenthic invertebrates will have obvious implications for the diversity of this benthic community. Indeed, observations that epifaunal communities had been altered in heavily fished areas provided some of the first indications of the potential long term effects of fishing on benthos. For example, the disappearance of reefs of the calcareous tube-building worm, *Sabellaria spinulosa,* and their replacement by small polychaete communities indicated that dredging activity had caused measurable changes in the Wadden Sea benthic community (Riesen and Reise 1982). Despite this evidence, the long history of fishing activity in European waters suggests that other areas which supported biogenic, epibenthic communities may already have been altered.

Many long-lived epifaunal organisms perform a structural role within benthic communities, providing a microhabitat for a large number of species

(Nalesso *et al.* 1995). Loss of such structures will affect the survivorship of any associated species and prolong the recolonization process. Calcareous algae of the genus *Lithothamnion* (maerl) are amongst the oldest marine plants in Europe and provide a substratum that takes hundreds of years to accumulate (Potin *et al.* 1990). The branching structure of each thallus provides a unique habitat for a diverse community of animals, including commercial species such as scallops, *Pecten maximus.* Not surprisingly, scallop dredging in this habitat causes destruction of the interstices between the thalli and causes long term changes to the composition of the associated benthic fauna (Hall-Spencer 1995).

There are few accounts of the physical contact of stationary gears (gillnets, tangle nets, pots) having measurable effects on benthic biota, as the area of sea bed affected by each gear is almost insignificant compared with the widespread effects of mobile fishing gears. A recent study evaluated the effects of pot deployment and retrieval on supposedly fragile epifauna that are the subject of conservation interest in northern Europe (Eno *et al.* 1996). Not surprisingly, pots that landed on or were hauled through beds of the foliose bryozoan, *Pentapora foliacea,* caused physical damage to the colonies. However, contrary to expectations, sea pens, *Pennatula phosphorea, Virgularia mirabilis* and *Funiculina quadrangularis,* and sea fans, *Eunicella verrucosa,* were found to be less vulnerable than anticipated (Eno *et al.* 1996).

Many of the mobile epibenthic invertebrate fauna of the European Continental Shelf are scavengers of both discards and damaged fauna, and their presence is often indicative of areas of trawl disturbance (Berghahn 1990; Britton and Morton 1994; Collie *et al.* 1997; Kaiser and Spencer 1996; Ramsay *et al.* 1997a). After the initial disturbance or the arrival of a food fall on the sea bed, a succession of scavenger aggregation occurs that relates to their background abundance, speed of movement, and the prevailing current conditions (Nickell and Moore 1992; Ramsay *et al.* 1996; Sainte-Marie 1986; Sainte-Marie and Hargrave 1987). Experiments using traps baited with either dead fish or swimming crabs (animals typically killed by trawling) revealed distinct feeding preferences among different scavenger species. Hermit crabs preferred dead fish and avoided pots baited with dead crabs, whereas whelks showed the opposite responses (Ramsay *et al.* 1997b).

THE EFFECT OF DEMERSAL TRAWLS ON FINFISH ASSEMBLAGES

The direct effects of trawling on target species is clear and has resulted in high levels of fishing effort on most of the important European stocks. The development of the heavy beam trawl in the 1960s allowed the introduction of a targeted flatfish beam trawl fishery in an area of the southern North Sea that had already experienced constant otter trawling effort for many years previously (Millner and Whiting 1996; Rijnsdorp and Leewen 1996) *(Figure 2)*. Another important direct effect of fishing is that it has provided food for other species in the ecosystem by discarding unwanted bycatch and by killing benthic animals in the passage of the gear.

Recent studies of long time-series of data, some taken in research vessel cruises before the first World War, have revealed patterns in fish abundance which cannot always be associated with the deleterious effects of commercial fisheries (Daan *et al.* 1990; Rijnsdorp *et al.* 1996; Walker and Heessen 1996). One group that is considered vulnerable to the effects of increased fishing effort are the elasmobranchs, which generally have low fecundity and high age and length at maturity. However, not all species appear equally sensitive, and those with a relatively low length at maturity such as the starry ray, *Raja radiata*, have proved to be resilient (Brander 1981; ICES 1996; Walker and Heessen 1996). Survival experiments using fish bycatch taken from beam trawls have shown mortality rates of up to 40% for *Raja neavus*, compared with higher rates of 60 to 90% for dragonet, *Callionymus lyra*, and for plaice and dab, *Limanda limanda* (Kaiser and Spencer 1995).

In the 1960s and 1970s an increase in growth rate was reported for both plaice and sole (Bannister 1978; Rijnsdorp and Beek 1991) which could not be related to changes in temperature, but which did coincide with increases in both beam trawl effort and eutrophication in coastal waters. There is some evidence that eutrophication has enhanced populations of polychaetes and brittle stars in coastal waters, thereby increasing the food supply for fish (Duineveld *et al.* 1987; Heessen and Daan 1996; Rijnsdorp and Leewen 1996). Some of the most important consequences for the production of demersal benthic organisms result from the presence on the sea bed of (1) damaged or dead organisms resulting from the passage of the trawl and (2) discarded target and nontarget species

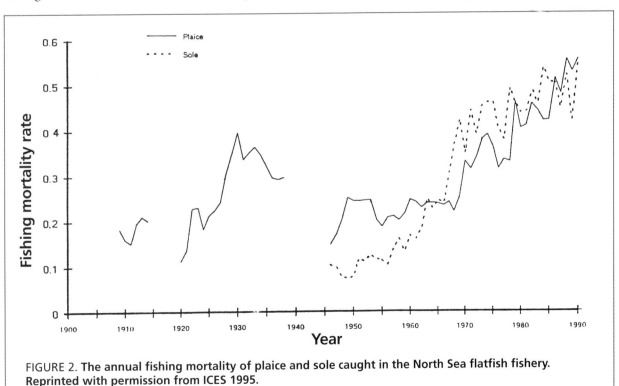

FIGURE 2. **The annual fishing mortality of plaice and sole caught in the North Sea flatfish fishery. Reprinted with permission from ICES 1995.**

(bycatch) (ICES 1995). It is estimated that 475,000 mt of fish, offal, and benthic invertebrates are discarded in the North Sea annually (Camphuysen *et al.* 1993). Kaiser and Spencer (1994) observed 35 times as many fish aggregating over a recently beam trawled line compared with adjacent unfished areas, which implied that fish moved into areas of disturbance. Similarly, gadoids were observed to aggregate around newly disturbed pits in sandy sediments (Hall *et al.* 1993). Analysis of plaice and sole growth rate confirmed that increases for intermediate plaice size classes (15–30 cm) may have been due to a combination of beam trawl and eutrophication effects because of the spatial overlap of these effects and of these fish size classes (Rijnsdorp and Leewen 1996; Rijnsdorp and Millner 1996). Increases in mean length at age for sole since the 1960s was significantly correlated with increased beam trawl effort (Millner and Whiting 1996). Although the small mouth size of sole suggests that this species may not be able to benefit directly from damaged benthos, the longer term effect of trawling would tend to encourage smaller opportunistic benthic invertebrates, which form a large part of its diet. As the fishery operates outside the 12-mile limit, these effects would tend to benefit older individuals *(Figure 3;* Millner and Whiting 1996).

Dietary analyses of gurnards (*Trigla* spp.) and whiting *(Merlangius merlangus)* caught on recently beam trawled and undisturbed areas also revealed that both species consumed significantly greater numbers of the amphipod, *Ampelisca spinipes*, within the fished area. This amphipod constructs a tube that protrudes from the surface of the sea bed, which makes it vulnerable to contact with bottom fishing gear. Interestingly, gurnards normally eat large prey items such as shrimps, *Crangon* spp., and swimming crabs, *Liocarcinus* spp., but preferentially selected *A. spinipes* when feeding within the trawl tracks.

This switch in diet implied that large numbers of amphipods were made available to predatory fish as a result of trawling (Hughes and Croy 1993). Adult queen scallops, *Aequipecten opercularis,* do not occur in the diet of whiting under normal circumstances. However, the distinctive orange gonads of these bivalves were recorded in whiting stomach contents after trawling, indicating that these molluscs had been damaged by the trawl (Kaiser and Spencer

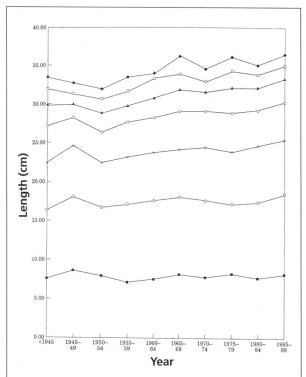

FIGURE 3. **Trends in mean length at age for female sole by five-year periods. Age is measured at the end of each year's growth for age zero (bottom of plot) to age six (top of plot). Reprinted with permission from Millnerand Whiting 1996.**

1994). Large numbers of the bivalve *A. islandica* are damaged by trawling at times of intensive otter trawling in Kiel Bay, and at these times this species is common in the stomach of cod, *Gadus morhua* (Arntz and Weber 1970).

Similar responses to fishing disturbance were also recorded for dab, which were attracted to animals damaged by the trawl within 20 minutes of its passage and increased to three times their former abundance after 24 h (Kaiser and Spencer 1996). In addition, the diet of dab captured in the trawled area consisted mainly of the oral discs of the brittle star, *Amphiura* spp., in contrast to those in adjacent undisturbed areas, which consumed only brittle star arms (Kaiser and Ramsay 1997).

CHANGES IN STRUCTURE OF DEMERSAL ASSEMBLAGES

Whereas populations of seabirds have shown clear responses to the extra food resources made available by discarding (Furness 1996), the consequences of discards, bycatch and animals damaged on the sea bed for other populations of benthic scavengers is less well understood. Increases in the abundance of small and nontarget species of fish (e.g. Norway pout, *Trisopterus esmarkii*, and dabs) have been linked to several environmental and human factors. Fisheries in the North Sea have removed a large proportion of major predatory species such as cod, thereby reducing predator pressure and competition from juveniles (ICES 1995). Analysis of groundfish assemblage data from the early part of the century in the northern North Sea showed that, although differences in community structure could be detected, the nontarget assemblage appeared to have remained relatively unchanged, despite a century of intensive fishing activity (Greenstreet and Hall 1996).

Recent efforts to understand changes to assemblage structure (ICES 1995) have concentrated on developing new ways of identifying patterns in species relative abundance. The nature of diversity indices suggests that no single index can convey all the information that is necessary when interpreting community dynamics, and that a number of different descriptors are often required to cover all aspects of observed variability (e.g. Warwick and Clark 1991, Rogers *et al.* 1998b). In this context the biomass or abundance size spectrum has proved a useful tool in the analysis of temporal patterns in fish populations, where changes in gradient of the log-linear transformation reflect changes in size composition of populations (Pope 1989; Pope and Knights 1982). A good example of this relationship was shown by Pope (1989) using the mean catch by size group of fish caught during the UK's North Sea groundfish survey (1979–89) and the USA's trawl survey on Georges Bank, which has been operating since 1963 *(Figure 4)*. In both areas, increased fishing pressure on larger fish resulted in a change in slope of the abundance/size class relationship and an increased abundance of smaller fish. On Georges Bank, this pattern was partly disguised by the replacement of some larger commercial species by other similar sized, but lightly fished species, such as elasmobranchs (Pope 1989; Rice and Gislason 1996). In the North Sea the progressive decline in abundance of large fish since the 1970s was attributed to increasing exploitation rates (Rice and Gislason 1996), yet the presence of areas without larger fish

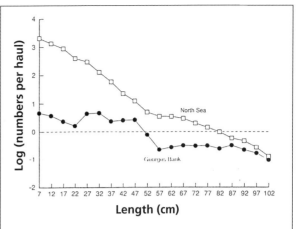

FIGURE 4. **Comparison of the total finfish catch at length per trawl haul on Georges Bank and in the North Sea. Reprinted with permission from Pope (1989).**

does not necessarily implicate fishing effort as the cause. Beam trawl survey data over a large area of the European continental shelf highlighted areas in the southern bight of the North Sea that were dominated by small individuals of large flatfish species (dab and plaice), which may be present in response to fishing activity. In other areas, however, there were sites with similar population structure which normally supported an abundance of juvenile fish and where the harmful effects of trawling were not apparent and not implicated (Rogers *et al.* 1998a). These results confirm the problem of interpreting changes in community structure and identifying a specific environmental or human factor as the cause (Daan *et al.* 1990).

CONCLUSIONS

Despite the long and relatively well-documented history of fishing in European waters, it is still very difficult to attribute the cause of long term population changes for all but a few of the most obvious cases. The variation in reproductive success of marine species is still the most destabilizing factor in exploited fish populations and is crucial in setting year class strength of all other benthic marine fauna (Daan *et al.* 1990). Analysis of long term data sets provides a useful insight into possible long term changes in target species associated with bottom fishing activity and can at least provide correlative associations with a range of factors, where clear causal relationships are more difficult to achieve. Recent history of fishing disturbance can be inferred from studies of species vulnerable to trawl damage, such as the extent of arm loss of starfish (*Asterias rubens*) and damage to the shell of *A. islandica* (Gaspar *et al.* 1994; Witbaard and Klein 1994). The observation by Pauly et al. (1998) that worldwide commercial exploitation of marine stocks has resulted in the exploitation of organisms at lower trophic levels suggests that direct and indirect threats to invertebrate infauna and epifauna will increase. Monitoring changes to these important functional groups is unlikely to be achieved as a byproduct of current surveys and will require targeted sampling programs. At the level of the entire finfish assemblage, spatial trends in structure need further interpretation using new indices of diversity (Rice and Gislason 1996) and, crucially, must be related to fishing effort data of higher resolution. Recent progress with mapping the microdistribution of beam trawlers during fishing operations has revealed the highly patchy distribution of the fleets, suggesting that corresponding data on population structure are required (Rijnsdorp and Leewen 1996).

ACKNOWLEDGMENTS

This work was funded by the Ministry of Agriculture, Fisheries and Food, UK under mou 'A'.

REFERENCES

Arntz, W. E., and W. Weber. 1970. *Cyprina islandica* (Mollusca: Bivalvia) als Nahrung von Dorsch und Kliesche in der Kieler Bucht. *Berichte der Deutschen Wissenschaftlichen Kommission für Meeresforschung* 21:193-209.

Atkinson, R. J. A., and R. D. M. Nash. 1990. Some preliminary observations on the burrows of *Callianassa subterranea* (Montagu) Decapoda: Thalassinidea) from the west coast of Scotland. *Journal of Natural History* 24:403-413.

Bannister, R. C. A. 1978. Changes in plaice stocks and plaice fisheries in the North Sea. *Rapp. P.v. Reun. Cons. perm. int. Explor. Mer* 172:86-101.

Beek, F. A. v., P. I. v. Leeuwen, and A. D. Rijnsdorp. 1990. On the survival of plaice and sole discards in the otter trawl and beam trawl fisheries in the North Sea. *Netherlands Journal of Sea Research* 26:151-160.

Berghahn, R. 1990. On the potential impact of shrimping on trophic relationships in the Wadden Sea. Pp. 130-140 in M. Barnes and R. N. Gibson, eds. *Trophic relationships in the marine environment.* Proceedings of the 24th European Marine Biology Symposium. Aberdeen University Press, Aberdeen.

Bergman, M. J. N., and M. Hup. 1992. Direct effects of beam trawling on macrofauna in a sandy sediment in the southern North Sea. *ICES Journal of Marine Science* 49:5-11.

Beukema, J. J. 1995. Long-term effects of mechanical harvesting of lugworms *Arenicola marina* on the zoobenthic community of a tidal flat in the Wadden Sea. *Netherlands Journal of Sea Research* 33:219-227.

Brander, K. 1981. Disappearance of common skate *Raia batis* from the Irish Sea. *Nature* 290:48-49.

Britton, J. C., and B. Morton. 1994. Marine carrion and scavengers. *Oceanography and Marine Biology: an Annual Review* 32:369-434.

Caddy, J. F. 1973. Underwater observations on tracks of dredges and trawls and some effects of dredging on a scallop ground. *Journal of the Fisheries Research Board of Canada* 30:173-180.

Camphuysen, C. J., K. Ensor, R. W. Furness, S. Garthe, O. Huppop, G. Leaper, H. Offringa, and M. L. Tasker. 1993. Seabirds feeding on discards in winter in the North Sea. Netherlands Institute for Sea Research, Den Burg, Texel.

Cole, H. A. 1971. The heavy tickler chain—right or wrong? *World Fishing* 10/1971:8-10.

Collie, J. S., G. A. Escanero, and P. C. Valentine. 1997. Effects of bottom fishing on the benthic megafauna of Georges Bank. *Mar. Ecol. Prog. Ser.* 155:159-172.

Daan, N., P. J. Bromley, J. R. G. Hislop, and N. A. Nielsen. 1990. Ecology of North Sea fish. *Netherlands Journal of Sea Research* 26:343-386.

Dare, P. J., D. Key, and P. M. Connor. 1993. The efficiency of spring-loaded dredges used in the western English Channel fishery for scallops, *Pecten maximus* (L.). International Council for the Exploration of the Sea 1993\B:15. 8 pp.

Duineveld, G. C. A., A. Künitzer, A., and R. P. Heyman. 1987. *Amphiura filiformis* (Ophiuroidea: Echinodermata) in the North Sea. Distribution, present and former abundance and size composition. *Netherlands Journal of Sea Research* 21:317-329.

Eno, N. C., D. MacDonald, and S. C. Amos. 1996. A study on the effects of fish (Crustacea/Mollusc) traps on benthic habitats and species. In *Report to European Commission Directorate General XIV*, Studies Contract 94/076. 43 pp.

Fenchel, T. 1996. Worm burrows and oxic microniches in marine sediments. 1. Spatial and temporal scales. *Marine Biology* 127:289-295.

Furness, R. W. 1996. A review of seabird responses to natural or fisheries-induced changes in food supply. Pp. 168-173 in S. P. R. Greenstreet and M. L. Tasker, eds., *Aquatic predators and their prey*. Blackwell Scientific Publications, Oxford.

Gaspar, M. B., C. A. Richardson, and C. C. Monteiro, C. C. 1994. The effects of dredging on shell formation in the razor clam *Ensis siliqua* from Barrinha, southern Portugal. *Journal of the Marine Biological Association of the United Kingdom* 74:927-938.

Gislason, H. and T. Helgason. 1985. Species interaction in assessments of fish stocks, with special application to the North Sea. *Dana* 5:1-44.

Greenstreet, S. P. R. and S. J. Hall. 1996 Fishing and the ground-fish assemblage structure in the north-western North Sea: an analysis of long-term and spatial trends. *Journal of Animal Ecology* 65:577-598.

Hall, S. J., D. J. Basford, and M. R. Robertson. 1990. The impact of hydraulic dredging for razor clams *Ensis* sp. on an infaunal community. *Netherlands Journal of Sea Research* 27:119-125.

Hall, S. J., and M. J. C. Harding. 1997. Physical disturbance and marine benthic communities: the effects of mechanical harvesting of cockles on non-target benthic infauna. *Journal of Applied Ecology* 34:497-517.

Hall, S. J., D. Raffaelli, and S. F. Thrush. 1993. Patchiness and disturbance in shallow water benthic assemblages. Pp. 333-376 in P. S. Giller, A. G. Hildrew, and D. Raffaeilli, eds., *Aquatic Ecology*. Blackwell Science, Oxford.

Hall-Spencer, J. 1995. Evaluation of the direct impact of fishing gears on the substratum and on the benthos. European Commission, Brussels.

Harden-Jones, F. R., and P. Scholes. 1974. The effect of door-to-door tickler chain on the catch-rate of plaice (*Pleuronectes platessa* L.) taken by an otter trawl. *Journal du Conseil International pour l'exploration de la Mer* 35:210-212.

Heessen, H. J. L., and N. Daan. 1996. Long-term trends in ten nontarget North Sea fish species. *ICES Journal of Marine Science* 53:1063-1078.

Hughes, R. N., and M. I. Croy. 1993. An experimental analysis of frequency-dependent predation (switching) in the 15-spined stickleback, *Spinachia spinachia*. *Journal of Animal Ecology* 62:341-352.

ICES. 1995. *Report of the Study Group on Ecosystem Effects of Fishing Activities*. ICES Cooperative Research Report. No. 200. ICES: Copenhagen.

ICES. 1996. Report of the working group on ecosystem effects of fishing activities. *ICES C.M.* 1996/Assess/Env:1.

Jennings, S. and M. J. Kaiser. 1998. The effects of fishing on marine ecosystems. *Advances in Marine Biology*. In Press.

Jones, J. (1992). Environmental impact of trawling on the seabed: a review. *New Zealand Journal of Marine and Freshwater Research* 26:59-67.

Kaiser, M. J., and B. E. Spencer. 1994. Fish scavenging behaviour in recently trawled areas. *Marine Ecology Progress Series* 112:41-49.

Kaiser, M. J. and B. D. Spencer. 1995. Survival of benthos from beam trawls. *Marine Ecology Progress Series* 126:31-38.

Kaiser, M. J., and B. E. Spencer. 1996. The effects of beam-trawl disturbance on infaunal communities in different habitats. *Journal of Animal Ecology* 65:348-358.

Kaiser, M. J., D. B. Edwards, and B. E. Spencer. 1996. A study of the effects of commercial clam cultivation and harvesting on benthic infauna. *Aquatic Living Resources* 9:57-63.

Kaiser, M. J., and K. Ramsay. 1997. Opportunistic feeding by dabs within areas of trawl disturbance: possible implications for increased survival. *Marine Ecology Progress Series*, 152:307-310.

Krost, P., M. Bernhard, F. Werner, and W. Hukreide. 1990. Otter trawl tracks in Kiel Bay (Western Baltic) mapped by side scan sonar. *Meeresforschung* 32:344-353.

Millner, R. S. and C. L. Whiting. 1996. Long-term changes in growth and population abundance of sole in the North Sea from 1940 to the present. *ICES Journal Marine Science* 53:1185-1195.

Nalesso, R. C., L. F. L. Duarte, I. Rierozzi, I. and E. F. Enumo. 1995. Tube epifauna of the polychaete *Phyllochaetopterus socialis* Claparède. *Estuarine, Coastal and Shelf Science* 41:91-100.

Nickell, T. D., and P. G. Moore. 1992. The behavioural ecology of epibenthic scavenging invertebrates in the Clyde Sea area: laboratory experiments on attractions to bait in moving water, underwater TV observations *in situ* and general conclusions. *Journal of Experimental Marine Biology and Ecology* 159:15-35.

Pauly, D., V. Christensen, J. Dalsgaard, R. Froese, and F. Torres, Jr. 1998. Fishing down marine food webs. *Science* 279:860-863.

Polet, H., W. Blom, and W. Thiele. 1994. An inventory of vessels and gear types engaged in the Belgian, Dutch and German bottom trawling. Pp. 7-20 in S. J. De Groot and H. J. Lindeboom, eds., *Environmental impact of bottom gears on benthic fauna in relation to natural resources management and protection of the North Sea*. Netherlands Institute for Sea Research, Den Burg, Texel.

Pope, J. G. 1989. Fisheries research and management for the North Sea: the next hundred years. *Dana* 8:33-43.

Pope, J. G. and B. J. Knights. 1982. Comparison of the length distributions of combined catches of all demersal fishes in surveys in the North Sea and at Faroe Bank. Pp. 116-118 in M. C. Merccer, *Canadian Special Publication of Fisheries and Aquatic Sciences*, 59.

Potin, P., J. Y. Floc'h, C. Augris, and J. Cabioch. 1990. Annual growth rate of the calcareous red alga *Lithothamnion corallioides* (Corallinales, Rhodophyta) in the Bay of Brest, France. *Hydrobiologia* 204:263-267.

Ramsay, K., M. J. Kaiser, and R. N. Hughes. 1996. Changes in hermit crab feeding patterns in response to trawling disturbance. *Marine Ecology Progress Series* 144:63-72.

Ramsay, K., M. J. Kaiser, and R. N. Hughes. 1997a. A field study of intraspecific competition for food in hermit crabs (*Pagurus bernhardus*). *Estuarine Coastal and Shelf Science* 44:213-220.

Ramsay, K., M. J. Kaiser, P. G. Moore, and R. N. Hughes. 1997b. Consumption of fisheries discards by benthic scavengers: utilisation of energy subsidies in different marine habitats. *Journal of Animal Ecology* 66:884-896.

Rice, J. and H. Gislason. 1996. Patterns of change in the size spectra of numbers and diversity of the North Sea assemblage, as reflected in surveys and models. *ICES Journal Marine Science* 53:1214-1225.

Riesen, W., and K. Reise. 1982. Macrobenthos of the subtidal Wadden Sea: revisited after 55 years. *Helgolander Meeresuntersuchungen* 35:409-423.

Rijnsdorp, A. D. and F. A. Van Beek. 1991. Changes in growth of North Sea plaice (*Pleuronectes platessa* L.) and sole (*Solea solea* L.). *Netherlands Journal of Sea Research* 27:441-457.

Rijnsdorp, A. D. and P. I. Van Leewen. 1996. Changes in growth of North Sea plaice since 1950 in relation to density, eutrophication, beam trawl effort, and temperature. *ICES Journal Marine Science* 53:1199-1213.

Rijnsdorp, A. D., P. I. Van Leewen, N. Daan, and H. J. L. Heessen. 1996. Changes in abundance of demersal fish species in the North Sea between 1906-1909 and 1990-1995. *ICES Journal of Marine Science*, 53:1054-1062.

Rijnsdorp, A. D. and R. S. Millner. 1996. Trends in population dynamics and expoloitation of North Sea plaice (*Pleuronectes platessa* L.) since the late 1800s. *ICES Journal Marine Science* 53:1170-1184.

Rogers, S. I., A. D. Rijnsdorp, U. Damm, and W. Vanhee. 1998a. Demersal fish populations in the coastal waters of the UK and Continental N.W. Europe from beam trawl survey data collected from 1990 to 1995. *Journal of Sea Research* 39:79-102.

Rogers, S. I., D. Maxwell, A. D. Rijnsdorp, U. Damm and W. Vanhee, 1998b. Fishing effects in northeast Atlantic shelf seas: patterns in fishing effort, diversity and community structure. IV. Can comparisons of species diversity be used to assess human impacts on coastal demersal fish faunas in the Northeast Atlantic? *Fisheries Research*. In press.

Rowden, A. A., and M. B. Jones. 1993. Critical evaluation of sediment turnover estimates for Callianassidae (Decapoda: Thalassinidea). *Journal of Experimental Marine Biology and Ecology* 173:265-272.

Sainte-Marie, B. 1986. Effect of bait size and sampling time on the attraction of the lysianassid amphipods *Anonyx sarsi* Steele and Brunel and *Orchomenella pinguis* (Boeck). *Journal of Experimental Marine Biology and Ecology* 99:63-77.

Sainte-Marie, B., and B. T. Hargrave. 1987. Estimation of scavenger abundance and distance of attraction to bait. *Marine Biology* 94:431-443.

Shepherd, S. A. 1983. The epifauna of megaripples: species' adaptations and population responses to disturbance. *Australian Journal of Ecology* 8:3-8.

Walker, P. A. and H. J. L. Heessen. 1996. Long-term changes in ray populations in the North Sea. *ICES Journal Marine Science* 53:1085-1093.

Warwick, R. M. and K. R. Clarke. 1991. A comparison of some methods for analysing changes in benthic community structure. *Journal of Experimental Marine Biological Ecology* 71:225-244.

Witbaard, R., and R. Klein, R. 1994. Long-term trends on the effects of the southern North Sea beam trawl fishery on the bivalve mollusc *Arctica islandica* L. (Mollusca, bivalvia). *ICES Journal of Marine Science* 51:99-105.

Wood, H. 1956. Fisheries of the United Kingdom. Pp. 10-80 in M. Graham, ed. *Sea Fisheries: Their Investigation in the United Kingdom*. Arnold, London.

Fishermen's Perspectives on their Gear and on Fish Habitats

Bottom Trawling on
Soft Substrates

Frank Mirarchi

F/V CHRISTOPHER ANDREW, SCITUATE, MASSACHUSETTS

I am a dragger fisherman from Scituate, Massachusetts. I feel somewhat ill at ease making this presentation because I have spent 35 years at the top of the ocean, but not one minute underneath it looking at what my gear does. I consider myself to be a fairly astute observer, even though I am not a scientist. I look at the facts as analytically as I possibly can and try to attribute the causes to those facts and to come up with a theory as to why things are. My thoughts reflect my many years on the ocean. Naturally, the waxing and waning of fish populations are high on the list of things that I think about.

For an illustration of a bottom trawl, see Smolowitz Figure 3 (page 49). The primary difference between hard and smooth bottom trawls is the cables (or ground gear, as they are known in the trade) between the doors and the net. The purpose of the ground gear in a hard bottom trawl is to get over irregularities in the substrate. In contrast, its purpose in a smooth bottom trawl is to herd fish into the path of the net to maximize the catch per unit effort.

I would like to make some observations on this type of gear. Where does trawling occur? How are trawls rigged and used in this region? How has trawling changed since the 1960s, when I started fishing? What can we learn from the groundfish decline and recent partial recovery? I will address these topics in turn.

The assumption that fishing is comprehensive and covers all areas of the bottom of the ocean is not a correct one. This may be more the case with smooth

bottom trawling than with other strategies of fishing, because we are limited by the nature of the bottom that we can fish over.

I frequently fish in the area around Stellwagen Bank. The top of Stellwagen Bank ranges from pebbles to gravel to sand, and it has its own particular community of organisms. Previous talks have illustrated better than I can the types of epibenthic organisms that live there, but I do know a lot about the fish that live there. The primary fish species on the top of Stellwagen Bank is yellowtail flounder, a species that has been in significant decline in recent years, but is now showing some remarkable signs of recovery. The western edge of Stellwagen Bank is very steep, and the sediment grades very rapidly from the sand to muds and silts to soft mud in what is known as Stellwagen Basin. Stellwagen Basin has its own particular assemblage of fish species. The most commonly occurring flatfish species there and the primary target of smooth bottom fishermen is American plaice or dab. Thus, within a space of literally a couple of miles there exist two totally dissimilar habitats with two totally different assemblages of fish.

Plots of my actual tows in this area over about two years of fishing time show the non-uniform distribution of where I fish (Figure 1). The most productive areas are the ones I have towed down the most. I frequently tow along the edge of the bank, I tow on top of the bank, and I tow in the basin. There are large areas where I do not fish because they have rocky bottoms. We simply do not fish in areas that damage the net. Thus, fishing activity is, by nature, specific to certain areas. If all fishing activity were compiled into a unified database, such as a geographic information system, a pattern of high usage areas would emerge. This could provide higher resolution data than is presently available and might become a useful tool for analysis or management.

My first point, then, is that fishing does not take place uniformly everywhere. It takes place more in some areas than in others. Fishing is driven by bottom substrate type and by fish abundance and the value of fish species.

The second point that I would like to raise deals with the gear. The assumption that all fishing gear is alike and has an equal impact on the sea bed is not

true. Furthermore, the impact on the sea bed is probably not uniform throughout the trawl system. The doors (or trawl boards) weigh about 500 pounds apiece and are by far the heaviest part of the trawl system. They are steel, so their specific gravity is in the 6 to 7 range. They do not lose much weight in water, and they obviously have a much higher impact on the sea bed than the cable.

The cables that connect the net to the doors are steel cable inside ⅝-inch diameter plastic coat (the same as what Bill Gell uses in his rockhopper). Strung on the cables are rubber cookies with a specific gravity of about 1.25. The purpose of this gear configuration is to herd fish and to get the gear to

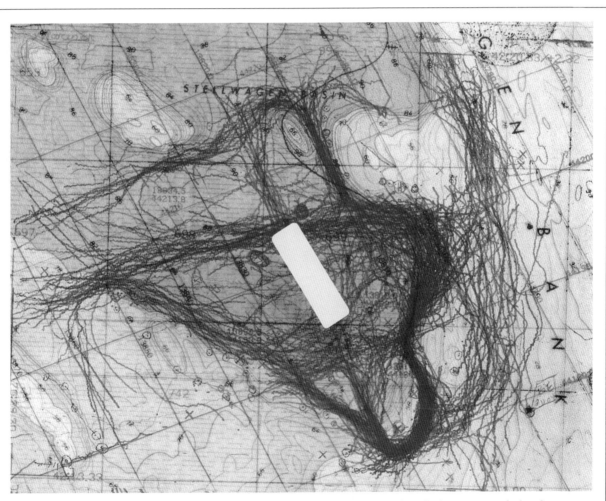

FIGURE 1. **A section of a bathymetric chart of Stellwagen Bank, overlaid with the tows made by the author's vessel over a two-year period, as taken from the vessel's plotter. It is a hard copy plotter, which uses a pen to trace onto a piece of paper the latitude and longitude position generated by the Global Positioning System. The density of tows is proportional to the number of lines on the chart. The blank rectangle near the center is an area where the plotter's pen wore through the paper, causing the author to apply a piece of opaque tape. The small circled dots mark rocky areas that the author avoided. Darker background shading indicates deeper water. The figure spans about seven nautical miles, vertically.**

ride lighter on the bottom. The cookies can rotate on the cable, but I doubt that they do that in actual fishing operation. There is definitely an impact on the sea bed by towing the gear. I tow 300 feet of this on each side of my net or a total of 600 feet of this material on the sea bed. Since the distance between the doors during a tow is about 200 feet, the ground cables and net form a deep parabola when in use.

Part of the trawl system is the sweep of the net. The sweep is an assembly of chain or cable that is usually strung with 4 to 6 inch diameter rubber discs. The lower edge of the trawl's netting is attached to the sweep. There are two main varieties of sweeps used in smooth bottom trawls. In a very light net such as is used in the squid fishery, there would be loops, or bights, of chain that are suspended from a ⅝-inch steel cable (see Carr and Milliken Figure 3b, page 102). This gear is intended to skim along the sea bed with only two or three links of the middle of the chain touching the bottom. The net has slightly negative buoyancy. When the chain bights contact the sea bed, they remove part of the chain's weight until the net has neutral buoyancy, ideally with the sweep gliding a few inches above the sea floor. This type of gear is used for squid or scup, species that swim slightly off the sea bed. It is not used for flounders and is not a rig I would use on my tows around Stellwagen Bank.

For the flounder fishery, the trawl sweep is significantly heavier and is designed to hug the bottom much more closely. Instead of cable in the middle, there is chain of ½ inch diameter, which probably weighs about five pounds per foot. On the chain are the ubiquitous rubber cookies (see Carr and Milliken Figure 3c, page 102), and the purpose of the sweep is to follow the contour of the bottom. The sweep is nice and flexible and heavy enough that basically everything in its path is swept into the net. This is not a rockhopper. It is not intended to go over any obstructions, but is intended to catch flatfish or flounders, which lie in contact with the sea bed. This is typical of the rig used on smooth bottom on or around Stellwagen Bank.

We have seen a significant change in the abundance of fish over time. Groundfish have gone from great abundance 30 years ago to critically reduced abundance about 10 years ago. Questions have been raised as to why. Is it overfishing? Is it habitat destruction? Is it sunspots? Is it something we do not understand at all? In recent years, since Amendments 5 and 7 to the groundfish management plan have been implemented, fishing rates have diminished significantly. For this year, 1997, fishing effort has been reduced to a level 50% lower than our basis years. Now, fish are beginning to come back. Is the recovery driven by habitat recovery? Is it driven by fishing mortality reductions? I cannot answer the question. At this point I do not think anybody can answer the question. Mortality-driven causes and habitat-driven causes of fish depletion are probably both linked xto the level of fishing activity. It is difficult, maybe impossible, to weigh their relative contributions.

In the 1960s and 1970s, fishing in Massachusetts Bay and Stellwagen Bank was characterized by small (< 65-foot) "day draggers" fishing areas that were limited to smooth bottom. Imprecise navigation precluded access to complex topography. Probably less than 50% of the area was fished. Boats were limited by weather conditions. During November through February, we averaged only 10 to 12 fishing days per month. Typically, day boats averaged 10 hours per day when they were actually towing their gear across the sea bed. Throughout the 1960s and 1970s, we averaged about 210 fishing days per year.

I have made an estimate of the area swept by

FIGURE 2. **Calculation of bottom area swept by a smooth bottom trawl.**

Assumptions:

- path swept by door = 5 feet (ft)
- spread between doors = 200 feet
- towing speed = 3 nautical miles/hour (n mi/hr)
- time with gear on bottom = 10 hours/day
- time fishing per year = 210 days
- time to repeat each tow = 1 month

Area swept by doors alone = 5 ft/door x 2 doors x 3 n mi/hr x 6076 ft/n mi x10 hr/day x 210 days per year = 1,822,800 ft²/day = 0.049 n mi²/day x 210 days/year = 10.29 n mi²/year ÷ 12 = 0.86 n mi²/year

Area swept by entire trawl = 200 ft x 3 n mi/hr x 6076 ft/n mi x 10 hr/day = 36,456,000 ft²/day = 0.987 n mi²/day x 210 days/year = 207.27 n mi²/year ÷ 12 = 17.3 n mi²/year each smooth bottom trawl under these conditions, considering both the entire trawl system from door to door and the doors alone (Figure 2). I estimate that in each year the doors traveled over a total of about 10 square nautical miles of sea floor and the entire trawl traveled over about 200 square nautical miles. Since draggers habitually repeat the same tows at least once a month, however, the total area of sea bed affected is only about 8% of those figures, or less than one square nautical mile for the doors and about 17 square nautical miles for the entire trawl.

During the next two decades (the 1980s and 1990s until Amendment 5 to the groundfish plan commenced in May 1994), unprecedented changes in fishing patterns occurred. For example, the Hague Line decision (1984) and haddock protection closures (around 1988) diverted large boats inshore. New technology, such as rockhopper sweeps, polyvalent doors, monofilament gillnets, and precision navigation, opened 100% of the bottom area to fishing activity. The sea scallop meat count requirement brought large scallopers inshore seeking to legitimize their sub-legal offshore catches with larger, although scarce, inshore product.

Large draggers and scallopers fish about 20 hours per day at sea. Thus, one 10-day trip by an "offshore" boat could equal two months of day boat activity. Coupled with the broader area access provided by rock hopper gear and precision navigation, it is probably correct that the entire Gulf of Maine was swept by fishing gear at least once annually.

Presently, in 1997, which is the second year of Amendment 7 to the groundfish plan, things again have dramatically changed. Fishing time appears to be below the 50% reduction prescribed in the days at sea program. Enormous areas of once heavily trawled bottom are now obstructed by lobster pots. A much higher percentage of groundfish catch is now taken by hooks and gillnets.

Technology has not been reversed. Despite some regulatory efforts, such as banning pair trawls and soon "street sweeper" trawls, fishermen continue to have access to risk prone areas. Limits now are provided more by regulation or obstructing fishing gear than by fear of lost or damaged equipment.

Changes in fish abundance and catchability, probably a consequence of the noted shifts in effort

and access, are now becoming manifest. The New England Fishery Management Council's Multispecies Monitoring Committee finds that fishing mortality rates are declining on all five principal groundfish stocks (just not fast enough for Gulf of Maine cod). Fishermen report improving catches per unit effort on cod, haddock, yellowtail, and winter flounder.

The combination of recent and historic events provides a murky signal regarding the contribution of habitat alteration to both fish depletion and fish recovery. At the time of peak activity, about 1984 to 1994, effort was several times that of the preceding decades. Power and technology penetrated any refuges the fish might have enjoyed. Large fish and spawning aggregations were specifically targeted. By 1993, my catch per unit effort dropped to an all time low of 50 pounds per towing hour.

My guess is that the primary culprit for the decline in catch per unit effort was the removal of spawning stock biomass by fishing. However, I cannot exclude the possibility of contributions from other factors related to fishing, such as disruption of spawning activities, disturbance of shelter for juveniles, alteration of primary food production, resuspension of sediment, or some other unknowns. The incipient recovery in fishing productivity, as distinct from a fish *stock* recovery, is more revealing. In 1996, my catch doubled to about 100 pounds per towing hour (still far below my catch rate in the 1960s and 1970s, which was 200 to 250 pounds per towing hour). Small aggregations of spawning cod began to reappear in the traditional areas, areas that were fished exceptionally heavily because of their earlier productivity. This suggests that either the areas' attributes that attracted fish in the first place were unchanged by fishing or whatever changes did occur were reversed over time.

Another point I would like to make is that there is certainly room for modification to trawl gear as a mitigation strategy. What I have described is typical traditional gear that has evolved over time and was developed solely for the purpose of catching fish, with minimal regulatory control. The criterion for success was to catch more fish at lower cost. Nobody ever gave a thought to bycatch and habitat when this gear was invented.

Recently, growing concern over undesirable

consequences of fishing has led to the development and introduction of technological solutions. Thus far, attention has focused on bycatch. Nordmore grates, turtle excluder devices, bycatch reduction devices, raised foot ropes, net pingers, and escape panels are examples of devices intended to reduce catches of unwanted or protected species.

Similar advances are possible to mitigate habitat impacts. With the exception of mollusks, most marine animals can probably be herded into a net's path by stimuli other than the massive equipment in use today. As with most technology applied under uncertain knowledge, there has been a tendency to overbuild trawls. Using fish behavior, it would be possible to come up with gear that is less offensive to the bottom than the current gear is (and I do not believe that it is terribly offensive) and that can still catch fish effectively.

Much of the massive fishing equipment in use today is an artifact of declining catches. If Amendment 7 continues to allow depleted stocks to rebuild, catches will rebound to a point where fishermen can again support families with 300 horsepower engines or 50 gillnets.

My final point is that the patchiness of fishing lends itself to consideration of a management strategy using small closed areas. If it is possible to find some areas of critical habitat that need to be protected, they should not be fished. They can be defined out of the system, and people can fish around them.

Bottom Trawling on Hard Substrates

Bill Gell

F/V XIPHIAS, ADAMSVILLE, RHODE ISLAND

I am not really a hard bottom fisherman, but I am pinch hitting for Rodney Avila, who helped prepare my remarks. I have a short talk about rockhopper gear, a demonstration with a five-gallon bucket, and a videotape to show. My trawler is 65 feet long with 300 horsepower, so it would not really be considered a hard bottom trawler at all. Most hard bottom trawlers have at least 600 horsepower.

There are many assumptions that trawling on the ocean bottom is harmful. One of the so-called demons is the rock hopper. I would like to dispel some misconceptions about rock hopper gear. Rock hoppers are simply larger rubber discs that are added to the footrope of a trawl, spaced every 18 inches or so, with 3- to 4-inch rubber discs in between (see Carr and Milliken Figure 4b, page 103). Rock hopper discs are usually 12 inches in diameter, though some are bigger, and they do not rotate. Some people that do not understand bottom trawl fishing gear are very afraid of this gear. They believe that this gear plows over the ocean floor, destroying everything in its path.

I know from my own use of the rockhopper that its purpose is not so much to get over rocky bottom— its purpose is mainly to increase the quality of the catch. Over the last few years, fishermen have had some pretty significant quota cutbacks in one of my target species, fluke (or summer flounder). Since the sushi market for fluke has developed, and since we can only land 200 to 300 or 400 pounds a day (depending on what state we land it in), the quality of the catch is really important, so that we get top price. Dragging on smooth bottom for fluke usually catches a lot of skates, which are kind of prickly. They scale the fluke up, ruining its appearance. So, we use rockhoppers to hold the footrope of the net above the skates to reduce their bycatch. This way we can catch a clean trawl of high quality fluke. We use it in other places as well, basically to avoid bycatch and reduce the work of sorting the catch.

I have a demonstration of just how heavy rock hopper gear is and how it affects the bottom. I brought some of what are called cookies—rubber disks that are punched out of rubber tires. This is the same material that the rockhopper cookies are cut from. I did not bring any rockhoppers because they are too big for this demonstration. I brought a five-gallon bucket of water, and I also brought a fully scientific scale that is totally calibrated. We can see that the cookies weigh four pounds in air. But when I put them in the bucket of water and fully submerge them, they weigh something less than half a pound—four tenths of a pound in my test yesterday. So it looks like about a 90% reduction in weight. Even though these are quite bulky and heavy out of the water, they are pretty light in the water.

When the rockhoppers are rigged for fishing, there is a cable running through them. I use 5/8-inch cable with plastic coating, and I use some chains, dropper chains and so on. The sweep that I use is 60 feet long and weighs out of water 400 to 500 pounds. In the water it probably weighs not a heck of a lot more than 100 pounds. So, common sense shows that it wouldn't have as much impact on the bottom as people expect.

I also brought a videotape that shows just how the rockhopper operates on the bottom. The tape comes from Frank Avila, Rodney Avila's cousin and a friend of mine. He owns a boat named the *Play Time*, a boat that is about like mine, and fishes out of New Bedford. In the videotape, he is dog fishing east of Round Shoal Channel (between Monomoy and Nantucket Island) in an experimental fishery on a bottom with sand ridges.

EDITORS' NOTE: *At the conference, Mr. Gell played a videotape that shows a trawl's rockhoppers holding the footrope of the net up off the bottom and allowing flounders to slip underneath.*

Gillnet Fishing

John Williamson

FORMER COMMERCIAL FISHERMAN, KENNEBUNK, MAINE

I did my initial apprenticeship as a fisherman in Maine in the 1970s, and I started out on bottom trawl vessels. Then I had the occasion to go to Alaska to fish for three years and learned drift gillnetting there. I came back to New England and started working on sink gillnet vessels. I consider myself a fixed gear fisherman, and as far as impacts are concerned, I think that there are impacts to marine mammals from fixed gear that we as a society must learn to manage.

I am going to give a very brief description of gillnetting, from a fisherman's point of view. Here in New England there are two main types of gillnet in use. For bottom fishing, we use sink gillnets, which tend the bottom. The other type of gillnet used in New England is pelagic surface nets such as for mackerel, but sink gillnets are the predominant gill-net type. There are two subtypes within sink gillnets: (1) stand-up gear, which is primarily for cod, haddock, pollock, and hake, and (2) tie-down gear, which is used to target flounders or monkfish.

The basic construction of the sink gillnet is as follows. It is weighted on the bottom, with lead woven onto the bottom line of the gillnet, and there are floats on the top that keep the upper edge of the gillnet off the bottom (see Smolowitz Figure 4, page 50). There are about 12 feet of mesh in between the top and bottom. The mesh comes in various sizes, with six-inch mesh the most common. The standard length for a gillnet is 300 feet. We tie these gillnets together in strings, and here in New England people fish from four net strings up to, more typically, 20 net strings, over a mile long. They are like a curtain sitting on the bottom hanging up into the water column about 12 feet and maybe a mile along the sea floor.

A tie-down gillnet is a variation used for flounders or monkfish. Typically, the float line is tied to the lead line at six-foot intervals by a three to four foot length of twine. That way the float line floats close to the bottom, and the net forms a limp bag in between. Tie-down nets for flounder are usually made of 6.5- to 8-inch mesh, while 10- to 12-inch mesh is used for monkfish. For flounder and monkfish, fine gauge monofilament usually works better than heavy gauge monofilament.

The secret to the gillnet is that it is cryptic. It disappears when it is in the water because it is made out of monofilament, so a fish cannot see the net when it is swimming along. When it tries to swim through the net, it gets caught around the head.

The soak duration of a gillnet—the length of time that it is left in the water before being hauled—depends on the species that is being targeted. For stand-up gear, the target is codfish or pollock, and the net would be hauled daily. A 24-hour soak is most typical for this gear, but some people, especially offshore gillnetters, fish stand-up gear on a 12-hour soak. For tie-down gear, the target is flounder or monkfish, and the soaks are longer, sometimes as long as four nights. Both flounders and monkfish tend to stay alive when caught in the gillnet. Unlike cod and haddock and pollock, they are not dependent on water flow over the gills, so they continue to live in the net for a number of days.

My experience with gillnets is primarily with cod, haddock, and pollock, so I tend to fish on structures on the bottom. I look for changes in bottom topography for places to put my gillnets. I have a net that is three quarters of a mile or a mile long, and I look for large structures to fish on. Those macro structures might be edges or a series of pinnacles or gullies. The reason for looking for those macro structures is that I look for backwashes or eddies from the constant tidal movement of water. The backwash is going to create opportunities for bait fish to feed, and the fish that I am targeting are feeding on those bait fish. There is a greater abundance in back eddies. I try to place the net in such places where cod or pollock are going to be swimming up under those bait fish and feeding on them. Also, when fish are spawning, we tend to find spawning activity in the backwash from hard bottom structure, which creates sand pockets. Fish seek out those areas for spawning, and if I am targeting the fish during spawning season, I would be looking for those bottom profiles.

Often the most productive pieces of bottom are where the bottom type changes from mud to gravel and sand or from mud to hard bottom. As Frank Mirarchi showed in his towing plots (see Mirarchi Figure 1, page 81), he also tends to tow along edges between the soft bottom and the hard bottom,

because that is where fish tend to be, especially when they are moving.

When you go out and do this daily, you realize that within the macro structures are smaller structures, or micro structures, where the fish tend to be more abundant. When I haul a mile-long gillnet, I will get a smattering of fish all through it, but there will be spots where there will be small groupings of fish. I will be looking at my electronic depth recorder as the net comes aboard and will notice that the groupings of fish associate with very small changes in general habitat. Those changes might be just a large rock, or a cobble patch, or a pipe clay patch.

Pipe clay *(Figure 1)* is something that most of us fishermen are familiar with. In our area, between Cape Ann and Cape Elizabeth, we find these hardened pipe-like structures in mud deposits. The deposits seem to be shaped by organisms burrowing in the mud, and I understand that the shapes are hardened by iron precipitating out in layers on the surfaces. These shapes create very complex bottoms, which we find in large patches. We know where the pipe clay is because we snag pieces of it in our gillnets. The patches tend to be multiple acres in size in

FIGURE 1.
A sample of pipe clay collected by a gillnetter. This piece measures about 24 cm across. This type of pipe clay is very irregularly shaped; another type is in the form of smooth pipes, one of which is illustrated in Valentine Figure 2, page120. Photograph by Peter Auster.

soft bottom habitat where there is a high concentration of brittle stars and other invertebrates. These pipe clay patches are good places to catch groundfish.

I would like to speak for some of the fishermen in my area. One of their concerns is that this type of habitat is diminishing. They associate the decrease with increased trawling over the years. The ability of mobile gear to work on the edges of pipe clay has gradually degraded the size of these areas of pipe clay. Over the course of a couple of decades, that traffic also seems to have caused changes in bottom contours, so that topographic features that we used to set our nets on have gradually disappeared. We wonder what effect that has.

I have been speaking as a fisherman. I want to take a minute now to speak as a fisheries manager, a member of the New England Fishery Management Council. I am very painfully aware that the Magnuson Act is only 20 years old. As far as I am concerned, fisheries management worldwide is at the very crudest beginnings, especially here in the United States. Up until now our primary tool has been counting fish, but counting fish is trying to manage the aggregate for fishing impacts. In a lot of ways that is like trying to swat flies with a baseball bat. We know as fishermen that there are a lot of components that make up the overfishing equation. These include things like forage and the species that make up the forage for commercial species, and also spawning. We have to address the productivity of the environment and invest in that productivity. That will pay dividends for all of us as fishermen.

Scallop Dredge Fishing

James Kendall

NEW BEDFORD SEAFOOD COALITION, NEW BEDFORD, MASSACHUSETTS

I would like to give a scalloper's perspective, and what I would like to present is basically anecdotal evidence. I looked in the dictionary (Webster's Office Edition), and I found these definitions for "evidence," a noun. One definition is "facts or signs on which a conclusion can be based." A second part to that definition is "an indication." "Anecdote," another noun, is defined as "a short interesting or humorous account of a real or fictitious incident." Anecdotal is an adjective with the same meaning. I hope my comments will be viewed at least as one of these.

It is unusual for a fisherman to come before a group like this to present what he has seen and learned during his years of experience at sea. I should say *hopefully* learned, for very often fishermen see things, but for various reasons we do not always learn from the experience. I was a fisherman for 32 years, and I chose to fish for the Atlantic sea scallop (*Placopecten magellanicus*). Unfortunately, I cannot fish any longer due to an injury.

In the scallop fishery, there are basically two fishing styles. There is a hard bottom fishery and a soft bottom fishery. These are fairly obvious terms: the hard bottom boats fish in hard rocky areas, while the soft bottom boats frequent softer sandy areas. The dredges for the two fishing styles have the same general design (see Smolowitz Figure 2, page 48), but for hard bottom scalloping the bale is heavier and stronger with different shoes, and rock chains are added to keep rocks out. A boat rigged up for soft bottom would certainly not tow on hard bottom on the

same trip unless the crew changed gear during the trip.

Another term for a scallop dredge used by the industry for years is a scallop rake. A "channel boat" is the term in New Bedford for a scallop vessel that usually fishes in the Great South Channel. It is also called a rock boat or a hard bottom boat. The men are called channel men or channel guys. The northern edge of Georges Bank is another low long piece of hard bottom edge, and in-between the two places is the soft bottom.

Although some boats cross over between fishing styles, some almost never change styles. This is true for the men as well. Some never get the hang of one style or the other, while others are good at both. Scallopers probably change styles of fishing more nowadays out of need, since we have lost a good portion of scalloping grounds due to the groundfish closures that started in late 1994, particularly on Georges Bank. The closures represent approximately 40% of the sea floor on Georges Bank, but they are probably closer to 60% of the bottom that we used to go scalloping on and nearly 75% of the landings. So the closures have had quite an impact on us.

I had fished with both styles of New Bedford scallopers over the years until 1972, when I joined the company that I was with for the next 24 years. The owner of that company was a well known soft bottom man. We did not have many occasions to fish the hard bottom until the owner built a second boat for the company, the *Nordic Pride*, which I had the pleasure of running for eight years. We set a stock record for New Bedford boats on both our first and third trips. We were fond of saying that we earned a million dollars on one set of chain bags that first year. I am not sure of the exact amount of truth in that claim, but it was close.

The captain then was Carl Acorn, one of the best soft bottom men around. He taught me most of what he knew, but probably not everything. I have always felt that he kept a little bit back as an edge.

Over the years I had the occasion to change my style. I ended up working into harder and harder bottom. It was a learning process that was not easy. I believe it forced me to pay more attention to what I was seeing, and it helped me learn a lot by being observant. I was good at what I did when I was scalloping.

Over the 15 years I was captain, I managed to fish virtually every part of Georges Bank, as well as much of the Mid-Atlantic area, as far south as Cape Hatteras. During all this time I kept written records of each and every tow that I made. I would mark down my position from the beginning of my tow to the point where I turned around or, if it was a straight tow, to the end of the tow. I kept the bearings of each tow and the results of each, along with notes to describe the catch, the bycatch, the bottom characteristics, and the weather and sea state. In later years I was able to record water temperatures as well. I required my mates to do the same.

I can dig out those notes today and return to the first tow I ever made. Some of those Loran bearings are no longer used, but I can still come pretty close. I could replicate those tows down to within a few feet of where they started, and I could give an idea of what I would find that would be pretty close to the actual catch. The catch will vary, and the bycatch will vary, but not so much that it will be surprising.

This is not just supposition on my part. I had many occasions during my years as a captain to do exactly what I have just described. At times I would find that something had in fact changed when I returned to a tow, but it was more likely to be much the same or changed for the better rather than for the worse. Some of the most prolific areas of yesterday remain the best areas today. Several of my former mates are captains who are still fishing for scallops today and still fishing in many of these same areas. We feel that the bottom is still there, and the fishery is still there to go through various natural changes.

When I first started fishing in the early 1960s, scallop gear was much smaller and lighter than today's dredges and chainbags. The gear changed significantly by the late 1960s and has remained fairly constant since then with 15-foot dredges the norm. While this might seem to be a destructive trend, the reason for the change was that the newer, larger, and more powerful boats would literally fly a lighter dredge up off the ocean bottom, much like a kite or a glider. Even with today's larger and heavier dredges, were it not for a pressure plate that adds downward force similar to a spoiler on an automobile, this would still occur. This principle is much the same for an otter trawl door. It depends on the correct angle of the door to obtain the spread required to keep the net open, as well as to keep it in contact with the ocean floor. To bury or plow the sea bed with either configuration would be more akin to dragging an anchor.

Scallop dredges do not tend the sea bed by virtue of their size and weight alone. With this gear, as well as with a lot of other towed gear including trawls, speed plays an important role. A lot of people seem to feel that faster tows do more damage to the bottom. The fact is that if fishermen tow too fast, they will actually fly the gear right up off the bottom much as with a kite, because the gear becomes functionally weightless. All we want to do is get down low enough to skip along the bottom and get the scallops out of the sand or off along the sand waves. The steel frame rides on the bottom without digging in like a lot of people suppose.

I am not suggesting that the act of scalloping on the ocean floor does not create an impact upon it, but I am suggesting that it may not be the adverse one so easily assumed. I believe that there are several different time frames that should be considered as part of the entire equation. There is the immediate effect, the short term effect, and perhaps most importantly, the long term results. Before anyone says we have all the answers, perhaps we should know all the questions. The truth is that we have little in the way of actual studies to show short term effects on the sea floor by scallop dredges. This lack of scientific evidence is further exacerbated by the absence of studies to show the longer range outcomes.

One such study of a bottom trawl conducted by the Massachusetts Division of Marine Fisheries off Duxbury Beach found no fresh damage to lobsters and negligible habitat impact (MDMF 1989). Admittedly, this was a study of a trawl track, and not of a scallop dredge track, but I do not know of a conclusive study of a scallop dredge. Those studies that I have seen raise more questions than they answer. No one has any hard bottom evidence on scallop fishing gear. Maybe we need to look into this and see what scallopers are actually doing down there.

One thing that seems fairly certain to me is that if the scallop dredges and/or trawl nets were responsible for as much habitat destruction as has been attributed to them, there would be no need for this conference. Mother Nature created the diversity of Georges Bank eons ago, but apparently she is not done with it yet. She still likes to dabble with the bank as she chooses. In the form of severe storms, she caused some of the most startling changes to the ocean bottom that I have witnessed.

One big change that I observed happened on the northern edge of Georges Bank. Scallopers started seeing a strange sort of bycatch in the early 1980s. I could only describe it by saying that it looked like a lot of little sand castles. I brought a sample in and was told by someone in Woods Hole that it was a tube worm. We could barely fish the area because of this. If we towed, our drags came up completely filled with them. This animal had taken over, and then it disappeared over night. We had a huge storm with winds of 75 to 80 miles per hour. The boats stopped fishing. I was the first to start back fishing when the winds started to diminish. When I set out, I was catching 7 to 8 bushels of scallops per side per tow in the same area. There wasn't a tube worm left. So, storms can have a major impact out there. Perhaps the old adage "time heals all wounds" applies to the ocean bottom as well.

Over the years, I have seen certain areas go fallow for one reason or another, so that there were not enough scallops to warrant us fishing there. The southwest part of Georges Bank was one such area. We stopped fishing it for seven or eight years because the abundance was too low. When the meat count regulation came along and set a maximum number of meats per pound, we needed to find a few large

scallops to mix in with the small ones to meet the meat count requirements, so we began to fish there again. In a short period of time we began to see signs of juvenile scallop recruitment, and soon afterwards the area was able to provide an abundance that I had not seen there in about 12 years. Could this be the New England equivalent of the Dover sole fishery in the North Sea, where the fishery actually has improved with increased trawling effort (see Rogers *et al.,* this volume)?

There are other questions that go begging in the headlong rush to attribute blame to one fishing gear type or another. Some of these are identified in a report by Valentine and Lough (1991) as part of a study by the U.S. Geological Survey. Among some of the questions they raise are the following: What is the impact of physical disturbance of the sea bed by fishing gear, and does this disturbance have a positive or negative effect, or no impact, on the fishery? Does this activity oxygenate the sediment, release buried nutrients, damage herring egg beds, or adversely affect juvenile fish and scallops? I would add another question: What role does fishing disturbance play upon the predators or upon the diseases that are quick to take advantage of concentrations of a species?

A significant recent development has been that scallopers have been forced by changing management plans to change the manner in which we fish and to fish in ways that are not of our own choosing. The suspension of the meat count requirement in 1994 has removed one of the most important regulatory pressures. We no longer need to fish on very low abundances of scallops solely to find some big ones to meet the meat count. But will this be offset by the need to concentrate on less-productive fishing areas due to permanent area closures for groundfish?

I believe that area closures are a great opportunity to enhance and replenish much of the resource. The correct way to do this would be with rotational closures that would maximize both the growth and the yield of the affected species, while minimizing the impacts on the affected habitat. If done properly, rotational closures could lessen the impact on any given area, while protecting the habitat and its resources at the most crucial stages, when there is an abundance of small scallops. Farmers long ago learned of the value of rotating their crops and their fields. Perhaps we need to learn from their experience.

When we had more bottom to work with, we would rotate on our own. We would move off an area when the catch was dropping off to another area where we hoped it was higher. We would work a bottom pretty hard, then we would leave it alone for a while, and when we came back, usually we would see an abundance of scallops start to return. The current closed areas demonstrate the same point. People are now poaching inside these closed areas because the abundance of scallops in there is *tremendous*. Scallopers are risking fines of over $100,000 because the growth of scallops in these closed areas in the last two years has been so phenomenal.

As a parting thought, I would like to raise questions about what once might have seemed to be a foregone conclusion. There is a reference to the possible effects of bottom trawling upon historic herring spawning grounds in the most comprehensive study since 1970 of these spawning grounds (Valentine and Lough 1991). This survey was taken during the period October 7–12, 1991. The gravel bottom was reported to be extensively trawled and dredged for groundfish and scallops, and as best as I can judge, much of it continues to be open to the trawl sector. In 136 dredge samples of the area, no herring eggs were found, and no herring larvae were found in samples of the water column. This was viewed as an indication that the eastern Georges Bank population of herring had not recovered from its earlier collapse. Now herring is considered recovered, and the recovery occurred while scalloping continued in the herring spawning areas. Towing in those areas cannot be much of a problem for herring.

EDITORS' NOTE: *At the conference, Mr. Kendall showed a videotape of a research scallop dredge fishing on sandy bottom. The dredge was eight feet wide, about half the size of a standard dredge, and weighed several thousand pounds in air, according to Mr. Kendall. The tape showed the dredge behaving in the manner that Mr. Kendall describes above—skipping over the bottom and staying close to it without digging down into it. Readers wishing to see the videotape should contact Arne Carr of the Massachusetts Division of Marine Fisheries in Pocasset, Massachusetts.*

REFERENCES

MDMF. 1989. The impact of bottom trawling on American lobsters off Duxbury Beach, MA (October 1, 1989). Massachusetts Division of Marine Fisheries. Boston, MA.

Rogers, S.I., M.J. Kaiser, and S. Jennings. **This volume.** Ecosystem effects of demersal fishing: a European perspective.

Valentine, P.C. and R.G. Lough. 1991. The sea floor environment and the fishery of eastern Georges Bank; the influence of geologic and oceanographic environmental factors on the abundance and distribution of fisheries resources of the northeastern United States continental shelf. U.S. Geological Survey Open-File Report 91-439. 25pp.

Lobster Trap Fishing

Thomas Morrell

F/V PATTI M, QUINCY, MASSACHUSETTS

I have been lobster fishing for 34 years. I fish out of Boston now. I will explain how lobster traps (or pots) work and how lobstermen fish them.

If the first person to trap lobsters, from 150 or 200 years ago, could be resurrected and brought back today, he would recognize the traps that we use. The design is the same, and lobster traps are basically the same, except for a change in materials from wood to wire. Lobster traps have two entrances for lobsters to crawl in, one on each side of the trap, each with a head or funnel-shaped webbing. We put bricks inside the trap for weight, and we put bait inside, either on a little spike or inside a bait bag that hangs from the top. The trap just sits there on the bottom, and we hope that a lobster comes by and senses the bait and crawls in. When it does, it enters the first compartment, called the kitchen. Then we hope that it crawls through another funnel into the back compartment, which we call the parlor. It has to squeeze to get in there, and then the opening closes after it, and it is trapped (see Smolowitz Figure 5, page 51).

If the lobster does not feel like crawling around and climbing into a trap, it can make that decision. At certain times of the year, when the water temperature gets colder, the lobsters do not move very much. Then we can almost drop a trap on its head, and if it has hidden and does not want to move, it is not going to move. That is why most of the lobster fishing in our area is done in the warmer months. We catch most of our lobsters between April and January. Although the air is cold in December and January,

that is when the water temperature is just starting to get cold. The coldest month for water is in March.

Most of the lobstermen are using wire traps now. We used to use wood traps years ago. When we would lose a wood trap, within a year the wood would disintegrate because of worm infestation, and then it did not have any effect on the bottom at all. But now most of the fishermen have changed to vinyl-covered wire, which lasts much longer in the water.

We have added escape vents to the traps so that small lobsters can get out. The escape vents started out being 1 or 1½ inches high. Then we went to 1⅝ inches, and now we are up to 1⅞ inches in the state of Massachusetts. If we use a slightly smaller escape vent of 1¾ inches instead, our traps will come up literally half full of lobsters. Most of the lobstermen use 1⅞ inches and do not see many shorts (sublegal lobsters). We see some shorts, but not as many as we would if we had a smaller vent size. Now the federal managers are talking about increasing further to 1¹⁵⁄₁₆ inches. A lot of legal-sized lobsters get out of vents that big, especially when the lobsters are shedding. Right after they shed, their shells are really soft, so when they get in the trap, they can just squeeze right out the vents.

The advantages of these escape vents have been increased by using biodegradable hog rings to hold them on. The hog rings are just a little ring or clip of soft steel. They hold the escape vent (with its opening of 1⅞ inches) over a larger opening (about 6 inches by 4 inches). After a year in the water, the hog rings disintegrate, giving lobsters the much larger hole to climb out. The purpose of this is to make sure that lost traps do not keep on catching and killing lobsters for ever. One of the surprising things is that even when the hog rings fall apart, giving lobsters an opening plenty big to crawl out, often they stay inside. I have hauled lots of traps with the vents open, but with all kinds of shorts just hanging around inside the trap, and I wonder why they don't just climb out. I guess they try to find places to hide down there on the bottom, and they make the trap almost like their home. They keep coming in the trap and climbing out the vent, and then one day they just grow a little bit too big and then they never go back over the side of the boat again because they have grown to legal size.

Most lobstermen fish their traps in trawls of between 10 and 25 pots. Some of the offshore guys fish 50-pot trawls. We have a buoy on the first trap at the end of the trawl and then roughly 100 feet of line in between each trap and then another buoy on the last trap. By fishing trawls instead of single traps, we can recover our gear if buoys get cut off by a boat. The electronics that we have nowadays can pinpoint us within feet of where we lost our traps. We then throw a big grapple over the side, and we usually can grapple up our gear. But if a buoy gets cut off on a single trap, it is pretty hard to get that back.

The lobstermen that I hang around with do not loose much gear from boats accidentally knocking over their buoys. The draggers, of course, will dispute that because they tow up a lot of ghost pots, I am sure, along with some of the good pots. But we try

to get along with the draggers and try to stay out of the way. We are all fighting for the same kind of bottom. We try to get that edge. The inshore lobstermen probably do not go more than two or three miles from the coast, but most of the guys who have been lobstering for a lot of years fish a little further out. We fish out in all of Massachusetts Bay and the edge of Stellwagen Bank and other places. We try to look for little edges. We try to keep away from where the draggers' tows are. We watch for that and learn where they are and try to keep out of the way.

As for the impact of lobster traps on the sea bottom, I feel that traps are the least intrusive of all fishing methods. Wood traps disintegrate and decay, posing no threat to lobsters. With biodegradable escape vent rings, wire traps become hideaways, not prisons, regardless of a lobster's size. Traps create a passive fishing industry and pose no threat to the sea floor.

In conclusion, I will point out changes that I have observed in the bottom over the years. About 20 years ago, I found that most of the lobsters that I got were on hard bottom. Gradually more and more of my fishing has been done on soft bottom. In the last five years, I have not fished hardly any gear at all on hard bottom. The lobsters just are not present on the hard bottom like they used to be. Lobstermen have to fish out in the mud, which of course causes problems with the draggers because that is where they tow. We are all fighting for the same piece of bottom.

Bottom Longline Fishing

Mark Leach

F/V SEA HOLLY, HARWICH, MASSACHUSETTS, CAPE COD COMMERCIAL HOOK FISHERMEN'S ASSOCIATION

I started fishing in 1975, and I am 40 years old. I am basically a tub trawler (longliner), and just recently I have started doing some lobstering, as well. I got my feet wet fishing by working on the deck of a North Shore lobsterman's boat in 1975 while I was attending the University of Massachusetts at Amherst, and I started longlining in 1985.

There are two different approaches to bottom longlining in New England. In the more conventional tub trawl system, fishermen use what they call stuck gear. That means that the hooks are fixed at six-foot intervals onto lines of parachute cord, and the lines are stored in tubs when they are not fishing. The tubs containing the lines are brought to shore at the end of each trip for rebaiting. The other approach uses wire cable instead of parachute cord, and the wire is stored on a big drum on the boat. When the gear is being set, monofilament gangions with baited hooks are snapped onto the wire as it pays off the drum, and as the gear is hauled and the wire is rewound onto the drum, the gangions are removed for rebaiting. I have had a cable boat and fished with snap-on gear in the past, but I own a tub trawler now, which I purchased in 1984. Both approaches to longlining set the gear similarly along the ocean floor (see Smolowitz Figure 6, on page 52).

Tub trawlers employ baiters on shore to bait the hooks. Some baiters are former fishermen who made the choice to work onshore after a good career in fishing. They often can continue making a good income on the shore helping guys like myself get their gear baited. One fellow who baits for me in Chatham is Tiggy Poluso, who is a former tub trawler himself. He taught a lot of the guys down in Chatham the ins and outs of the industry, and we all owe him a tremendous debt of gratitude for passing on his secrets on to us.

Another form of hook fishing—jigging—is done without longlines. Jigging is done either with a pole or with a hand line, usually without bait. The fisherman drops the jig over the side and fishes just off the bottom with a silver jig and a couple of "bugs" (teasers or lures with hooks) attached to the line. If he is lucky he will hook up, and the result will be a nice cod fish. Jigging tends to catch a slightly larger run of fish than tub trawling. It is the oldest fishery that I know of.

Like Boston Harbor and Gloucester, Stage Harbor in Chatham used to be full of schooners that took dories out and harvested codfish with hand lines. Fishing this way went back to the Portuguese. Boats came over and fished the northwest Atlantic before the settlement of Cape Cod and before the settlement of Massachusetts by the Pilgrims.

I consider hook fishing to be a very clean fishery with an extremely high quality of product, particularly from the day boat. Fish are caught in the morning and landed on the dock that night, providing an unsurpassed quality, which I am sure a lot of restaurants would be more than willing to attest to.

The Cape Cod Commercial Hook Fishermen's Association has gotten itself involved with a lawsuit against the National Marine Fisheries Service (NMFS). We filed the lawsuit in June 1996 and charged that

Amendment 7 to the groundfish management plan fails to comply with the Magnuson Act because it ignores the different habitat impacts of different gear types. We feel that NMFS should be more active in protecting the habitats for fish, and we hope that the Sustainable Fisheries Act will force NMFS and the New England Fishery Management Council to do this. I have heard charges that the hook fishermen are just making an allocation argument and are looking to get their piece of the pie and to kick everyone else out. But habitat has long been critical to the hook fishermen, well before the advent of modern electronics.

The dual function of the sounding lead is an indication of the importance of habitat. Tiggy Poluso explained to me how he and generations of hook fishermen before him used the sounding lead to decide where to set gear. They would jam a type of wax onto the end of a heavy piece of lead weighing around 5 to 10 pounds. When dead reckoning had taken them close to the fishing grounds, they would throw the sounding lead overboard with a line. The purpose was not only to gauge the depth of water with marks on the line, but also to make a stamp onto the wax end of the lead as it hit the sea floor. It would not pick up pieces of the bottom (though I suppose at times it could) but rather would bring back an imprint of the material on the bottom.

What fishermen looked for was mussel beds, shell fragments, and things of that nature that indicate a fertile bottom that would hold cod fish. If they did not see the right impressions in the wax, they would not set their hooks until they found it. Of course, now we use GPS and Loran for navigation, and we have a much better way of pinpointing these critical habitat areas. But I just want to make the point that critical habitat has been essential to the success of hook fishermen all along, even to this day. We cannot fish just anywhere with hooks; we have to set our gear on the right kind of bottom, where fish aggregate.

I want to mention some of the things that we find when we are looking for this critical habitat. A few animals get hooked in our gear, and the ones that I am going to mention occur in places where we see the best fishing for cod and haddock. Horse mussels, for example, occur in large beds in places. A lot of other animals come attached to the horse mussels,

such as regular razor clams, some barnacles, small scallops, and Icelandic scallops. What we call a lemon *(Figure 1)* is sometimes attached to mussels, often to rocks or gravel as well. Scientists tell me they call it a stalked sea squirt. To us it looks like a lemon, and it has an attachment vine. The strength of the stalk is about the same as a tomato to its vine, so it is very fragile. Another piece of habitat we call pork fat, and another we call a fig. They are both species of sea squirts without stalks. We use funny little terms, but when these come up on the hooks, especially the lemons, we know we are in a good spot. When we start getting a couple of lemons, then we are getting into some good fishing. It is really important to notice all the animals that attach to the rocks. Hard rocky bottom is essential for these benthic flora and fauna to survive.

I want to talk a little about the current conditions from a hook fisherman's perspective. We notice that there are very few hang downs any more. A hang down is a place where the gear snags as we are hauling it back in. We just do not hang down any more in places where we used to. We believe it is because the rocky hard bottom has been destroyed by mobile gear. Jiggers do not loose their jigs anymore. Jiggers tend to fish on wrecks and specifically look for wrecks. I know some excellent jiggers who can not find the wrecks anymore that they used to fish on. We, as longliners, like to go over a wreck, but we

FIGURE 1. **Lemons or stalked sea squirts,** ***Boltenia ovifera.*** **These indicators of good cod fishing rarely come up on bottom longlines any more.** Photograph by Jon Witman.

PRINTED IN COLOR ON PAGE 160.

are looking more for runs of mussel beds and things of that nature.

It is harder and harder to find the good habitat. The good habitat is shrinking. Good areas used to be five microseconds long, and now they are only three microseconds long. We catch nothing on either end of our longline in places where we used to get fish all the way through. We perceive the problem to be that large draggers are towing on this bottom and removing the mussels and other bottom critters that make good habitat for the fish we target. A good illustration of the effect of draggers is provided by the pictures from the U.S. Geological Survey of an untowed area on a hard gravel bottom, compared to a towed area (see Collie Figures 9a and 9b, pages 61 and 159). It is as clear as night and day to us. There is nothing left here on these bottoms, where we used to have mussel beds, lemons, figs, pork fat, and other animals. We are very concerned because we believe that this is reducing the productivity of the ocean and the abundance of fish.

Minimizing Fishing Gear Impacts to the Sea Floor

Conservation Engineering: Options to Minimize Fishing's Impacts to the Sea Floor

H. Arnold Carr and Henry Milliken

MASSACHUSETTS DIVISION OF MARINE FISHERIES, POCASSET, MASSACHUSETTS

Commercial fishing in New England waters has undergone significant technological advances within the past 20 years. Mobile fishing or trawling has been a very fortunate recipient of advancing technology. Three critical areas of improvement are navigation, vessel capability, and fishing gear. Fishing vessel captains have increased their ability to navigate accurately in inclement weather and tow precisely around trawl net tearing hazards. The towing power of commercial vessels as well as their seaworthiness and increased hydraulic capability render the modern dragger a highly efficient fishing unit. Couple these improvements with major advances in trawl gear design, and the result is that each fishing vessel has vastly increased its catch capability during the past 20 years.

HOW TRAWLS INTERACT WITH THE SEA FLOOR

In order to consider the impact of fishing gear on the sea bottom and benthos, one must understand the design of the gear and consider recent advances in trawl design. The physical impact of trawling on the sea floor is primarily the result of two parts of the trawl: the trawl doors and the trawl sweep.

The trawl doors, mounted ahead and on each side of the net, spread the mouth of the net laterally across the sea floor. The spreading action of the doors results from the angle at which they are mounted, which creates hydrodynamic forces to push them

apart and also to push them toward the sea bed (in concert with the doors' weight). On sea bottom of finer sediment size, such as sand or mud, each door usually leaves a continuous narrow trench. These can remain in evidence for a considerable time period in areas where wave action and currents are low. A number of scientists, including ourselves, have documented trawl door tracks from high resolution side scan sonar in many places in the western North Atlantic (Figure 1). The doors also create a silt cloud on bottoms containing fine particulates (Figure 2). The cloud is a functional part of the operation, as it aids in herding fish into the mouth of the trawl. The action and impact of the door on rocky or more irregular bottom depends on the type and size of door, but doors do impact the rocks and bottom material in a jarring manner and do jump distances of 1 to 2 meters (m).

The second part of the trawl that impacts the sea bottom is the sweep. The sweep is the bottom of the net mouth and is attached to the net's footrope (Figure 3a). The sweep acts to collect marine animals that lie or gather before it. The configuration of the sweep varies considerably depending on what fish species and what bottom type are targeted by the fishing operation. This element of the trawl system largely determines where the gear will be fished, especially in regard to bottom type.

The simplest and lightest sweep is a chain sweep, which consists of chain attached in loops to the footrope (Figure 3b). Cookies or rubber discs made from old automobile tires (Figure 3c) can be tightly strung

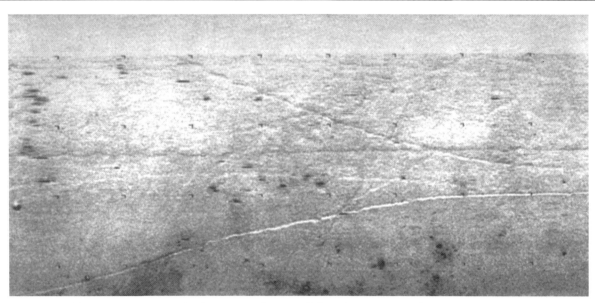

FIGURE 1. **Side scan sonar record taken at 100 kHz. Each lane has a range of 100 m. The sonagram was taken at the Massachusetts Bay Disposal Site and shows small targets as well as long narrow trenches left by otter trawl doors. Such marks are commonly seen on sand or mud sea floors throughout New England coastal waters. Sonagram courtesy of American Underwater Search and Survey.**

together to provide a sweep that enables a trawl net to fish on soft and slightly irregular bottom and to maintain consistent contact with the bottom. Cookies vary in diameter from about 4 inches to 12 inches. Two other sweep configurations common to New England allow trawling on much more irregular bottom. The roller sweep *(Figure 4a)* has the capability of rolling over the bottom, since the rollers are free to rotate. The diameter of rollers can be as large as 36 inches. Rollers are more common on European trawls than on New England trawls.

In this region, roller sweeps have largely given way to the rockhopper. Rockhopper gear *(Figure 4b)* has larger "rubbers" spaced amid smaller diameter ones; the larger rubbers are fixed in position and do not rotate. The rockhopper was first designed in Europe about 20 years ago. Improvements to its design since then now enable trawls to easily hop over rocks as large as one meter in diameter without snagging the net. This is dependent, however, on the power of the vessel and the size and structure of the rockhopper sweep.

In addition to the physical evidence of trawling impacts recorded by sonar or underwater video systems, we have made some direct observations of trawl impacts. The impact of the trawl does vary with the

type of trawl and how it is operated. Two examples of directly observed trawl impacts follow. By SCUBA diving off Falmouth, Massachusetts, during the height of trawling for squid, we have observed trenches left by the trawl door. At the same time, we observed luxuriant beds of decorator worms (*Diopatra cupraea*). These worms are quite fragile and were heavily impacted where the trawl doors had recently passed. The second example was north of Jeffreys Ledge in the Gulf of Maine. Looking from a submersible, we saw a large boulder, estimated to be about 1 × 1.5 m, at one end of a deep, 4-m-long trench that was clearly formed by the boulder being pushed or pulled along the sea floor, apparently by a trawler.

Innovation is a vital part of fishing, especially trawling. A new sweep design known as the street sweeper *(Figure 4c)* surfaced in about 1995 in Massachusetts. The main component of this type of sweep is the brushes used in terrestrial street sweepers. This design has become popular since its introduction, probably because it is lighter than rockhopper gear, so towing efficiency for the vessel is increased. The street sweeper can probably fish much rougher bottom than other sweep designs. The diameter of the individual "brush" was initially about 18 inches, but now brushes up to 31 inches in diameter are in use.

Unsubstantiated reports suggest that the landed catch from vessels that use this gear is quite high.

OPTIONS TO MINIMIZE UNDESIRED EFFECTS OF TRAWLS

Advances in fishing technology also present opportunities to render gear more selective of nontargeted species and juveniles of target species and less impacting on the benthos. The following four solution categories are worthy of consideration:

a) target certain species and modify gear appropriately;

b) encourage the use of lighter sweeps;

c) reduce the sea bottom available to trawlers that fish very irregular terrain; and

d) opt for stationary gear over mobile gear.

Target certain species and modify gear appropriately —This is an option in certain fisheries. One example is the small mesh whiting fishery that occurs in Cape Cod Bay and Massachusetts Bay. This fishery ceased in 1994 because of high bycatch of regulated species, particularly American plaice. An experimental fishery was permitted during the fall of 1996 and 1997 using a raised footrope trawl *(Figure 3a)*. The raised footrope trawl has 42-inch-long chains connecting the sweep to the footrope of the trawl. This design makes the trawl fish about 18–24 inches off the

bottom. The trawl still catches whiting because this species occurs slightly above the sea floor, but it allows flatfish and other bottom-tending species to slip under the footrope and avoid capture.

With this sweep design, the bycatch of regulated groundfish species was reduced to less than 5% of the total catch, the maximum allowed for a fishery that uses mesh smaller than six inches. Measured as a function of unit time fishing, the raised footrope trawl reduced the regulated bycatch from over 200 pounds per hour to less than 30 pounds per hour.

The raised footrope trawl was not designed to reduce the impact of trawling on the bottom, but it does have that effect. Underwater videotapes and observations in flume tanks have both confirmed that the raised footrope sweep has much less contact with the bottom than the traditional cookie sweep that

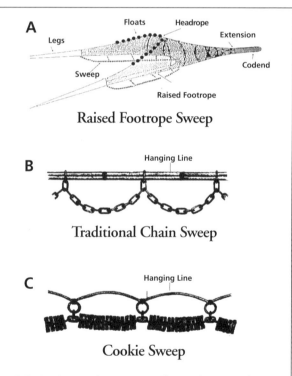

FIGURE 3. **Trawl sweep configurations used on smooth bottoms. (A) A trawl net with the sweep modified by the addition of light dropper chains. These allow the footrope to rise off the sea bottom. The net then tends the sea bottom with less impact. Drawn by Henry Milliken. (B) The traditional chain sweep used by New England commercial trawlers prior to advanced design. Drawn by Paul Shuman. (C) A cookie sweep commonly used by New England trawlers to fish smooth mud or sand bottom. Drawn by Paul Shuman.**

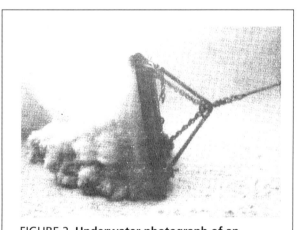

FIGURE 2. **Underwater photograph of an otter trawl door showing the angular spreading action and typical sediment cloud stirred up by the combination of the contact of the door on the sea bottom and the hydrodynamic forces associated with the moving door. Photo courtesy of Fisheries Research Service, Aberdeen Marine Laboratory, Aberdeen, Scotland.**

it replaces. Furthermore, because the raised footrope design keeps the trawl up off the bottom, it allows trawling in rough cobble areas that would snag and tear a trawl with a cookie sweep (Dave Dutra, personal communication). It will also be useful if the purpose is to catch cod and haddock without catching flatfish.

Encourage the use of lighter sweeps—The size and composition of some sweep elements, such as rockhopper or roller gear, can be changed or eliminated to reduce bottom impact. As Captain Frank Mirarchi mentioned, reducing the diameter of cookies to four inches can mean lighter, less impacting trawl gear. It has been quite effective in catching flatfish.

Reduce the sea bottom available to trawlers that fish very irregular terrain—This is also an effective option to reduce impact. There are two ways to accomplish this: area restrictions or sweep restrictions. The former, area restrictions, can be the more difficult of the two to enforce. Restrictions on gear or sweep type can reduce the ability to trawl in more irregular sea floors. An example of such a restriction is the action of the Massachusetts Division of Marine Fisheries about 10 years ago to prohibit fishing in state waters with disks, rollers, or rockhoppers greater than 18 inches in diameter. This action still allows a trawler to fish rough bottom, but the restriction has reduced fishing on very rough bottom.

Opt for stationary gear over mobile gear—The last option to reduce impacts of mobile gear on the sea bottom recognizes the generally benign effect on the environment of stationary gear, such as longlines and fish pots. This option would certainly eliminate the impact of trawling, but would the economic cost and political consequences of converting to stationary gear allow it?

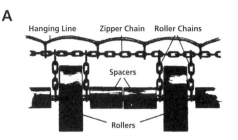

Roller Gear

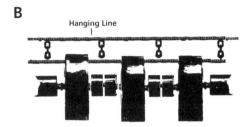

Rockhopper Gear

Street Sweeper Gear

FIGURE 4. Trawl sweep configurations that enable trawlers to fish rocky or irregular bottom. (A) Roller gear, the first innovation that allowed rough bottom trawling. The rollers are made of rubber and spin. Drawn by Paul Shuman. (B) One version of rockhopper gear. The large vertical rubbers are fixed. This gear has a remarkable ability to twist or spring (hop) over rocks more than one meter in diameter. Drawn by Paul Shuman. (C) Three brushes as used in a street sweeper sweep, a relatively new development of increasing popularity. The individual brushes are fixed and essentially replace the large vertical rubbers shown in Figure 4b. Photograph by Henry Milliken.

Implications of the Essential Fish Habitat Provisions of the Magnuson-Stevens Act

Jonathan M. Kurland

NOAA / NATIONAL MARINE FISHERIES SERVICE, GLOUCESTER, MASSACHUSETTS

The 1996 amendments to the Magnuson-Stevens Fishery Conservation and Management Act included substantial new provisions to protect "essential fish habitat" (EFH). I will explain what these changes were, what they mean, and how they are being implemented in New England, to provide some context for the discussion about the effects of fishing gear on habitat.

The Magnuson Act requirements for habitat information before the 1996 amendments were fairly general. The Act required that each fishery management plan (FMP) must "include readily available information regarding the significance of habitat to the fishery and assessment as to the effects which changes to that habitat may have upon the fishery." Fishery management plans needed to include information about habitat and potential threats, but the law called no attention to important habitat areas and did not require any specific measures to protect habitat.

The Sustainable Fisheries Act amended this language, so the new Magnuson-Stevens Act includes a mandatory requirement that each FMP must do three things: "describe and identify essential fish habitat for the fishery..., minimize to the extent practicable adverse effects on such habitat caused by fishing, and identify other actions to encourage the conservation and enhancement of such habitat." Existing FMPs are supposed to be amended to include these provisions by October 11, 1998, which is two years after enactment of the new requirements.

What is EFH? The statutory definition is quite broad: "The term 'essential fish habitat' means those waters and substrate necessary to fish for spawning, breeding, feeding, or growth to maturity." The National Marine Fisheries Service (NMFS) is interpreting this definition to mean that "waters" refers to the physical, chemical, and biological properties of the water column; "substrate" includes sediment, hard bottom, vegetation, and structures under water; "necessary" is the habitat required to support a sustainable fishery; and "spawning, breeding, feeding, or growth to maturity" covers the entire life cycle of managed species. Since EFH is interpreted to include the full life cycle, EFH may be designated in state or federal waters, so it can include estuaries and coastal areas in addition to offshore habitats.

EFH must be designated for all federally managed species. In New England this includes the existing FMPs for groundfish, scallops, and Atlantic salmon, plus the new FMPs being developed by the New England Fishery Management Council for monkfish and sea herring. Management of the lobster fishery is being transferred to the Atlantic States Marine Fisheries Commission, so EFH probably will not need to be designated for lobster, since the Magnuson-Stevens

Act does not apply to interstate FMPs prepared by the Commission.

Designation of EFH will occur through the New England Council using the Council's process to ensure thorough public input and review. A technical team comprised of Council and NMFS staff, the Atlantic States Marine Fisheries Commission, state agency biologists, and other experts will review and synthesize existing literature, databases, and other information and develop draft EFH documents for consideration by the Council's Habitat Committee. The Habitat Committee will be the primary forum for public and industry input on the designation of EFH. The Committee will scope out the issues that need to be addressed and will guide development of FMP amendments for the Council. Once the Habitat Committee has a draft EFH designation, NMFS will review that document and provide technical recommendations, which will fulfill the statutory requirement for NMFS to provide the Councils with recommendations regarding EFH. A public hearing will then be held to receive public comments on both the Council's draft designation of EFH and NMFS' draft EFH recommendations. Following any necessary revisions, the EFH amendments will be transmitted to the full Council for a vote and then submitted to the Secretary of Commerce for approval.

One of the advantages of designating EFH is that federal agencies will be required to consult with NMFS regarding any action they authorize, fund, or undertake that may adversely affect EFH. In addition, NMFS is required to provide conservation recommendations to both federal and state agencies to minimize the effects of their actions on EFH. Although NMFS' recommendations are not mandatory, the federal agency must respond in writing for each action to describe measures the agency will take to protect EFH and to explain its reasons for not accepting any of the recommendations.

Fishery Management Councils will also have an opportunity to comment on proposed actions that could harm EFH. Under the Magnuson-Stevens Act, Councils may comment on any federal or state action that could harm EFH, and Councils must comment if a proposed action is likely to substantially affect the habitat of an anadromous species. These provisions offer the Councils an opportunity to have input on activities such as dredging, industrial discharges, marina development, coastal construction projects, and other actions that may harm EFH and managed species.

The key phrase in the Magnuson-Stevens Act regarding the effects of fishing gear on habitat is the requirement that FMPs must "minimize to the extent practicable adverse effects on EFH caused by fishing." Any management measures to regulate gear impacts on EFH will be restricted to federally managed fishing activities (in federal or state waters), because the Magnuson-Stevens Act only applies to fisheries covered by federal FMPs. So how will the Council and NMFS determine what measures are "practicable" to alleviate any identified gear impacts?

NMFS' regulations to implement the EFH provisions require the Councils to consider three issues to determine what types of management measures are "practicable:" (1) whether and to what extent the fishing activity is adversely impacting EFH, including the fishery; (2) the nature and extent of the adverse effect on EFH; and importantly (3) the long and short term costs as well as benefits to the fishery and its EFH. The regulations also require that each FMP include an assessment of the potential adverse effects of all gear types used in waters designated as EFH. Of course, any decisions on gear modifications, restrictions, closed areas, and so on, may involve fundamentally allocative decisions between gear sectors. These decisions will be made by the Fishery Management Council, through their committees, public hearings, and opportunities for written and verbal public comment.

In closing, I would like to emphasize a few points. First, as the Council amends its FMPs, there will be many opportunities to comment on the designation of EFH for each species and any associated management measures. Secondly, for those who may be unsure of the benefits of designating and protecting essential habitats, the overall goal of the EFH provisions is to facilitate more of an ecosystem-based approach to fishery management, whereby habitat protection and harvest management are better coordinated in an effort to enhance the sustainability of marine fisheries. Finally, regarding gear impacts, it is very important for those who are concerned about these issues—both the effects of fishing on habitat and the effects of gear management measures on fishermen—to stay involved in this process.

EDITORS' NOTE: *The author updated this paper to reflect the requirements of NMFS' December 19, 1997 interim final rule on EFH, which provides guidelines for the Councils to use in developing EFH amendments.*

Short Takes: Additional Observations by Fishermen and Scientists

The Effect of Dredge Harvesting on Eastern Oysters and the Associated Benthic Community

Richard Langan

JACKSON ESTUARINE LABORATORY, UNIVERSITY OF NEW HAMPSHIRE, DURHAM, NEW HAMPSHIRE

INTRODUCTION

A study was conducted in 1994 to determine the effects of dredge harvesting on oyster populations and the benthic community associated with the oyster bed. The study area was located in the Piscataqua River, which divides the states of Maine and New Hampshire. An oyster bed approximately 18 acres in size is located in the river channel and is divided nearly equally by state jurisdictional lines *(Figure 1)*.

Differences in regulations between the two states provided a unique study opportunity. At the time of the study, the State of Maine classified the area as "restricted for depuration" and allowed commercial harvesting, whereas New Hampshire had placed a "prohibited" classification on the area many years prior to the study and did not allow commercial harvesting. The Maine side of the bed had been harvested using a small oyster dredge two days per week on average for five years prior to the study, while the New Hampshire side had not been harvested by any method for many years. The dredge used in the area is 30 inches wide and weighs approximately 60 lbs. The bottom-tending portion of the dredge has blunt, two-inch teeth spaced approximately three inches apart and a chain mesh bag. The different state regulations with regard to harvesting allowed a well-controlled study of the effect of dredge harvesting both on the oysters and on the associated benthic invertebrates. In addition to effects on the oysters and benthos, the amount of suspended sediment that is added to the water column as a result of harvesting was also studied.

METHODS

Six random samples of oysters were collected by SCUBA divers on each side of the river using a 0.25 m² quadrat. All oysters were counted and measured. Five random grab samples were collected on each side of the river using a custom made 0.0625 m² grab

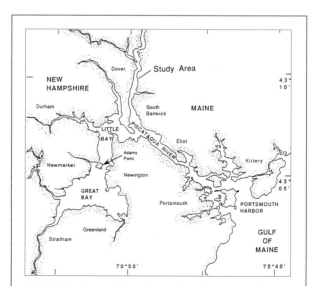

FIGURE 1. **Map of the Great Bay Estuary and the Piscataqua River, showing the location of the oyster bed sampled in this study. The boundary between New Hampshire and Maine bisects the bed.**

sampler. All samples were processed through a 500 µ sieve, and epifaunal and infaunal species were identified and enumerated. Additionally, near bottom water samples collected using a submersible pump in the tracks of the passing dredge were analyzed to assess the impact of the dredge on suspended sediment concentrations. Samples were filtered through 0.45 µ glass fiber filters, which were dried at 80°C and weighed to determine suspended particle concentration.

RESULTS AND DISCUSSION

Results of the oyster sampling are presented in Figure 2. On the Maine (dredge harvested) side of the river, oyster populations showed a normal size distribution and good recent recruitment, while on the New Hampshire (unharvested) side, the size frequency of oysters was skewed toward older, larger individuals and recruitment was poor. The higher recruitment of young of the year individuals on the Maine side may be due

to the action of the dredge in turning over oyster shells and removing silt, resulting in clean, exposed substrate for the larvae to settle on. Since the larger oysters are being removed on the Maine side, the population on the New Hampshire side has more larger, older oysters, as well as what appears to be lower recruitment, perhaps due to accumulation of silt on the shells.

Results of the analysis of the benthic community are shown in Figures 3 and 4. Oligochaetes were just about equally abundant on both sides of the line. Polychaete density was slightly higher on the New Hampshire side. Crustacea and mollusks were more numerous on the Maine side. The number of species per replicate ranged from 31 to 39 on the Maine side, slightly higher than in New Hampshire, which had from 26 to 37 species per replicate. No significant differences (ANOVA) between the two areas were found in the number, species richness or diversity

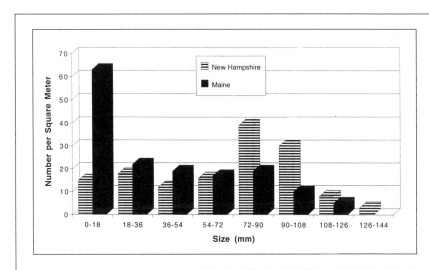

FIGURE 2. **Size class distribution of oysters collected using standard quadrats on the Maine and New Hampshire sides of the Piscataqua River.**

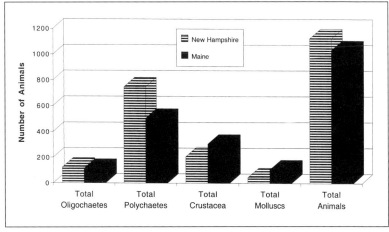

FIGURE 3. **Density of major taxonomic groups of macro invertebrates in grab samples from Maine and New Hampshire.**

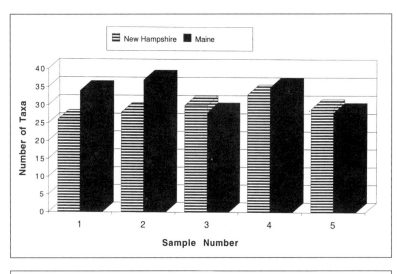

FIGURE 4. **Number of benthic macro invertebrate taxa per sample in grab samples from Maine and New Hampshire.**

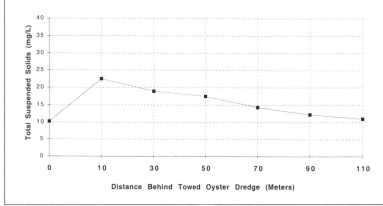

FIGURE 5. **Suspended sediment concentration in the Piscataqua River relative to distance behind a towed oyster dredge.**

of epifaunal and infaunal invertebrates, indicating that dredge harvesting has no detectable effect on the benthic community.

Results of the analysis of suspended sediments resulting from the harvesting activities are presented in Figure 5. The ambient suspended sediment concentration before passage of the dredge was approximately 10 milligrams per liter (mg/l). At a distance of 10 m behind the dredge, the sediment concentration increased to slightly greater than 20 mg/l. At a distance of 30 m behind the dredge, the concentration remained at about 20 mg/l. Suspended sediment concentration began to decline at a distance of 50 m and dropped progressively at 70 m and 90 m. At a distance of 110 m behind the dredge, the sediment concentration had returned to near-ambient concentrations.

These results indicate that the impact of the dredge on suspended sediment concentration was localized and not very large. The effect of towing this type of gear will ultimately depend upon on the amount of sediment covering the bed prior to harvesting. Towing this gear on an oyster bed that has not been harvested recently and has an accumulation of silt will probably result in a greater amount of resuspension from dredging than was found in this study.

In conclusion, the results of this study indicate that this type of mobile fishing gear did not cause negative impact on either the habitat or the targeted species.

Another Approach to
Scallop Production, Habitat Concerns,
and Biodiversity

Richard Taylor

F/V MY MARIE, GLOUCESTER, MASSACHUSETTS

For me, fishing has always been about production. Production has been the name of the game: a gang of men working as hard as possible, landing as much as possible for other people to eat. I began scalloping in 1968, and I have an old boat, a wreck or an antique depending on your point of view, that has in effect outlived the species it was designed to catch. More recently I have begun to grow scallops in cages with funding from the National Marine Fisheries Service. I have had a lot of time to think, out there towing when there is not a lot to catch. There must be a better way. Below are some of my thoughts about increasing scallop production.

Standard gear for the scallop fishery is a 15-foot-wide scallop dredge with a two-inch steel frame and a chain bag, which weighs well over a ton empty *(Figure 1)*. The crewman in the photograph provides a good sense of scale (see also Smolowitz Figure 2, page 48). This gear is used on about 250 large vessels on the east coast and on 18 vessels in Alaska. Most of the boats tow two of these dredges. Alaska allows only 18 scallop permits, while the east coast has over 250 permits in an area roughly comparable in size.

The area covered by offshore scallop vessels on the east coast is indicated for 1993 in Figure 2. The vessels fish over a considerable area, and it is not the same area each trip or each year. Since the end of 1994, three large offshore areas (shaded in *Figure 2*) have been closed to the scallop fleet to help rebuild groundfish stocks. These closures cover only about 20% of the area normally fished for scallops, but account for over 50% of the scallop landings, so they have an enormous impact on the fishery.

Landings for the scallop fishery for the last 50 years show a lot of year-to-year variation *(Figure 3)*. A boom and bust pattern is clearly evident. The precise cause of the peaks in recruitment is unknown. With the larger number of vessels in the more recent boom cycles, there are high landings, but the duration of periods of good production has declined. Note, for contrast, the long period of good production after 1945. Now we catch scallops faster, because fishing pressure is high. Once the scallops are found, they are rapidly harvested, many at a small size, so that total tonnage is less than it might be if the small scallops had been allowed to grow. Landings in 1996 have declined significantly to around 7,000 to 8,000 tons, lower than at any time since the early 1970s.

Since 1968, when I started fishing, not only has the world population nearly doubled, but the fisheries production worldwide has also doubled, from about 50,000 metric tons to around 100,000 metric tons. But as I look ahead, I expect the human population to increase more rapidly than fisheries production with our current methods, at least in this region. That puts us in a crunch.

My primary concern is not so much for the impacts of dredges on the sea floor, but for techniques that can increase production of scallops. Perhaps

FIGURE 1. **15-foot scallop dredge on the stern of a commercial scallop vessel. Photograph by Bill DuPaul, Virginia Institute of Marine Science.**

there is a solution that will address both problems. My current project involves growing scallops in wire mesh cages similar to large lobster traps—five-foot cubes with shelves. Sea scallops grow about an inch a year in shell height and take about three years in the cage to reach marketable size.

Close inspection of sea scallop shells reveals edges that are razor thin, sharp, and fragile. The frequency of shell damage that I see in small scallops harvested by dredges is high (see examples in *Figure 4*; see also Shepard and Auster 1991) and is cause for concern. Ring size of scallop bags has been increased to allow escapement of smaller scallops, but it is not easy on small scallops to go through the steel rings of a dredge moving at four to five miles per hour. Many show chipped edges and shell repair, presumably from the earlier times when they have been run over by fishing gear and not caught. Each time this happened, the scallop has had to reallocate its energy budget to repair the thin outer shell edge, because until they can close their shells, they are more vulnerable to predators. Only afterwards can energy be shifted back to meat growth.

People do not eat scallop shells, and we do not care what the shells look like, but we like the scallop meat. I believe that we lose meat production every time a small scallop is damaged and forced to shift its energy budget in that way. This belief was supported by my observations on a recent sea scallop tagging cruise conducted by the National Oceanic and Atmospheric Administration (NOAA). The cruise sampled scallops from Georges Bank on both sides of the Hague Line in late summer 1997. Scallops from the U.S. side and inside closed area II (where scalloping has been prohibited since 1994) had noticeably greater shell height and meat size than scallops of the same year class from the Canadian side (where low-level scalloping is still occurring). Production would be increased if small scallops were protected from mobile fishing gear until they are ready for market. They should should be allowed to grow.

Part of my reading has led me to examine the approaches in Japan. The Japanese ran up against the limits of their marine resources before the U.S. did and have had some time to develop strategies to increase production. They now catch newly settled scallops (spat) and keep them in a protected environment away from predators for about a year. The fastest growing 10% are selected and kept for two years in contained grow-out culture until ready for market. The other 90% are reseeded in areas that

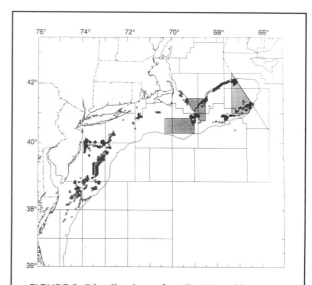

FIGURE 2. **Distribution of scalloping effort in 1993 off the U.S. east coast, as observed from the Domestic Sea Sampling Program. Source: NEFSC 1997.**

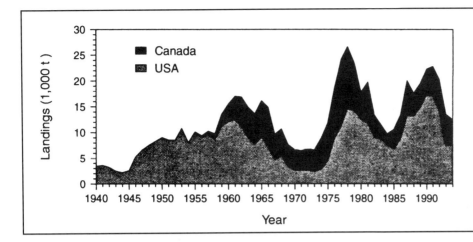

FIGURE 3. **U.S. Atlantic sea scallop landings, 1940 to 1994. Source: NMFS 1996.**

are not opened to the dredge fishery until year four. Production from these two methods (hanging culture and reseeding to the wild) has been about equal (Ito and Bykuno 1990). Once rotational fishing areas are established, there is always an adult year class for the boats to work on and follow-on year classes growing in protected areas, to be brought into the fishery in the years ahead. Japanese production has soared since these methods were introduced *(Figure 5)*.

The Japanese have set aside a much smaller area for scallop seeding than the thousands of square miles that our east coast scallop fleet covers, but production from the Japanese method is much higher. The two countries report landings in different units, so they must be converted for a comparison. Japanese landings *(Figure 5)* are presented in whole live weight, while the U.S. landings *(Figure 3)* are in wet meat weight. It takes about 10 to 15 pounds of live weight to produce one pound of scallop meat. In 1996 Japanese

FIGURE 4. **Examples of shell edge damage and repair in small scallops collected from commercial scallop dredges. Photograph by Richard Taylor.**

production totaled about 550,000 metric tons (mt) or about 35,000 to 45,000 mt of meat, at least five times the U.S. landings (H. Ito pers. comm.). Note that records from both countries show low production in the early 1970s before the 200-mile limits

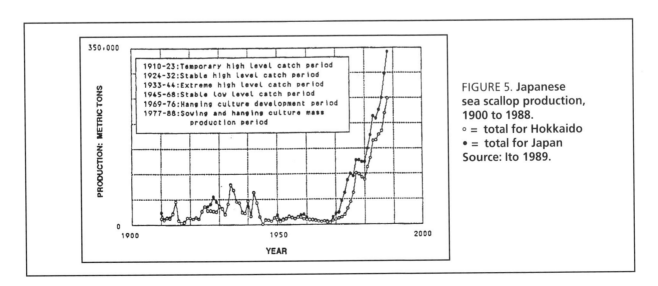

FIGURE 5. **Japanese sea scallop production, 1900 to 1988.**
○ = total for Hokkaido
● = total for Japan
Source: Ito 1989.

were established. The Japanese production is the result of careful planning and reseeding. Ours comes from a fluctuating resource. Our fishery management concerns are about over exploitation and the politics of scarcity. Japan is building abundance. Similar methods have been successfully instituted both in New Zealand (Anon. 1995; Bull 1990) and more recently in the Magdalen Islands in the Gulf of St. Lawrence.

What does all this have to with the impact on the bottom? Suppose we succeed in rebuilding the depleted fisheries in our region and have a viable habitat to produce the maximum sustainable amount of marine life for human consumption. If we pick cod, for example, we might get 100 million pounds a year over the range. That sounds like a huge number because it is so much larger than what we are landing now. But even that is only two pounds of cod fish (flesh, bones, guts, and all) per person per year for the population between Boston and Washington. So the sustainable catch from our local ocean will not feed our numbers, even with all the other species added in. I believe that this country is going to have to set aside areas for intensive cultivation to meet our food demands and put larger areas aside for stock and habitat reserves.

One of the other current concerns is maintaining biodiversity. In closing, I want to use an example from the land. As a society, we do not expect much biodiversity in a wheat field. We actively get rid of pests and weeds in order to put bread and other staples in the supermarket. The other side of it is that farmers do not drive wheat combines across the rest of the prairie or through the forest looking for wheat. I believe that it is possible to greatly increase scallop production by applying proven methods on a small percent of the continental shelf. This would benefit the habitat on the remainder of the shelf by eliminating the need to search large areas of the sea floor with scallop gear.

I firmly believe that in the long run the U.S. is going to have to follow the Japanese approach to marine protein production. This approach will work with scallops, and although it is clearly more difficult with other species, the U.S. needs to move toward intense production in some areas and keep others as reserves.

REFERENCES

Anonymous. 1995. Model Fishery Setting the Pace. *Seafood New Zealand.* May:8-13. The N.Z. Seafood Industry Magazine, Ltd., Wellington, NZ.

Bull, M. 1990. Enhancement and management of New Zealand's southern scallop fishery. Pp. 253-263 in M. C. L. Dredge, W. F. Zacharin, and L. M. Joll, eds. *Proceedings of the Australasian Scallop Workshop 1988*. Hobart, Australia.

Ito, H. 1989. Successful HOTAC methods for developing scallop sowing culture in the Nemuro District of East Hokkaido, Northern Japan. Pp. 107-116 in *Proceeding of the 15th US-Japan Conference on Marine Ranching 1989*, NMFS Technical Memorandum No. 102.

Ito, S. and A. Bykuno. 1990. History of scallop culture in Japan. Pp. 166-181 in M. C. L. Dredge, W. F. Zacharin, and L. M. Joll, eds. *Proceedings of the Australasian Scallop Workshop 1988*. Hobart, Australia. Hobart, Australia.

NEFSC. 1997. Report of the 23rd Northeast Regional Stock Assessment Workshop (SAW) Stock Assessment Review Committee (SARC) Consensus Summary of Assessments. Northeast Fisheries Science Center Ref. Doc. 97-05. 209 pp.

NMFS. 1996. Our Living Oceans. Report on the Status of U.S. Living Marine Resources, 1995. U.S. Dep. Commer., NOAA Tech. Memo. NMFS-F/SPO-19. 160 pp.

Shepard, A.N. and P.J. Auster. 1991. Incidental (non-capture) damage to scallops caused by dragging on rock and sand substrates. Pp. 219-230 in S. E. Shumway and P. A. Sandifer, eds. *An International Compendium of Scallop Biology and Culture*. World Aquaculture Workshops, Number 1. World Aquaculture Society, Baton Rouge, LA.

Changes to the Sea Floor in the Chatham Area

Fred Bennett

F/V SEA BAG III, CHATHAM, MASSACHUSETTS

I am a longliner. I started my career back around thirty years ago, hauling a longline by hand and jigging cod. From longlining, I went to sea scalloping in the 1970s, and that enabled me to buy a much larger vessel. I bought a 55-foot stern trawler and started trawling on smooth bottom. When the smooth bottom fishery more or less failed, I switched to roller gear so that I could trawl on hard bottom. I used very large roller gear that was extremely heavy, and I continued with that for a number of years.

In 1987, I went back to hook fishing again, and I have done that ever since. I am the oldest hook fisherman in the Chatham area. My longlining has evolved into a more modern method, but the hooks are still baited by hand. I fish using four longlines, each about one mile long. The hooks are baited on land and fed out from a tub, so this is often referred to as tub trawling.

I have been observing for all these years that I have fished on the ocean, and there seems to be a really serious problem. The ocean is definitely at a low period in production in just about everything. There has been a little improvement in some stocks, but the ocean does not seem to be producing much for the amount of time and effort that the fishermen have had to give up in attempts to rebuild. I have concluded that the real problem is not the fishermen. The problem is the method used for harvesting because it destroys the critical habitat. I will describe several examples of habitat destruction.

One example is an area about 25 miles east-southeast of Chatham called the Peaks. When I first fished at the Peaks in the late 1960s, they were a row of hills running northwest to southeast for about a mile. I had a paper depth recorder, and on it I could watch the bottom go up and down. There were four big steep peaks whose height from bottom to top was about 10 fathoms, and there were several smaller hills as well. I would set my longline right across those peaks, because the fishing for cod was excellent. When I went back in 1987 after taking up longlining again, all I could find was a couple of little bumps in the bottom, just little hills, none higher than two to three fathoms. The fishing was not as good as before, though I still fish there at times. I do not know what happened to that topography, but I suspect that it was destroyed by the trawlers and scallopers that have fished there.

There is another area that used to be good hook fishing. Fishermen call it the Big Mussels, and it is to the east of the Fishing Rip. It used to be a huge expanse of horse mussels 2 to 3 miles wide and 6 to 7 miles long. The mussels were mixed in with other creatures, like crabs, anemones, and tube worms, and there was a lot of growth on the mussels. This showed that the bottom was relatively stable and had not been beaten up. One portion of the area, where I have been fishing on and off for 30 years, not only had big mussels, it also had peaks in it, steep sand hills in the western part near the north end.

For two years, this particular area was not available to me due to the presence of larger draggers fishing there. They were fishing very close to the Fishing Rip, less than half a mile from the rip, and they were catching flounders and cod and other fish. When

I had a chance to get back in there in April 1997, there was no one else fishing there. I was sure I was going to catch a lot of fish. I set my gear as usual from the south to the north over those peaks.

As in the past, I put a sash weight, a five-pound weight, on each side of the peak to drive my hook gear right to the bottom, so that none of it would be suspended in midwater between the peaks. When I went over where these peaks used to be, however, I looked on my depth sounder, and there was nothing there. I checked my GPS (Global Positioning System) and my Loran to make sure I was in the right place, and I was. Those hills were gone. I would guess they were seven fathoms high before, and they have been reduced to about two fathoms.

In addition to the hills disappearing, the mussels are gone from the Big Mussels. When I first started fishing there, there were so many mussels that with the older type gear, which was not very strong, they would actually cut through the ground line with their sharp edges. On a trip in April 1997, I spent quite a bit of time there, and I did not snag more than one mussel the whole time. In the past I would have caught many clumps. I noticed the lack of mussels as soon as I returned to hook fishing in 1987. Both scallopers and trawlers have towed in that area.

It is not just the horse mussels that have disappeared. A bed of blue mussels that used to be on the west side of the Fishing Rip is also mostly gone. Another creature that has mostly disappeared is one we call lemons (see Leach Figure 1, pages 97 and 160). Scientists call them stalked sea squirts. They indicated a good place for fishing, and they used to come up all the time in certain areas, often in clumps. Now I only see single lemons, and hardly any of those. I would estimate that they have declined by 98% since I started fishing. Corals have mostly disappeared, too, from the southwest part of the Great South Channel, the one place where I used to see them regularly. I saw the first piece in a very long time just recently.

Another bottom habitat that has been destroyed is the clay pipes. Thirty to forty years ago, there used to be a large area of clay pipes located about 30 miles southeast of Nantucket. The clay pipes were spread over about 25 square miles where the depth ranges from about 32 to 50 fathoms. We longliners would sometimes snag pieces of pipe and bring them up on our boats. I myself never saw any pieces longer than 6 or 8 inches, but I know a longliner who pulled up a two-foot-long section once. The pieces of clay pipe usually had various creatures on or in them, such as brittle stars, mussels, and pork fat (a sea squirt with no stalk). We had good cod fishing where the clay pipes used to be, but now the pipes have all been smashed into little pieces since scallopers started fishing there. We never see anything except tiny pieces of clay pipes from this area now. The clay pipes are wrecked there. There are still some fish to catch in that area, but it is not as good fishing as it used to be.

The rocks on the bottom have also changed over time. When I first started fishing back in the 1960s, rocks would come up with barnacles on them in clusters as big as my fist. There were thousands of them. The barnacles were bigger than you see now— up to an inch and a half wide at the base. The barnacles and other animals on the rocks, like anemones, brittle stars and tube worms, were signs of a fairly stable bottom that had not been towed too much. Now the rocks are mostly bare, or they have just a few white base plates to show where barnacles were sheared off. They have clearly been mashed by something.

All these signs of a healthy bottom have disappeared in thirty years, and they have disappeared more dramatically in the past ten years. These habitats had been there for generations previously, and the names for these places (the Peaks, the Big Mussels, the Lemons, and others) are ancient. I learned these names from people who fished there long before me, people who were old-timers in 1960, when I first came to Chatham. Hook fishing had occurred on these areas for at least 70 and probably more than 100 years with no decline.

In closing, I would like to say that I believe that science and industry must work together to create new ways of catching fish. Fisherman cannot continue with the same old otter trawl and the same old style of fishing. We have put ourselves out of a job. That is what we have been doing for a long time.

EDITORS' NOTE: *At the conference, Mr. Bennett showed specimens of horse mussels (Modiolus modiolus), "lemons" (stalked ascidians, Boltenia ovifera), a rock with a lot of whole barnacles attached, and a rock with only the base plates of barnacles attached.*

A Better Urchin Drag

Kristan Porter

F/V BLACK SHEEP, DOWNEAST DRAGGER'S ASSOCIATION, CUTLER, MAINE

I grew up in Cutler, Maine, which is just 15 miles from the Canadian border. I fish for scallops and sea urchins in the wintertime. In the summer, I fish for mahogany quahogs. I bought my own boat back in 1991, but I have been fishing since 1984. I want to describe an improved drag (or dredge) for sea urchins that has been developed in my area.

About the time that dragging for sea urchins started, it was kind of a savior for the scallop fishermen in our area because the scallops were on a down swing. But the bottom in the area is really rugged. The drag we were using for urchins is like a small scallop dredge. We were fishing with traditional 5/8-inch sweep chain on the drag. For the urchin fishery, the state of Maine requires us to use a drag no wider

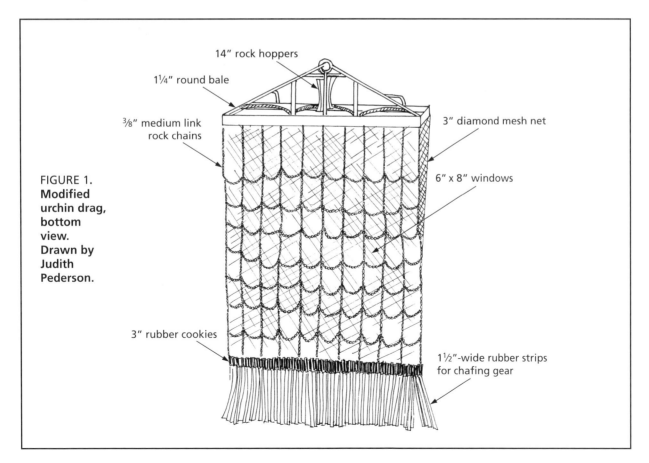

FIGURE 1.
Modified urchin drag, bottom view. Drawn by Judith Pederson.

14" rock hoppers

1¼" round bale

⅜" medium link rock chains

3" diamond mesh net

6" x 8" windows

3" rubber cookies

1½"-wide rubber strips for chafing gear

Short Takes: Additional Observations by Fishermen and Scientists **117** than five and a half feet. With traditional scallop gear, we were damaging some of the urchins, so we came up with a way to get a better product on the market and also fish the harder bottom.

The solution was a lighter urchin drag that was originally called a Green drag because a guy named John Green designed it. It is more like the beam trawl used in the North Sea. It has a smaller window and a smaller chain and a light head bale with rockhoppers (rubber discs) on the head bale. Some people use rock-hoppers on either side of the head bale to come up over the heavier bottom. Because we urchin draggers were tearing up our nets in the rocky bottom, we added rubber strips from tires. We put those over the bag in the front, looped them in, and used sheet rock screws to hold them in, so the jagged rocks would not rip our nets. On some bottoms these would not work—kelpy bottom and soft bottom—because we had to dig them out from under kelp. So we came up with a variation between the two drags.

The modified urchin drag is shown in Figure 1. Instead of rockhoppers along the bottom and the small cookies with the straight bottom, we put a sweep in like a traditional chain sweep. We also made smaller windows (the space between chains in the sweep), so rocks wouldn't get in and damage the product. This design seems to work well in our area because of the ruggedness of the bottom. Our catch has improved dramatically in quality and also in quantity because of the areas we can tow in. Some people also put wheels (rubber discs that rotate) on the drag. We can strap the wheels on for towing over certain types of bottom.

The Maine Sea Urchin Zone Council is now considering requiring lighter drags in the urchin fishery. Lighter urchin drags are good in some places but not good in others. We need to be able to use different drags for different types of bottom.

As I said earlier, I dredge for mahogany clams in the summer time. I have heard it said that once you dredge through an area, then it is dead and gone. That does not match my observations. I have been working on boats for many years, since I was old enough to go. About 10 years ago, when I was in high school, we were working on a bed of mahogany clams off Jonesport. Now in 1997, we are working on the same bed with a brand new set of clams, and we are having better landings now than we did then in that area. So, in some instances, dragging an area could enhance it instead of destroying it.

Brief Notes on Habitat Geology and Clay Pipe Habitat on Stellwagen Bank

Page Valentine

U.S. GEOLOGICAL SURVEY, WOODS HOLE, MASSACHUSETTS

In our studies of sea floor habitats, my colleagues and I use both biological and geological approaches. We call our studies "habitat geology," a term coined by a biologist friend of mine. We view it as the study of sea floor materials and biological and geological processes that influence where species live. Some of the factors that we consider are the following:

1) composition of the sea bed, which ranges from mud to sand, gravel, bedrock, and shell beds;

2) shape and steepness of the bottom;

3) roughness of the bottom, which is enhanced by the presence of cobbles, boulders, sand waves and ripples, burrows into the bottom, and species that extend above the bottom;

4) bottom currents generated by storm waves and tides, which can move sediment and expose or cover habitats; and

5) the way in which the sea bed is utilized by species.

In addition, we take into account the impact of sea bed disturbance by bottom fishing trawls and dredges. Habitats characterized by attached and burrowing species that protrude above the sea bed appear to be most vulnerable to disturbance.

Our continuing studies of the large gravel patch that covers the northeastern edge of Georges Bank show the importance of that habitat to herring, scallops, and juvenile cod (Valentine and Lough 1991; Collie

et al. 1997). In Massachusetts Bay, we have mapped the Massachusetts Bay Disposal Site and noted the rapid colonization by lobsters of the piles of rock that dramatically altered the natural habitats when they were dumped there in 1992 and 1993 (Valentine *et al.* 1996).

Recently, we have documented an unusual habitat type that is referred to as "clay pipe" (also known as "pipe clay"). Clay pipes are pieces of hard fine-grained sediment having irregular shapes that usually are lying scattered on the sea floor. Some pieces are hollow and pipe-like, but many pieces are curved fragments of broken pipe walls. There is some question regarding their origin, but it is likely that they are derived from the walls of former burrows into soft mud (made by crabs, fish, and burrowing anemones) that have hardened and been eroded from the sea bed. Clay pipes lying on the sea bed provide primary bottom roughness that is enhanced by the voids inside the pipes.

There is anecdotal evidence from fishermen that clay pipe is a rich groundfish habitat and that many sites no longer exist because they have been destroyed by dredging and trawling. Historical sites apparently were present both north and south of Cape Ann, but recent attempts to find them have been unsuccessful. In our studies of Stellwagen Bank over the past several years, we had not observed clay pipes until Ellie Dorsey of the Conservation Law Foundation gave us a site location she had obtained from a gillnet fisherman. We visited that site in 1996 and adjacent sites in 1997 *(Figure 1)* and documented the clay pipes using video and still photography. They lie in 60 m of water on gravel sea bed and appear to be undisturbed, as the pipes are covered with various attached species *(Figure 2)*. The rough bottom and the presence of gillnets may prevent bottom trawling in this region.

These clay pipe sites have not been mapped fully, but they might be large enough to be appropriate for further detailed study.

There are several questions that could be considered in regard to the study and management of clay pipe habitat. Is clay pipe really an unusually productive groundfish habitat, and why? Is it accessible and vulnerable to trawling and dredging, and is it worth protecting? If clay pipe is a valued groundfish habitat, would it be possible and advisable to restore and expand this habitat type by depositing artificial clay pipes at favorable sites?

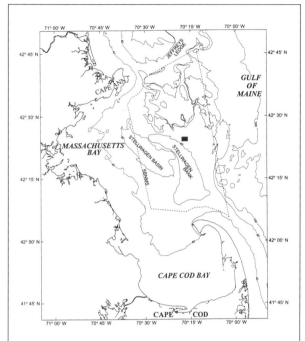

FIGURE 1. **Location of clay pipes observed on the sea floor. Depth contours in meters.**

REFERENCES

Collie, J.S., G.A. Escanero, and P.C. Valentine. 1997. Effects of bottom fishing on the benthic megafauna of Georges Bank. *Mar. Ecol. Prog. Ser.* 155:159-172.

Valentine, P.C., and R.G. Lough. 1991. *The sea floor environment and the fishery of eastern Georges Bank; the influence of geologic and oceanographic environmental factors on the abundance and distribution of fisheries resources of the northeastern United States continental shelf.* U.S. Geological Survey Open-File Report 91-439. 25p.

Valentine, P.C., W.W. Danforth, E.T. Roworth, and S.T. Stillman. 1996. *Maps showing topography, backscatter, and interpretation of sea floor features in the Massachusetts Bay Disposal Site region off Boston, Massachusetts.* U.S. Geological Survey Open-File Report 96-273, scale 1:10,000 and 1:12,500, 2 sheets.

FIGURE 2. **A clay pipe photographed on the sea floor in an apparently undisturbed location. Photograph by Page Valentine and Dann Blackwood.**

Observations of a
Fisherman and Spotter Pilot
in the Gulf of Maine

Bill Doughty

F/VS TORI T, PROWLER, PURSUIT, CLOSER LOOK, ORR'S ISLAND, MAINE

I have been a fisherman for a long time, beginning with fishing for lobster, herring, pogies and bait fish in Casco Bay, Maine. I have been in many different fisheries and have seen a lot of changes during that time. Humans have been blamed for many changes that I do not think they are responsible for. The ocean is not stagnant. For example, right now there is more biomass than ever before, but it is in different species than it used to be.

I have used fixed gear and seine gear, but most of my experience is with mobile gear. I started with a 100 horsepower engine, and the most powerful I have ever used was 600 horsepower. I have fished from 40 to 140 fathoms, and I match the gear to different target species. I learned how not to lose gear and how to make gear very forgiving on the bottom, which is necessary for fishing in the Gulf of Maine.

When I was 14 and in the herring business, I learned how to fly. I have flown over the same ledges for 37 years as a spotter for herring and pogies, and I have also flown offshore for swordfish and tuna. I have seen the inner shore habitat change. For example, from the air, I have seen changes in the kelp beds covering the rocks. Sea urchins stripped the kelp, sea moss, and other algae off the rocks. This happened because there are so many cormorants now. Cormorants feed on cunner, which are not fished commercially (although I did use them as lobster bait when I was a kid). Because cunner is the natural predator of urchins, when cunner decreased, sea urchin populations took off. Man has brought it back into balance again by harvesting the urchins, so now kelp is covering the rocks again. I see it when I fly over.

Cormorant populations have increased so much that they are moving inland. I was in Rangely, Maine recently at elevation 1467 feet above sea level, and I counted 14 cormorants in Mooselookmeguntic Lake. Eider ducks are also increasing in number and are eating up all the mussels in salt water. They are moving inland as well. Lakes close to sea level have literally hundreds of cormorants and eider ducks.

Another change I have observed over the last 30 years is pollution moving offshore in the form of visible cloudiness in the water. Sunlight is necessary for producing food in the ocean, but if the water is cloudy, light can not penetrate very deep. People need to start asking hard questions. What are we doing? Where is the pollution coming from?

I am most familiar with Maine, and I can describe how far the mud line (the line of cloudy water) has moved offshore. Years ago, I could see down 20 fathoms from the boat as well as when I was flying, just 16 miles from the Large Navigational Buoy at the Portland Light Ship site. Now, there is no clear water until much further out, at Cashes Ledge. This makes spotting for fish more difficult. It is necessary to look outside the mud line or else look for fish that are finning at the surface if you want to find them from the air.

Since white water rafting became popular, I have noticed a phenomenon, especially in Penobscot Bay. A mud cloud extends all the way out over Jeffreys Banks and Outerfalls and all the way to the Dories (Three Dory Ridge). There are two rivers that bring the mud down, the Kennebec and the Penobscot. In the past, natural spring floods would end and the mud cloud in the ocean would clear up sometime in June. Now from May to October there are rafters every day, requiring the dams to be opened for a while every day. This creates a mud cloud in the ocean all summer long.

In the late 1960s and early 1970s, I starting seeing the phenomenon of a pink slime. It started showing up on our cables at first, and then it was visible in the water column. We took a sample to Bowdoin College and got it identified as a species of alga. I do not remember its name. Industry has cleaned up its act, and the rivers are cleaner now, but this slime is still here. It was only inshore at first, and now it is everywhere—offshore and all over the coast. I am surprised that others have not mentioned it. What is this slime? And what is its effect? I believe that mobile gear keeps the slime stirred up. I have seen bottoms go "sour" without mobile gear, which drives fish away, and I attribute it to this slime.

I think man is an extremely small part of what goes on in the ocean, which is a great deal. With trawling, very little of the ocean really gets touched, in spite of the miles that are towed. Fishermen trawl over exactly the same bottom repeatedly, as Frank Mirachi's plotter showed (see Mirarchi Figure 1, page 81). Draggers will tow a piece of bottom hundreds of times in a year, and it stays productive. Contrary to what people think, big trawlers are not turning the bottom over

and over. There are all kinds of things that keep us from towing for miles, such as wrecks and other bottom features. Rockhopper gear is getting a very bad shake. When I started trawling, fishermen used wooden rollers and wooden spacers on the sweep to target redfish (ocean perch). Redfish live on the hardest bottom that you can get, and we made those sweeps to get over the rough bottom. I believe that rockhopper gear is no worse than the old wooden rollers.

Incidentally, redfish are taking over the bottom and a lot of the humps in Maine since the late 1980s when 5 1/2 inch mesh was required in trawls. I cannot give a scientific reason, but redfish are an extremely bad neighbor as far as groundfish are concerned. Years ago when you caught redfish, you would not get any groundfish with them until you got into the deeper water.

To conclude, I would like to say that science could be better served by using fishermen to help with sampling and research. By working together, we fishermen might get over our distrust of scientists. Several years ago, I offered the use of any one of my boats (which have diversified from longlining, dragging, and scalloping) for scientific purposes. I have also offered to take observers in my airplane. Anybody is very welcome. I think it would be very advantageous for people to see the mud line and the other things I can see from the air. I would really like to work closer with scientists. Fishermen are people who have learned a lot about the bottom out of sheer necessity. Scientists and managers are not utilizing the commercial fishing industry in the way that they should.

Post-settlement Survivorship of Juvenile Atlantic Cod and the Design of Marine Protected Areas

James Lindholm[1,2], Peter Auster[2], Les Kaufman[1] and Matthias Ruth[1]

1) BOSTON UNIVERSITY, BOSTON MA
2) NOAA'S NATIONAL UNDERSEA RESEARCH CENTER FOR THE NORTHWEST ATLANTIC
AND GREAT LAKES, GROTON CT

This paper describes one component of an ongoing research effort to assess the effects of fishing on habitat and the role of marine protected areas (MPAs) as tools for conservation and management. The purpose of this study is to formulate a model that describes post-settlement survivorship of juveniles as one of the critical components in the life history of demersal fish. Here we use the model to investigate the importance of sea floor habitat in fish survivorship.

First, we review the life history of a demersal fish, Atlantic cod (*Gadus morhua*). Cod eggs are released into the water column by spawning females and are subsequently fertilized. The eggs remain in the water column during development, eventually hatching into pelagic larvae which, in turn, metamorphose into pelagic juveniles. Roughly four months after spawning, the pelagic juveniles settle to the sea floor and transition to demersal juveniles. Historically, most scientific research has been dedicated to pelagic processes, such as predation on the various pelagic stages, in an attempt to explain annual fluctuations in fish populations (for example, see Anderson 1988). Much attention has also been paid to protection of brood stock through controls on fishing, such as effort limitations and gear type and size restrictions. Less attention has been given to small-scale processes affecting population dynamics immediately following settlement to the sea floor (Auster 1988). Early benthic phase fish are subject to a suite of potential predators, and mortality is sufficient to significantly modify population size (Sissenwine 1984; Sogard 1997). We focus here on juvenile fish in the first year after settlement. We show that protecting the quality of sea floor habitat utilized by settled juveniles will lead to improved recruitment to harvested populations.

Following settlement, juvenile cod seek shelter in a variety of sea floor habitats that serve as refuges from predation (Lough *et al.* 1989; Gotceitas and Brown 1993; Gotceitas *et al.* 1995; Tupper and Boutilier 1995a,b; Fraser *et al.* 1996). Sea floor habitat complexity, for the purpose of this study, is the vertical relief or cover provided by the physical substrate and by any emergent biogenic structures. In gravel, cobble, and boulder areas, biogenic structure is provided by emergent epifauna such as hydroids, sponges, and anemones. In areas of sand and mud, structure is provided by a variety of emergent tube-dwelling organisms, by burrows and depressions, and by sand waves and shell aggregations created by physical processes (Auster *et al.* 1991, 1995, 1998). As it is dragged across the bottom, mobile fishing gear used to catch demersal fish and shellfish (such as otter trawls, beam trawls, and scallop dredges) reduces much of the vertical relief provided by different substrates and associated emergent epifauna (Langton 1994; Auster *et al.* 1996; Schwinghamer *et al.* 1996; Auster and Langton, in press; Collie, this volume; Gordon *et al.*, this volume; Freese *et al.*, in prep). Loss of habitat complexity leads to increased predation on recently settled cod (Lough *et al.* 1989; Tupper and Boutilier 1995a,b; Gotceitas and Brown 1997; Lindholm *et al.*, in prep.). If we can identify areas of critical sea floor habitat and protect it from alterations by fishing activities, we should be able to improve post-settlement survivorship and subsequent recruitment to surrounding populations.

Much is unknown about the behavior and population dynamics of juvenile cod in the northwest Atlantic. We employ computer modeling to apply data from small-scale laboratory and field studies to population-level processes and responses. With models of this type, we can organize existing information and explore the implications of our knowledge relatively easily, although at this stage we cannot provide predictions of the size of any particular year class of fish. The output from computer models can be used to drive future research in the laboratory and field, as well as to inform discussions of a system's behavior with policy makers and the fishing industry.

The model presented here uses equations modified from Beverton and Holt (1957) and Ruth (1995). It is concerned only with the fate of juvenile fish following settlement to the sea floor. The model simulates a population divided into sixteen regions in a 4 × 4 matrix, where the habitat in each region is either protected from fishing disturbance as an MPA or not. An MPA is interpreted as any region or combination of regions in which the sea floor has achieved a measure of complexity commensurate with an epifaunal community undisturbed by fishing activities. Habitat complexity is considered to be uniform within any region. We assume density-dependent mortality rates with an S-shaped relationship between local density of settled fish and natural mortality. Juvenile fish in regions that are not MPAs lack adequate cover to seek refuge from predation and therefore experience increased natural mortality. For this model, we assume mortality rates outside protected areas to be two to five times as high as inside (for more details, see Lindholm *et al.* 1998).

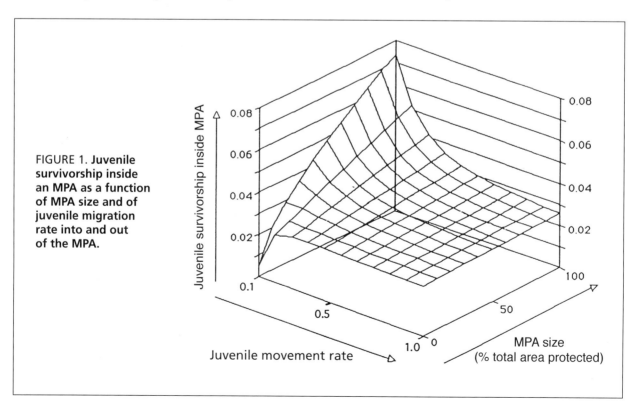

FIGURE 1. **Juvenile survivorship inside an MPA as a function of MPA size and of juvenile migration rate into and out of the MPA.**

Settlement of fish occurs uniformly to all sixteen cells of the model, and movement occurs both horizontally and vertically between adjoining cells. The model is run at a monthly time step, for a period of twelve months. Juvenile fish settle to the sea floor in the first period and are then subject to variable rates of natural mortality depending on the region to which they settle or migrate. We experiment with different values for each of the model parameters—number of fish settling, rates of mortality and movement, and MPA size and shape. The following three figures present the results from various runs of the model.

Figure 1 presents juvenile survivorship as a function of movement rate and MPA size. The vertical axis is juvenile survivorship within an MPA. On the left-horizontal axis juvenile movement rates into and out of the MPA varies from 0 (no movement) to 1 (movement of all fish in the region). Along the right-horizontal axis is the size of the MPA expressed as percent of total area protected. The result is a ramp or a response surface that suggests that the utility of an MPA is highly dependent on fish movement rates. Survivorship decreases rapidly with an increase in movement rate. This result highlights the importance of further research to determine actual juvenile fish movements in the field. For species or life history

stages in which movement rates are low, the utility of an MPA is very clear.

Figure 2 describes juvenile survivorship as a function of the number of fish settling to the sea floor. The shape of the response surface suggests that the utility of a protected area is very much dependent on the number of fish settling to the sea floor. As the number of settling fish increases in a given area, the sea floor habitat becomes saturated, and the benefits of the cover it provides are reduced. This is a very important point considering the critically low levels of many exploited fish populations in the Gulf of Maine and Georges Bank. The establishment of refuges designed to protect sea floor habitat may improve survivorship significantly at current low population sizes.

One obvious drawback of a protected area, from the perspective of the fishing community, is loss of access to previously fished areas. However, emigration of both juvenile and adult fish from protected areas may result in an increase in the number of harvestable fish in the areas immediately adjacent to MPAs. Quantifying the movement of biomass out of MPAs is problematic in the field, so modeling experiments such as this, which can easily explore such a question, are useful. In Figure 3a, the total number of individu-

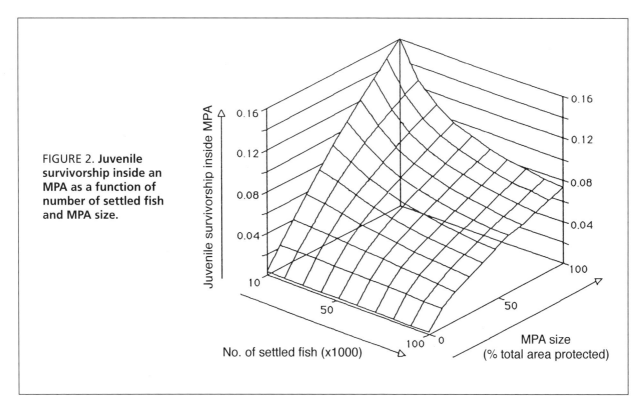

FIGURE 2. **Juvenile survivorship inside an MPA as a function of number of settled fish and MPA size.**

als surviving both within the refuge and outside the refuge are shown for a movement coefficient of 0.1 (10% of juvenile fish per region moving to adjacent regions per month). Survival within the MPA (Curve 1) increases nearly linearly with increasing MPA size. In contrast, survival in areas surrounding the MPA (Curve 2) is parabolic. Survival outside the MPA increases initially as MPA size increases such that an MPA which protects up to 30% of the sea floor habitat will produce more than double the number of

juvenile fish outside the MPA than in the absence of an MPA. Total survivorship in areas outside the MPA decreases as MPA size increases from 30% to 80% of the total area, but still remains higher than with no MPA.

The model suggests that the export of fish from an MPA is sensitive to the shape of the MPA in addition to its size. As additional regions are incorporated into the MPA incrementally, the total survivorship outside the MPA fluctuates with the configuration

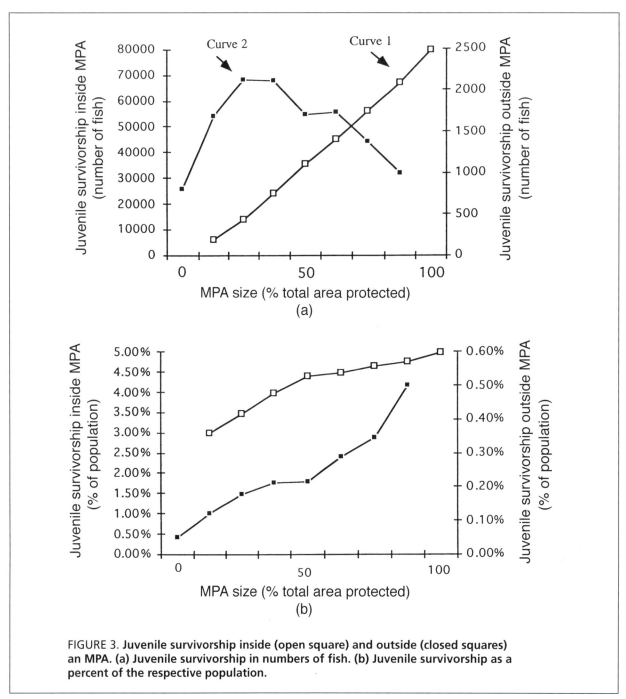

FIGURE 3. **Juvenile survivorship inside (open square) and outside (closed squares) an MPA. (a) Juvenile survivorship in numbers of fish. (b) Juvenile survivorship as a percent of the respective population.**

of the new portions of the MPA. Figure 3b depicts the survivorship of juvenile cod inside and outside an MPA as a percentage of the total respective populations. In Curve 2 at 50% habitat protected, the increase in survivorship levels off before increasing again. This pause in the increase in survivorship is likely the consequence of the perimeter-to-area ratio of the MPA and will be explored further in future modeling experiments.

This model is one step in an ongoing research process directed at understanding how different factors affect post-settlement survivorship of juvenile cod. We have ongoing laboratory and field experiments through which we hope to learn more about the associations of demersal fish with sea floor habitat. We anticipate that the combination of all three of these approaches—laboratory experiments, field studies, and computer modeling—will elucidate a critical component of fish population dynamics and lead to insights that are useful for management.

REFERENCES

Anderson, J.T. 1988. A review of size dependent survival during pre-recruit stages of fishes in relation to recruitment. *J. Northw. Atl. Fish. Sci.* 8:55-66

Auster, P. 1988. A review of the present state of understanding marine fish communities. *J. Northw. Atl. Fish. Sci.* 8:67-75.

Auster, P.J., R.J. Malatesta, S.C. LaRosa, R.A. Cooper, and L.L. Stewart. 1991. Microhabitat utilization by the megafaunal assemblage at a low relief outer continental shelf site- Middle Atlantic Bight, USA. *J. Northw. Atl. Fish. Sci.* 11:59-69.

Auster, P.J., R.J. Malatesta, and S.C. LaRosa. 1995. Patterns of microhabitat utilization by mobile megafauna on the southern New England (USA) Continental Shelf and Slope. *Mar. Ecol. Prog. Ser.* 127:77-85.

Auster, P.J., C. Michalopoulos, P.C. Valentine, and R.J. Malatesta. 1998. Delineating and monitoring habitat management units in a temperate deep-water marine protected area. Pp. 169-185 in N.W. Munro and J.H.M. Willison, eds. *Linking Protected Areas with Working Landscapes, Conserving Biodiversity.* Science and Management of Protected Areas Association, Wolfville, NS. In press.

Auster, P.J., R.J. Malatesta, R.W. Langton, L. Watling, P.C. Valentine, C.L.S. Donaldson, E.W. Langton, A.N. Shepard, and L.G. Babb. 1996. The impacts of mobile fishing gear on sea floor habitats in the Gulf of Maine (northwest Atlantic): implications for conservation of fish populations. *Rev. Fish. Sci.* 4:185-202.

Auster, P.J. and R.W. Langton. Indirect effects of fishing. In L.R. Benaka, ed. *Fish Habitats: Essential Fish Habitat and Rehabilitation.* American Fisheries Society Symposium 22. Bethesda, MD. In press.

Beverton, R.J.H. and S.J. Holt. 1957. On the dynamics of exploited fish populations. *Fishery Investigations* (series II) 19:1-533.

Collie, J. **This volume.** Studies in New England of fishing gear impacts on the sea floor.

Fraser, S., V. Gotceitas, and J.A. Brown. 1996. Interactions between age-classes of Atlantic cod and their distribution among bottom substrates. *Can. J. Fish. Aquat. Sci.* 53: 305-314.

Freese, L., P.J. Auster, J. Heifetz, and B. Wing. Impacts of trawling on sea floor habitat in the Gulf of Alaska: changes inhabitat structure and associated invertebrate taxa. In prep.

Gilbert, D.J. 1997. Towards a new recruitment paradigm for fish stocks. *Can. J. Fish. Aquat. Sci.* 54:969-977.

Gordon Jr., D.C., P. Schwinghamer, T.W. Rowell, J. Prena, K. Gilkinson, W.P. Vass, and D.L. McKeown. **This volume.** Studies in eastern Canada on the impact of mobile fishing gear on benthic habitat and communities.

Gotceitas, V. and J.A. Brown. 1993. Substrate selection by juvenile Atlantic cod (*Gadus morhua*): effects of predation risk. *Oecologia* 93:31-37.

Gotceitas, V., S. Fraser, and J.S. Brown. 1995. Habitat use by juvenile Atlantic cod (*Gadus morhua*) in the presence of an actively foraging and non-foraging predator. *Mar. Biol.* 123:421-430.

Langton, R.W. 1994. Fishing effect on demersal fish habitats. Pp.7-8 in R.W. Langton, J.B. Pearce, and J.A. Gibson, eds. *Selected Living Resources, Habitat Conditions, and Human Perturbations of the Gulf of Maine: Environmental and Ecological Considerations for Fishery Management.* NOAA Tech.Memo. NMFS-ME-106. Woods Hole, MA.

Lindholm, J., P.J. Auster, L. Kaufman, and M. Ruth. 1998. A modeling approach to the design of marine refugia for fishery management. Pp. 138-168 in N.W. Munro and J.H.M. Willison, eds. *Linking Protected Areas with Working Landscapes, Conserving Biodiversity.* Science and Management of Protected Areas Association, Wolfville, NS. In press.

Lindholm, J., P.J. Auster, and L. Kaufman. In prep. Habitat-mediated survivorship of 0-year Atlantic cod *(Gadus morhua)*. Submitted to *Mar. Ecol. Prog. Ser.*

Lough, R.G., P.C. Valentine, D.C. Potter, P.J. Auditore, G.R. Bolz, J.D. Neilson, and R.I. Perry. 1989. Ecology and distribution of juvenile cod and haddock in relation to sediment type and bottom currents on eastern Georges Bank. *Mar. Ecol. Prog. Ser.* 56:1-12.

Ruth, M. 1995. A system dynamics approach to modeling fisheries management issues: implications for spatial dynamics and resolution. *Sys. Dyn. Rev.* 11:233-243.

Sogard, S.M. 1997. Size-selective mortality in the juvenile stage of teleost fishes: a review. *Bull. Mar. Sci.* 60:1129-1157.

Schwinghamer, P. J.Y. Guigne, and W.C. Siu. 1996. Quantifying the impact of trawling on sea floor habitat structure using high resolution acoustics and chaos theory. *Can. J. Fish. Aquat. Sci.* 53:288-296.

Sissenwine, M.P. 1984. Why do fish populations vary? Pp. 59-94 in R.M. May, ed. *Exploitation of Marine Communities*. Springer-Verlag, NY.

Tupper, M. and R.G. Boutilier. 1995a. Effects of habitat on settlement, growth, and postsettlement survival of Atlantic cod *(Gadus morhua)*. *Can. J. Fish. Aquat. Sci.* 52:1834-1841.

Tupper, M. and R.G. Boutilier. 1995b. Size and priority at settlement determine growth and competitive success of newly settled Atlantic cod. *Can. J. Fish. Aquat. Sci.* 118:295-300.

Deep Sea Corals Off Nova Scotia

Mark Butler

ECOLOGY ACTION CENTRE, HALIFAX, NOVA SCOTIA

I work at the Ecology Action Centre, which is a local environmental group in Halifax. Prior to that, I worked for a while as a deckhand on inshore fixed gear fishing boats (lobster, gillnet, and hand line) and as a fisheries consultant. I am not a coral expert, and I am looking for more information from fishermen and scientists on the deep sea corals off Nova Scotia. I first learned about these corals from fishermen, who referred to them as coral trees. I want to credit Sanford Atwood (a longliner from Cape Sable Island) and Derek Jones, both of the Canadian Ocean Habitat Protection Society, as important sources of information, though they are not alone in knowing about the corals.

One reason that these corals are interesting is that they provide significant vertical extensions from the sea floor. People have seen coral trees that are around 2 meters (m) high, but there are suggestions that some get even taller. They are also extremely long-lived. Mike Risk, a scientist at Ontario's McMaster University, is doing some research on them and suggests that they might be 500 to 1,000 years old or more. He is doing carbon-14 dating on these corals and is trying to use them as a record of changes in water temperature and salinity in the past.

The Centre's interest began partly out of curiosity. We wanted to know what species of coral occur off Nova Scotia, where they are found, whether they provide fish habitat, such as protection for smaller fish, and also whether they are being endangered by fishing or threatened by other human activities. Right now in Canada, there is a lot of interest in oil and gas exploitation and pipelines, even aggregate extraction. How would these corals be affected by activities like that?

Approximately 20 different species of deep sea corals have been described off Nova Scotia. Most of them are colonial organisms made up of thousands of little polyps, each of which is like a tiny sea anemone. Corals are filter feeders. The two most commonly encountered species are both gorgonian corals, which are different from the reef-building corals that are found in the Caribbean. The first species is *Primnoa resedaeformis (Figure 1)* and is very dense. Fishermen call it a lot of things, including sea corn. The dead polyps on this species look like little Rice Krispies. When it has just been brought up from the bottom, it is colored bright orange from the living polyps on the outside. Without the polyps, it looks like petrified wood. The second species is *Paragorgia arborea (Figure 2)*. It is very light and grows to at least 2 m in length. The biggest piece I have seen, at the Archelaus Museum on Cape Sable Island, is 1 m long. Fishermen have various names for it—bubble gum coral, grapes, and strawberry trees.

Along with Heather Breeze and Dr. Derek Davis, I have started interviewing fishermen to find out what they know about these deep sea corals, in a project funded by the Nova Scotia Museum. We bring along a chart and ask the fishermen to identify where they catch corals, what species they catch, and what else they catch with the corals. Results show that, except for a couple of places, these corals occur out on the edge of the continental shelf in water deeper than 100 fathoms *(Figure 3,* Breeze *et al.* 1997). One area where they are quite common is in the Sable Island Gully, east of Sable Island. They also occur in a number of canyons along the Scotian Slope and in the channel between Georges Bank and Browns Bank. The corals live attached to a hard substrate. Since they are filter feeders, they have to be in areas where currents bring sufficient food to them. It appears that in some of these areas the food is coming off the continental shelf and running into the deeper canyons.

We have been told by longline fishermen that there used to be places where they could not set their longline gear because it would get hooked too badly in the coral trees. Now, they say they can go to the same areas and set their gear without worrying about getting hooked up. Fishermen have identified two locations in particular where corals have been severely damaged by the impact of dragging—along the Stone

Fence at the western edge of the Laurentian Channel (the eastern edge of the Scotian Shelf) and in the Northeast Channel between Browns and Georges Banks. Fishermen and fisheries observers have reported corals coming up in the cod ends of trawls, sometimes in large quantities. Fisheries data from the Department of Fisheries and Oceans also indicate that dragging occurs in areas where corals are found.

This information all suggests that these corals have been damaged, probably by dragging. Recovery from the damage can be expected to take decades or even centuries, given the long lifespans of the corals. The level of fishing activity off Nova Scotia has decreased substantially in the 1990s, compared to the three previous decades, but there are not currently any areas where corals are protected.

As to whether these corals provide fish habitat and how their loss affects overall fish productivity of the system, we have no definitive answers. Fishing is

FIGURE 1. **Two preserved specimens of *Primnoa resedaeformis*. The specimen on the left has lost its polyps, from which the species gets its common name, sea corn. Photograph by Derek S. Davis.**

FIGURE 2. **A specimen of *Paragorgia arborea* that now resides in George Townsend's living room. Townsend's father caught it while fishing on the Scotian Shelf. Photograph by Mark Butler.**

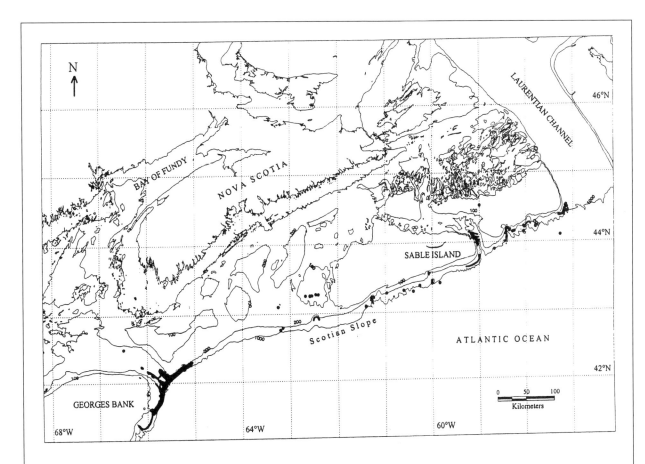

FIGURE 3. **Map of coral distribution (shaded areas), based on interviews with Nova Scotia fishermen and reports from museum and scientific collections of corals. Designed by Vladimir Kostylev. Reprinted with permission from Breeze *et al*. 1997.**

good in areas with corals, which suggests that there may be a link between the corals and commercially important fish species, or that the two groups prefer the same habitat, or both.

REFERENCE

Breeze, H. with D. S. Davis and M. Butler. 1997. *Distribution and status of deep sea corals off Nova Scotia.* Ecology Action Centre, Halifax, NS. 37 pp.

Observations on Lobster Trap Fishing

Jack Merrill

F/V BOTTOM DOLLAR, MAINE LOBSTERMEN'S ASSOCIATION, NORTHEAST HARBOR, MAINE

I am vice-president of the Maine Lobstermen's Association, and I live on Mount Desert Island, which is quite away up the coast in Maine. I have been lobster fishing with traps for 25 years. Like most people who live on the coast, I have fished in many different fisheries, but 95% to 100% of my income has come from lobstering.

The first thing that I want to talk about is this trash that I brought to show. It is essentially a collection of plastic bags, worn and tattered over time spent on the ocean bottom. It is either household garbage or industrial plastic. I have collected this trash over the last three weeks. It is plastic that comes up draped on my traps. This amount, enough to fill a small waste basket, is just from the last three weeks and just from one lobsterman. Multiplying that by three million traps, makes quite a statement as to what is out in the ocean. If all of the lobstermen on the coast of New England have been doing what I have been doing for the last 25 years, which is taking this trash to shore, then fishermen do a lot of cleaning of the ocean. I do not know what effect all this trash has on the marine environment. I do not know where it comes from. That is for someone else to determine, but there are days, especially if I cannot get out for a week or 10 days in the winter, when I can fill a five-gallon bucket with plastic trash from hauling my traps. When I bring it in, it goes to a landfill, which I guess is the right thing to do with it.

I want to make two points. First, there is a lot of trash out there in the ocean, and fishermen can help clean it up from the ocean floor. The second point is that when I started fishing 25 years ago, the old timers probably threw trash overboard at times. When they changed their oil, they would dump the used oil into the bilge and pump it overboard. That does not happen anymore. There has been a big change in attitude since those days. The fishermen today know they need a clean environment to work in. They want a clean ocean. That is important for everybody to understand. Although the plastic trash that I brought in from the last three weeks seems like a lot, I would say that over the years I have been fishing, I have been seeing less plastic trash overall and not more.

The second thing that I brought to show is a lobster trap that I pulled up recently that has been down on the sea floor for at least three years. I know it has been down that long because Maine started a trap limit two years ago with a tagging system. There is no tag on the trap, so it had to have been down for at least three years. There were a lot of things growing on the trap—scallops, barnacles, small mussel shells, kelp and a lot of white growth that I have been told is bryozoans.

Notice the hole in the trap. That is the biodegradable escape vent that Tom Morrell talked about earlier (see Morrell, this volume). The vent lifts up easily now that the hog rings have disintegrated, so that lobsters, crabs, and whatever else gets in the trap can crawl out. I have not touched the trap at all since I pulled it up. The bait bag is hanging where it was left. On the bottom of the trap, there are wooden runners, but only very little is left of one runner. The rest of the runner has been eaten by sea worms. I know a professor at the University of Maine who has been studying these worms (borers) because they can live by eating wood, which is very unusual. The point I want to make with this trap is that I would like to think that the lost gear from our fishery somehow becomes part of the ocean environment.

In 1988 I was involved in a study of "ghost traps" with Dr. Robert Bayer and some graduate students from the University of Maine. The study used time lapse photography taken from a fixed camera on the ocean bottom to monitor traps left in the water over a number of months. It showed conclusively that as soon as the bait was gone from the traps, there was virtually no observable marine activity around them. The study produced some of the most boring, uneventful film footage ever made.

A major change since I started fishing is that wire traps have now replaced wooden ones. When lobstermen lost wood traps, we would never get them back because they just disintegrated, leaving behind the synthetic heads and twine. But the wire on this trap shows hardly any evidence of rusting. I am going to take this trap home and fix it up and set it out again. The wire gear stays in a lot better condition than the wood gear did. It can be reused, even if it was lost for several years. When lobstermen haul up a lost trap, they call the original owner on the radio and return it to him. Traps get reused and recycled now. I have done a lot of different projects with scientists and divers, and I believe that there is much less ghost gear than there used to be.

The trap fishery is, of course, a passive fishery with minimal bycatch. Everything that is caught either goes to market or is returned to the ocean alive. I have recently become interested in determining the long term effects of millions of suspended ropes in the water column on early stages of marine life, particularly the development of phytoplankton and zooplankton that feed much larger animals. I will be trying to find scientific interest in determining these effects through the Maine Lobster Institute, located on the University of Maine campus.

REFERENCE

Morrell, T. **This volume.** Lobster trap fishing.

Sediment Resuspension by Bottom Fishing Gear

James H. Churchill

WOODS HOLE OCEANOGRAPHIC INSTITUTION, WOODS HOLE, MASSACHUSETTS

Underwater observations have revealed that, when trawl doors are towed at normal fishing speeds, they generate intense turbulent wakes which can, in turn, create highly turbid clouds of suspended sediment (Korotkow and Martyschewski 1977; Main and Sangster 1981, 1983; Wardle 1983). This phenomenon can have broad-reaching effects, encompassing the benthic and pelagic zones and extending far from the area of trawling. Here I will focus on sediment resuspension by trawling, touching on three points. First, I will give a brief review of my knowledge of this topic. Using this admittedly limited information base, I will consider what effects sediment resuspension by trawl gear may have on the marine environment. Finally, I will suggest studies that are needed to better understand the impact of resuspending sediment by bottom fishing gear.

My interest in this topic began more than a decade ago, when I was involved in a study of sediment transport from the New England continental shelf to the deep ocean. This study was motivated in part by an interest in contaminant movement over continental shelves. Fine sediments carry most of the contaminants that are introduced into the coastal ocean. Another interest of the study was the movement of organic carbon off the shelf. A significant fraction of the particulate organic carbon produced in the coastal ocean by photosynthesis is bound in fine particles. Because this carbon is largely derived from dissolved CO_2, a greenhouse gas, carbon-carrying particles can be thought of as tiny players in the

global warming game. They can act to mitigate global warming if carried off the shelf and buried in deep-sea sediments, in essence, permanently removing their carbon from the atmosphere.

As part of the study, my colleagues and I deployed instrumented moorings along a line extending across the New England shelf and down the continental slope into the deep ocean. On the shelf, the line was roughly centered within an area of fine grain sediment commonly referred to as the Mud Patch (*Figure 1*). Records from optical particle sensors revealed near-bottom patches of high turbidity that occurred during calm conditions and thus could not have been the result of sediment resuspension by bottom currents (Churchill *et al.* 1988). Suspecting trawling as a resuspension agent, I obtained records of trawling activity in the region of our moored array from the National Marine Fisheries Service (NMFS). These revealed that intense trawling often occurred near our particle sensors at times when the sensors detected high turbidity and companion sensor records showed weak currents and wave action. Similar findings have been reported by other researchers (Butman and Noble 1979; Wardle 1983; Bohlen and Winnick 1984). An unpublished but dramatic piece of anecdotal evidence was offered by the record of an optical sensor which showed a sharp peak in turbidity just before the sensor was hit by a trawl.

To assess the influence of trawling on shelf sediment movement, I developed a model to calculate the mean concentration of sediment put into suspension by trawling. This model utilized rates of sediment resuspension by trawls derived from the data collected in a near-shore study by Schubel *et al.* (1978). The model also required estimates of sediment settling and NMFS records of trawling activity in the region of interest. To estimate the mean concentration of sediment put into suspension by currents, I modified a model developed by Lyne *et al.* (1990), which utilized measurements of near-bottom currents, surface wave motions, and near-bottom particle concentrations.

Sample results from these models, comparing mean wintertime concentrations of trawl- and current-resuspended sediments over the Mud Patch, show that the overall impact of trawling on sediment resuspension is a strong function of bottom depth *(Figure 2)*. Currents are indicated as the dominant wintertime resuspension mechanism over the inner and middle shelf. Over the outer shelf, however, trawling is indicated as the principal agent effecting sediment resuspension. Clearly, these results, derived from data-driven models, should be viewed with a healthy measure of skepticism. Nevertheless, they strongly suggest that trawling can play an important (and in some regions, a dominant) role in raising bottom material into the water column.

Let us now consider the potential effects of sediment resuspension by trawling. One obvious effect is initiating horizontal movement of solid particles by exposing them to ocean currents. As noted above, the movement of fine particles off the shelf is of particular interest.

Based solely on the decline in sediment resuspension frequency with increasing depth off the shelf *(Figure 2)*, one would expect a mean transport of sediment from the outer shelf to the slope. This occurs because some portion of the sediment resuspended over the outer shelf will eventually settle out on the slope where resuspension events are rare (Csanady *et al.* 1988). A result is permanent (or at least quasi-permanent) removal of contaminants and organic carbon from the shelf environment. Calculations using current meter data and the models discussed above suggest that trawling is an important mechanism in initiating this type of off-shelf sediment transport from the Mud Patch (Churchill 1989).

From the viewpoint of maintaining a fishery, one of the most important potential effects of resuspension by trawling is delivering nutrients from the bottom into the euphotic zone, where photosynthesis

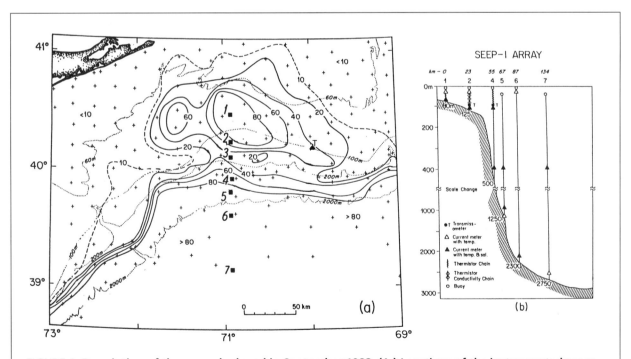

FIGURE 1. **Description of the array deployed in September 1983. (A.) Locations of the instrumented moorings (squares and triangle) on the continental shelf and slope south of New England. Solid and dashed contours give the percent of fine particles (silt and clay) in bottom sediment. These mark the "Mud Patch" region of fine bottom sediment discussed in the text. (B.) A cross-sectional view of the mooring array.**

occurs. In many areas of the continental shelf off the U.S. east coast, roughly half the nutrient supply for primary production is derived from upward transfer from sediments. Resuspension by trawling could significantly enhance the euphotic zone nutrient supply and primary production. However, the manner in which this occurs could produce side effects. For example, a significant nutrient input from trawl resuspension could alter the character of the lower food chain, favoring species which are better suited to pulsed nutrient supply.

Trawling could also influence the manner in which nutrients are regenerated in bottom sediment. An analogy can be made with tilling of an agricultural plot (Mayer *et al.* 1991). Nutrient regeneration within soils of untilled plots tends to be dominated by fungi. By contrast, in tilled fields, bacteria become a more important factor in nutrient regeneration. While fungi are not important in nutrient cycling within the ocean, trawling could produce a similar "downsizing" of the organisms effecting nutrient regeneration in marine sediments, reducing the importance of higher organisms (protozoans or animals)

and increasing the role of bacteria. Currently, however, there is little quantitative information on how sediment overturn by trawling, or other types of bottom fishing, alters bottom nutrient regeneration.

While it is clear that sediment resuspension by trawling likely impacts the shelf environment in numerous ways, understanding of the details of these is sketchy at best. Filling in the gaps in this understanding will require dedicated field studies. These must be done in the regions of interest, for it is clear that measurements related to sediment resuspension in shallow regions with sandy sediment are not likely to be applicable to deep regions with fine sediment.

From a sediment dynamics viewpoint, the most fundamental issues requiring study are the effects of trawling on suspended sediment load and sediment transport. Quantifying these effects requires determining the rate at which trawls resuspend sediment (i.e., the mass of sediment put into suspension per unit track length), the height of the sediment plumes generated by trawling and the time required for these to settle. These properties can be determined by measuring sediment concentration across a sediment

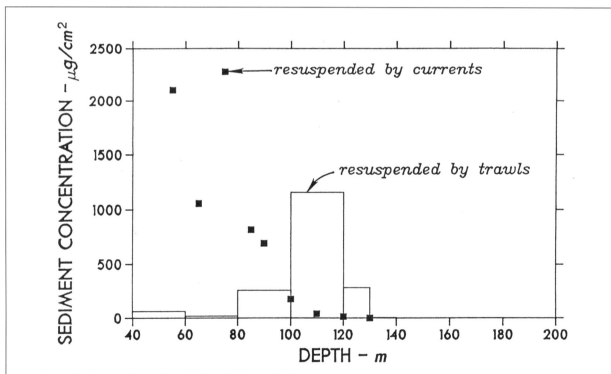

FIGURE 2. **Comparison of model predictions of the averaged mass of suspended sediment put into suspension by currents (squares) and trawling (histogram) as a function of bottom depth. Both sets of values are for sediment resuspended over the "Mud Patch" (shown in Figure 1) over the January through March time period (see Churchill 1989 for further details).**

plume segment at various times after its generation by a trawl. These measurements would likely require combining water sample collection with acoustical and optical sampling of sediment concentration. Following a plume segment will be problematical. It could be accomplished by marking the plume with drifters and dye and using shipboard velocity profile data (obtained with an acoustic Doppler current profiler) to further guide the plume tracking.

Investigating the effects of trawling on nutrient supply and on the resulting biological response will require still more involved techniques. My background as a physical oceanographer leaves me woefully unqualified to offer suggestions as to how these studies should be designed. Nonetheless, it is clear that, regardless of the design specifics, certain issues must be addressed. One is the effect of trawling in supplying the euphotic zone with nutrients. Does trawling significantly enhance nutrient levels in the euphotic zone? Is primary productivity appreciably increased? Does the pulsed nutrient supply by trawling benefit some species over others. If so, what is the ultimate effect on the ecosystem? Another issue of importance is the effect of trawling on nutrient regeneration in bottom sediments. Is the rate of nutrient regeneration significantly changed by trawl action? If so, how does this affect the benthic community?

Ideally, field studies on the effects of trawling should be directed at developing models which could be used to assess, with reasonable confidence, the impact of sediment resuspension by trawling on a specified ecosystem. However, whatever its goal, my experience is that any study on the effects of trawling is best done with input and cooperation of the fishing community and without *a priori* assumptions as to whether bottom fishing is harmful or beneficial to the marine environment.

ACKNOWLEDGMENTS: I extend my appreciation to Dr. Larry Mayer of the University of Maine for his critical reading of the manuscript.

REFERENCES

Bohlen, W. F. and K. B. Winnick. 1984. Observations of near-bottom suspended matter concentration at the FVP site central Long Island Sound predisposal material area;

18 April 1983—29 June 1983. Prepared for Science Applications International Corporation. Newport, Rhode Island. 100 pp.

Butman, B. and M. Noble. 1979. Observations of currents and bottom sediment mobility in the offshore middle Atlantic Bight, 1976-1977. Pp. 1-46 in H.J. Knebel, ed. *Middle Atlantic Outer Continental Shelf Environmental Studies, Vol. III: Geologic Studies*. Virginia Institute of Marine Science, Gloucester Point, VA.

Churchill, J. H., P. E. Biscaye and F. Aikman III. 1988. The character and motion of suspended particulate matter over the shelf-edge and upper slope off Cape Cod. *Cont. Shelf Res.* 8:789-809.

Churchill, J. H. 1989. The effect of commercial trawling on sediment resuspension and transport over the Middle Atlantic Bight continental shelf. *Cont. Shelf Res.* 9:841-864.

Csanady, G. T., J. H. Churchill and B. Butman. 1988. Near-bottom currents over the continental slope in the Mid-Atlantic Bight. *Cont. Shelf Res.* 8:653-671.

Korotkow, W. K. and W. N. Martyschewski. 1977. Results obtained by use of the underwater device "Atlant" for the study of how fish behave and how trawl net operate. *Fischerei-Forschung Schriftentreihe* 15:39-43.

Lyne, V. D., B. Butman and W. D. Grant. 1990. Sediment movement along the U.S. east coast continental shelf—II. Modeling suspended sediment concentration and transport rate during storms. *Cont. Shelf Res.* 10:429-460.

Main, J. and G. I. Sangster. 1981. *A study of sand clouds produced by trawl boards and their possible effect on fish capture*. Scottish Fisheries Research Report No. 20. Dept of Agriculture and Fisheries for Scotland. 19 pp.

Main, J. and G. I. Sangster. 1983. *Fish reactions to trawl gear—a study comparing light and heavy ground gear*. Scottish Fisheries Research Report No. 27. Dept of Agriculture and Fisheries for Scotland. 17 pp.

Mayer, L. M., D. F. Schick, R. H. Findlay and D. L. Rice. 1991. Effects of commercial dragging on sedimentary organic matter. *Mar. Environ. Res.* 31:249-261.

Schubel, J. R., H. H. Carter, R. E. Wilson, W. M. Wise, M. G. Heaton and M. G. Gross. 1978. *Field investigations of the nature, degree and extent of turbidity generated by open-water pipeline disposal operations*. Technical Report D-78-30. Marine Sciences Research Center, State University of New York, Stony Brook, NY. 245 pp.

Wardle, C. S. 1983. Fish reactions to towed fishing gears. Pp. 167-195 in A. G. MacDonald and I. G. Priede, eds. *Experimental Biology at Sea*. Academic Press, London.

"The Edge of the Bottom"— Heavily Trawled and Consistently Productive

Craig Pendleton

F/V SUSAN AND CAITLYN, NORTHWEST ATLANTIC MARINE ALLIANCE

I have made my living fishing for 29 years, mostly on bottom trawlers fishing out of Portland, Maine. I have trawled for shrimp and all the groundfish species, and I have also done some lobstering. I believe that trawling may not be appropriate for some areas because of negative effects to the bottom, but in many other areas trawling seems to have little or no effect, and it is a very good way to catch fish.

People should realize that there are places where trawling has gone on repeatedly and intensively for years and where fishing remains excellent. An example of such an area is what we call the "Edge of the Bottom." This area is located outside of Casco Bay, Maine, just a couple of miles outside of the Portland Sea Buoy (where the Portland Lightship used to be moored). The area is about 10 miles long and a mile wide, and the depth there ranges from 45 to 50 fathoms. We fish on a smooth muddy bottom that begins right where solid ledge drops off into the mud. We try to tow as close to the ledge as we can.

Bottom trawling has been going on in that area for decades with a predictable seasonal change in target prey. In winter, boats trawl for shrimp. In spring and early summer, they trawl for cod and dabs, with gray sole coming a little later. In summer and fall, they trawl for whiting, and some people target blackbacks and monkfish in December. So the area is trawled for one thing or another almost all months of the year. Different types of trawls are used for different targets, and the sweeps of these trawls vary from chain sweeps to cookie sweeps to rockhoppers and rollers.

The Edge of the Bottom was a good place to fish well before I started fishing, and it is still a good place to catch all these species. It is hard to accept that dragging is bad for the bottom there because the area has remained so productive. Of course, there have been good years and bad years for all of these species, but those cycles are evident everywhere in the Gulf of Maine. They are not caused by all the trawling on this piece of bottom.

I have fished in a few areas where I thought trawling was not appropriate, and my experience there was totally different from the Edge of the Bottom. The clearest example was when a few fishermen started dragging on Cashes Ledge in 1982 or 1983. At first we got nets full of kelp along with good amounts of big gray sole and huge cod. But soon, after only a few trips, we stopped catching kelp and we started tearing our nets on the rocks because the kelp no longer protected the nets. We probably should not have been dragging there because we tore off all the kelp. In addition, the large size of the fish there showed that it was a safe haven for them and that they were probably resident there.

Rockhoppers are allowing trawls to go in many areas where they had never gone before, places where fish were once safe. Today there are no more places where fish are safe. There need to be some places where no one fishes at all.

EDITORS' NOTE:
This paper was not presented at the 1997 conference.

Discussion

Summary of Discussion and Recommendations from the Conference

Eleanor M. Dorsey and Judith Pederson

In an effort to foster exchange among participants and develop a set of recommendations on future actions, a discussion period was held at the end of the conference, Effects of Fishing Gear on the Sea Floor of New England on May 30, 1997. The discussion was structured around two questions:

• What studies are needed in New England to improve our understanding of fishing gear effects and other disturbances on the sea floor?

• What insights have we gained from the conference presentations and discussions about research on and experience with fishing gear effects on the sea floor?

Approximately 60 of 150 participants attended the discussion session and shared information and observations of habitats and the relationship of habitats to fishery productivity. Although the intent of this session was specifically to identify research activities that would further understanding of sea floor habitats and fisheries, the exchange of information covered a broad spectrum of topics and reflected the experience of the scientists, fishermen, environmentalists, and fishery managers in attendance. The discussion ranged beyond the initial questions and fell into three categories: (1) general observations and assumptions, (2) recommendations for research, and (3) recommendations for fishery management

Time constraints precluded in-depth discussion on any one issue and there was no attempt to resolve contradictory observations. This summary focuses on themes that were identified as high priorities or were part of several recommendations. It also includes perspectives from a post-conference meeting of the conference steering committee. The conference discussion session was not taped and a number of participants could not attend. We have made every effort to capture the diverse viewpoints expressed during the day and to reflect the concerns and thoughtfulness of the attendees. A full list of comments and recommendations as recorded in writing at the conference discussion session is provided in Appendix 2.

GENERAL OBSERVATIONS

The provisions on essential fish habitat in the Magnuson-Stevens Fishery Conservation and Management Act of 1996 place new emphasis on fish habitats and will influence management decisions in the both the short and long term (Kurland, this volume). Participants at the discussion session noted that information on what constitutes essential fish habitat is limited, that scientists must help identify and describe habitats, and that decisions will have to be made based on incomplete information. One of the key recommendations was for fishermen's knowledge to be incorporated into the definition and identification of essential fish habitat and for fishermen to participate in designing research to better understand habitats and fish productivity.

A collaborative effort between scientists, managers and fishermen could translate fishermen's knowledge gained through years of observations into scientifically useful information. Some of the habitat features highlighted by fishermen in this volume are edges or transitions between different bottom types, rapid changes in topography, beds of benthic invertebrates (such as mussels and stalked ascidians), and special bottom structures (such as pipe clay and gravel pavement). These features occur on scales much smaller than the 10-minute latitude and longitude squares used for fish stock assessments. To use fishermen's knowledge of habitat effectively, habitat maps should depict small-scale features, such as substrate transitions, mussel beds, sea floor peaks, and clay pipe areas.

Several participants observed that different goals were expressed by various speakers at the conference. Some presentations focused on fishery productivity as the principal purpose for human use of marine ecosystems, whereas others stressed the preservation of biological diversity. Although these goals may not be mutually exclusive, they differ in emphasis and expectation.

Some presenters focused on the importance of biological diversity and stated that maintaining diversity at the sea floor benefits fisheries by increased structural heterogeneity and food availability. The protection of upright biota (such as sponges, algae, and bryozoans) not only provides refuge for early life history stages of harvested fish species, but also enhances prey for larval, juvenile and adult fish. Thus, scientists and fishermen with an interest in biological diversity and ecological functions of marine systems contended that maintaining a heterogeneous environment will improve fish populations. In addition, protecting benthic biodiversity might provide a buffer for fish populations if fishing regulations do not adequately control fishing mortality. This approach would suggest a change in emphasis for managers who currently use stock assessments as the principal consideration for management decisions. Another value expressed for biological diversity, apart from its contribution to robust fisheries, is the part that each species represents in the record of the evolution of life on this planet.

Those who emphasized marine productivity wanted research and management to focus on maximizing the yield of targeted species. An analogy to farming was used to frame the discussion. In agriculture, cultivation of the soil is used to increase yields of specific crops. Proponents of a focus on productivity were interested in processes and ecosystem components that enhance fishery productivity. For example, understanding how nutrient releases from sediment

disturbance affect primary productivity may ultimately help increase food for harvested fish. Another productivity-related question is to evaluate the role of trawling and dredging in reducing predators of targeted species through bycatch mortality or increased exposure to scavengers.

Throughout the discussion, many people remarked that we do not know what limits fish production. Without this understanding, it is difficult to evaluate the effect of natural disturbance, gear disturbance, predation, competition, weather, climate, and overfishing on fish productivity and habitat function. Another observation was that declines in fish stocks and alterations to sea floor habitats result from a single problem: too much fishing. Reduced fishing effort can be expected to result in increased fish stocks and improved bottom habitats

Several contradictory observations emerged at the conference. Some studies have shown fishing disturbance to reduce abundance, biomass, and diversity of some benthic invertebrates, while other studies and observations report increases in the abundance and biomass of other bottom species, notably scavengers, due to fishing. In this volume, sea scallop fishermen report both positive and negative effects of scallop dredging on the target species. Careful studies can help resolve these observed differences, and participants recommended further research on fundamental and applied questions.

RECOMMENDATIONS FOR RESEARCH

There was general agreement at the discussion session that a high priority for future studies should be to improve understanding of the relationship between carrying capacity of habitats and fishing productivity and to quantify that relationship. Another recommendation was to quantify the relationships between habitats and fish and to provide a scientific and technical basis for management decisions. In addition, a coordinated program to research the effects of fishing gear on habitats is needed. Such a program should, among other things, designate areas for research, develop methodologies, and study the importance of bottom structure. It was recommended that priorities be set for monitoring and research by focusing on the important areas and placing less effort on areas that are not important to fisheries. Studies should look at the effects in the short, middle, and long term and should integrate over the region for all populations. Furthermore, studies should focus at scales appropriate for individual fish, scales that are smaller than current management divisions.

A recurring theme throughout the discussion was the recommendation for fishermen and scientists to collaborate in identifying priority areas of research and developing research projects. Conducting fisheries-directed research is challenging because agencies that fund research, such as the National Science Foundation and the Office of Naval Research, encourage hypothesis-driven research rather than descriptive studies. Improved understanding of fishery habitats requires descriptive studies that may include fisher-

men's observations as well as hypothesis testing, and both should be reflected in agencies' funding priorities.

Another recommendation was for research to develop fishing gear that minimizes damage to sea floor habitats and to untargeted biota. Optimism was expressed that considerable improvements in this direction are possible.

RECOMMENDATIONS FOR MANAGEMENT

The conference did not attempt to address the management implications of fishing gear impacts to the sea floor, but some suggestions for management were made at the discussion session. A high priority was given to classifying the sea floor according to vulnerability to fishing gear, with input from both scientists and fishermen. Managers were urged to solicit increased input from fishermen and academic scientists, to establish protected areas, to re-examine appropriate scales for defining fish habitat, and to focus on productive and sensitive areas first. Several participants recommended the establishment of marine reserves. Permanent, seasonal, and rotating closed

---

Recommendations for Research

1. Investigate the relationship between sea floor habitats and fish productivity.

   • Develop a consistent assessment approach for evaluating habitats and habitat functions.

   • Develop methodologies for quantifying fishery productivity.

   • Evaluate the function of edges or transition areas to fisheries productivity.

   • Demonstrate that three-dimensional complexity results in higher fish productivity.

2. Demonstrate the effect of fishing gear on commercially important species. Several initiatives are needed; three are listed below.

   • Identify unfished areas to compare with fished areas.

   • Use fishing closures to gain insights into habitat recovery and fish use of habitats.

   • Improve estimates of trawl distribution and frequency using fishermen's records.

3. Map ecoregions of the sea floor as a first step in identifying important habitats.

4. Measure the productivity of fish regionwide because it is difficult to generalize from individual studies of habitat.

5. Improve fishing gear to minimize fishing mortality of non-target species, some of which provide habitat for target species.

6. Modify fishing gear to minimize damage to sea floor habitats.

Recommendations for Management

1. Classify the sea floor types according to vulnerability to fishing gear, using information from both fishermen and scientists.

2. Use fishery closures for research to separate the effects of fishing removals from fishing gear damage to habitats.

   • Determine whether closures should be permanent or rotating.

   • Look at effects over varying time and space scales.

   • Use fishermen records to identify trawled areas.

3. Consider zoning the sea floor (i.e. review land-use zoning and modify for the ocean bottom).

4. Improve economic valuation of marine ecosystems.

   • Include economic values for non-fisheries products and services.

   • Improve methods for valuing marine products.

---

areas were all suggested and would serve different purposes. Monitoring was recommended inside the existing fishery closures to examine their effects on fish and habitats. It was suggested that managers consider zoning the sea floor in a manner comparable to land use planning. This would be a major undertaking and would have to involve all the diverse interests in the use of the sea floor. Another recommendation was to improve the economic valuation of marine ecosystems, with the scope expanded to include values for other products and services than fisheries harvests. It was agreed that improved understanding of human impacts and natural disturbance is key to improving management decisions.

Appendices

Species List:
Scientific and Common Names
Used in this Volume

COMMON NAME	SCIENTIFIC NAME	TYPE OF ORGANISM
Ampeliscid amphipod	*Ampelisca* sp.	Amphipod
Ampeliscid amphipod	*Ampelisca spinipes**	Amphipod
Amphipod	*Erichthonius* spp.	Amphipod
Amphipod	*Unciola inermis*	Amphipod
Ascidian (Colonial)	*Aplidium pallidum*	Ascidian
Ascidian (Solitary)	*Ascidia collosa*	Ascidian
Barnacle	*Balanus* spp.	Barnacle
Basket star	*Gorgonocephalus arcticus*	Echinoderm
Bay scallop	*Aequipecten irradians*	Bivalve
Bivalve (Ocean quahog)	*Arctica islandica*	Bilvalve
Blackback flounder (Winter flounder)	*Pleuronectes americanus*	Finfish
Blood star	*Henricia sanguinolenta*	Echinoderm
Blue mussel	*Mytilus edulis*	Bivalve
Brachiopod	*Terebratulina septentrionalis*	Brachiopod
Brittle star	*Ophiura sarsi*	Echinoderm
Brittle star	*Amphiura* spp.*	Echinoderm
Bryozoan	*Idmidronea atlantica*	Bryozoan
Bryozoan	*Crisia* sp.	Bryozoan
Bryozoan	*Crisia eburnea*	Bryozoan
Bryozoan (encrusting)	*Parasmittina jeffreysi*	Bryozoan
Calcareous alga	*Lithothamnion* spp.*	Red alga
Calcareous tube building worm	*Sabellaria spinulosa**	Polychaete
Catfish (Wolffish)	*Anarhichas lupus*	Finfish
Cerianthid anemone	*Cerianthis borealis*	Cnidarian
Cockle	*Cerastoderma edule**	Bivalve
Cod	*Gadus morhua*	Finfish
Coralline alga	*Corallina officinalis*	Red alga
Cormorant (Double crested)	*Phalacrocorax auritus*	Bird
Crab (Jonah)	*Cancer borealis*	Crustacean

COMMON NAME	SCIENTIFIC NAME	TYPE OF ORGANISM
Cunner	*Tautogolabrus adspersus*	Finfish
Dab (American plaice)	*Hippoglossoides platessoides*	Finfish
Dab (European)	*Limanda limanda**	Finfish
Decorator worms	*Diopatra cupraea*	Polychaete
Dogfish	*Squalus acanthias*	Shark
Dover sole	*Solea solea**	Finfish
Dragonet	*Callionymus lyra**	Finfish
Eastern oyster	*Crassostrea virginica*	Bivalve
Eider duck	*Somateria mollissima*	Bird
Fluke (Summer flounder)	*Paralichtys dentatus*	Finfish
Foliose bryozoan	*Pentapora foliacea**	Bryozoan
Formaniniferan	*Bathysiphon* spp.	Foraminifera
Gaper clam (Soft-shelled)	*Mya arenaria*	Bivalve
Goosefish (Monkfish)	*Lophius americanus*	Finfish
Gorgonian coral (Grapes)	*Paragorgia arborea*	Cnidarian
Gorgorian coral (Sea corn)	*Primnoa resedaeformis*	Cnidarian
Green crab	*Carcinus maenas*	Crustacean
Grey sole (Witch flounder)	*Glyptocephalus cynoglossus*	Finfish
Gurnard	*Trigla* spp.*	Finfish
Haddock	*Melanogrammus aeglefinus*	Finfish
Hake (Red, silver and white)	Various genera	Finfish
Halibut	*Hippoglossus hippoglossus*	Finfish
Hard coral	Unknown species	Cnidarian
Heart urchin	*Echinocardium cordatum**	Echinoderm
Hermit crab	*Pagarus bernhardus**	Crustacean
Hermit crab	*Pagarus* spp.	Crustacean
Herring	*Clupea harengus*	Finfish
Horse mussel	*Modiolus modiolus*	Bivalve
Hydroids	Several genera	Cnidarian
Icelandic scallop	*Clinocardium pinnulateum*	Bivalve
Japanese scallop	*Patinopecten yessoensis*	Bivalve
Kelp	*Laminaria digitata*	Brown alga
Kelp	*Laminaria saccharina*	Brown alga
Lemon (Stalked sea squirt/ ascidian)	*Boltenia ovifera*	Ascidian
Little skate	*Raja erinacea*	Skate
Lobster (American)	*Homarus americanus*	Crustacean
Longhorn sculpin	*Myoxocephalus octodecimspinosus*	Finfish
Lugworm	*Arenicola marina*	Polychaete
Mackerel (Atlantic)	*Scomber scombrus*	Finfish
Maerl	*Lithothamnion* spp.	Red alga
Mahogany quahog (Ocean quahog)	*Arctica islandica*	Bivalve
Manila clam	*Tapes philippinarum**	Bivalve
Mantis shrimp	*Squilla amprisa*	Crustacean
Menhaden (Pogy)	*Brevoortia tyrannus*	Finfish
Mollusc	*Margarites sordidus*	Bivalve
Mollusc (Astarte)	*Astarte borealis*	Bivalve

COMMON NAME	SCIENTIFIC NAME	TYPE OF ORGANISM
Mollusc (Iceland cockle)	*Clinocardium ciliatum*	Bivalve
Mollusc (Northern cardita)	*Cyclocardium novangliae*	Bivalve
Monkfish (Goosefish)	*Lophius americanus*	Finfish
Northern pink shrimp	*Pandalus borealis*	Crustacean
Norway pout	*Trisopterus esmarkii**	Finfish
Nudibranch	*Aeolidia papillosa*	Gastropod
Ocean perch (redfish)	*Sebastes marinus*	Finfish
Ocean pout	*Macrozoarces americanus*	Finfish
Ocean quahog	*Arctica islandica*	Bivalve
Oligochaetes	Several genera	Annelid worm
Orange mounding sponge	*Myxilla fimbriata*	Sponge
Plaice (American)	*Hippoglossoides platessoides*	Finfish
Plaice (European)	*Pleuronectes platessa**	Finfish
Pogy (Menhaden)	*Brevoortia tyrannus*	Finfish
Pollock	*Pollachius virens*	Finfish
Polychaete	*Euphrosine borealis*	Polychaete worm
Polychaete (tube worm)	*Filagrana implexa*	Polychaete worm
Pork fat	Unknown species	Ascidian
Queen scallop	*Aequipecten opercularis**	Bivalve
Razor clam	*Ensis directus*	Bivalve
Razor clam	*Ensis siliqua**	Bivalve
Red hake	*Urophycis chuss*	Finfish
Redfish (Ocean perch)	*Sebastes marinus*	Finfish
Rockweed	*Fucus* sp.	Brown alga
Salmon (Atlantic)	*Salmo solar*	Finfish
Sand dollar	*Echinarachnius parma*	Echinoderm
Scallop (Atlantic sea)	*Placopecten magellanicus*	Bivalve
Scallop (European)	*Pecten maximus**	Bivalve
Scup	*Stenotomus chrysops*	Finfish
Sea anemone	*Metridium senile*	Cnidarian
Sea anemone (Northern red)	*Urticina crassicornis*	Cnidarian
Sea cucumber	*Cucumaria frondosa*	Echinoderm
Sea fan	*Eunicella verrucosa**	Cnidarian
Sea moss (Irish moss)	*Chrondrus crispus*	Red alga
Sea pen	*Pennatula aculeata*	Cnidarian
Sea pen	*Funiculina quadrangularis**	Cnidarian
Sea pen	*Pennulata phosphorea**	Cnidarian
Sea pen	*Virgularia mirabilis**	Cnidarian
Sea scallop (Atlantic)	*Placopecten magellanicus*	Bivalve
Sea star (Forbes)	*Asterias forbesi*	Echinoderm
Sea star (Northern)	*Asterias vulgaris*	Echinoderm
Sea urchin	*Strongylocentrotus droebachiensis*	Echinoderm
Sea urchin	*Strongylocentrotus pallidus*	Echinoderm
Sea worms (Wood boring worms)	*Toredo navalis*	Bivalve
Serpulid polychaete	*Spirorbis spirorbis*	Polychaete
Shrimp	*Crangon* spp.*	Crustacean

COMMON NAME	SCIENTIFIC NAME	TYPE OF ORGANISM
Shrimp	*Crangon crangon**	Crustacean
Shrimp (Northern pink)	*Pandalus borealis*	Crustacean
Silver hake (Whiting)	*Merluccius bilinearis*	Finfish
Skate	*Raja neavus**	Skate
Snake blenny	*Lumpenus lumpretaeformis*	Finfish
Snow crab	*Chionoecetes opilio*	Crustacean
Soft coral	*Alcgonium* spp.	Cnidarian
Soft coral	*Gersemia* sp.	Cnidarian
Sole	*Solea solea**	Finfish
Solitary ascidians	*Ascidia collosa*	Ascidian
Sponge	*Mycale lingua*	Sponge
Sponge (Orange mounding)	*Myxilla fimbriata*	Sponge
Sponge	*Iophon* sp.	Sponge
Sponge (Finger)	*Isodictya* spp.	Sponge
Sponge (Breadcrumb)	*Halichondria panicea*	Sponge
Sponge	*Hymedesmia* sp.	Sponge
Squid (Long-finned)	*Loligo pealei*	Mollusc
Squid (Short-finned)	*Illex illecebrosus*	Mollusc
Stalked sea squirt	*Boltenia ovifera*	Ascidian
Starfish	*Asterias rubens**	Echinoderm
Starry ray	*Raja radiata**	Skate
Summer flounder	*Paralichtys dentatus*	Finfish
Swimming crab	*Liocarcinus* spp.*	Crustacean
Swordfish	*Xiphias gladius*	Finfish
Tautog	*Tautoga onitis*	Finfish
Thalassinid shrimp	*Callianassa subterranea**	Crustacean
Toad crab	*Hyas coarctatus*	Crustacean
Tube dwelling anemone (Cerianthid)	*Cerianthis borealis*	Cnidarian
Tube worm	*Filograna implexa*	Polychaete
Tuna	*Thunnus* sp.	Finfish
Tunicate (Ascidian and sea squirt)	Several genera	Ascidian
Whelk	*Buccinum undatum**	Gastropod
White hake	*Urophycis tenuis*	Finfish
Whiting (European)	*Melangius melangus**	Finfish
Whiting (Silver hake)	*Merluccius bilinearis*	Finfish
Windowpane flounder	*Scophthalanus agnosus*	Finfish
Winter flounder	*Pleuronectes americanus*	Finfish
Witch Flounder	*Glyptocephalus cynoglossus*	Finfish
Wolffish (Catfish)	*Anarhichas lupus*	Finfish
Wood boring worm	*Toredo navalis*	Bivalve (Mollusc)
Yellowtail flounder	*Pleuronectes ferruginea*	Finfish

* Refers to organisms found in the northeastern Atlantic.

APPENDIX 2

Discussion Session Recommendations and Comments

Below is the list of recommendations and comments as recorded in writing at the discussion session that concluded the May 30, 1997 conference on Effects of Fishing Gear on the Sea Floor of New England. Recommendations in bold type were identified as high priority.

1. **There is a need to understand (a) the relationship between fishing productivity and habitat carrying capacity and (b) the effects of fishing on habitats.** Since habitat effects and fishing vary together, use closures for research to separate these two effects.

2. Add habitat considerations to gear development.

3. Look at gear impacts over short, medium, and long term.

4. Improve estimates of trawl frequency and distribution by using fishermen's records.

5. Investigate the function of "edges" (transition areas) to fish productivity in heavily trawled areas.

6. Prove there is a need to document this question first: What is the effect on commercially important species of fishing gear?

7. Consider zoning the ocean in a manner similar to land use zoning.

8. Differing goals for the ocean have been expressed at the conference: biological diversity and fishery productivity.

9. Minimize mortality of nontarget species because some provide habitat and food for target species.

10. Identify unfished areas to compare with fished areas.

11. Decisions will have to be made with imperfect knowledge.

12. Essential fish habitat regulations recognize that prey can be a component of habitat.

13. Recognize that there are other economic values from marine ecosystems in addition to harvested fish.

14. There is a need to demonstrate that three-dimensional complexity on the sea floor increases fish productivity.

15. Question: Can methods be developed for valuing marine products and services in addition to fish?

16. Set priorities for monitoring efforts: focus on important rather than representative areas.

17. Quantify effects of fishing on the sea floor.

18. Studies should measure the relationship between habitat and fish productivity on a regional scale because it is difficult to generalize from individual studies.

19. The scale of management is larger than the scale of fish populations.

20. Map sea floor ecoregions as a starting point for management.

21. **Classify sea bed types and determine which are most vulnerable to gear disturbance.**

22. Develop improved habitat understanding.

23. Develop an improved habitat assessment approach.

24. For the EFH deadlines, scientists need to help identify and describe habitats.

25. **Because we do not know what limits fish production, developing a research program to answer this question is a high priority.**

26. Decide the future of existing closed areas: should they be permanent or should they rotate? Permanent closures may create adjacent blighted areas.

27. Involve industry directly in research: find opportunities for collaboration, such as habitat of scallops.

28. Fishery closures must be unpopular to work.

29. There is only one problem: too much fishing. Reducing fishing effort will solve the problem.

Color Plates

The following eight pages reproduce in color some

of the figures in this volume. The color plates are labeled with

author's last name and figure number from the paper where the

figure appeared in black and white. The page number for

the black and white version of each color plate

is provided for quick reference.

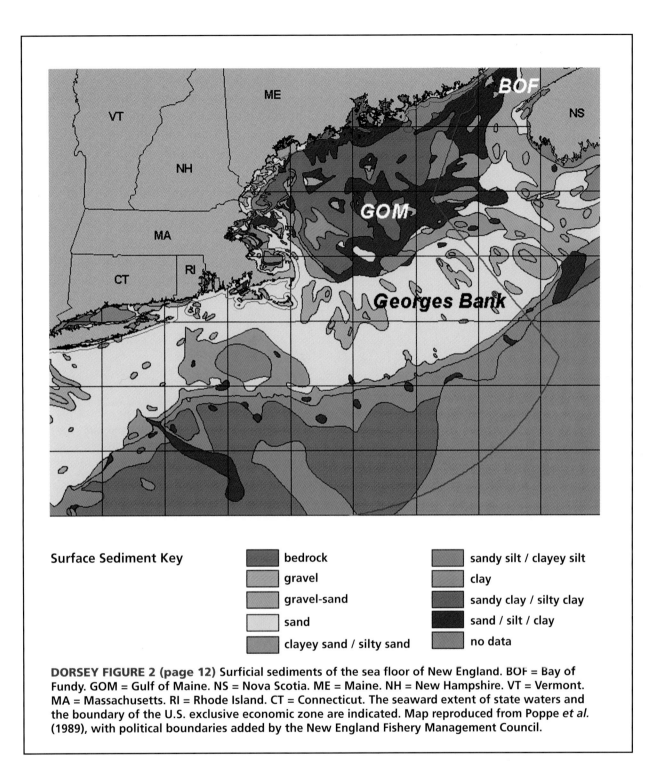

Surface Sediment Key

- bedrock
- gravel
- gravel-sand
- sand
- clayey sand / silty sand
- sandy silt / clayey silt
- clay
- sandy clay / silty clay
- sand / silt / clay
- no data

DORSEY FIGURE 2 (page 12) Surficial sediments of the sea floor of New England. BOF = Bay of Fundy. GOM = Gulf of Maine. NS = Nova Scotia. ME = Maine. NH = New Hampshire. VT = Vermont. MA = Massachusetts. RI = Rhode Island. CT = Connecticut. The seaward extent of state waters and the boundary of the U.S. exclusive economic zone are indicated. Map reproduced from Poppe *et al.* (1989), with political boundaries added by the New England Fishery Management Council.

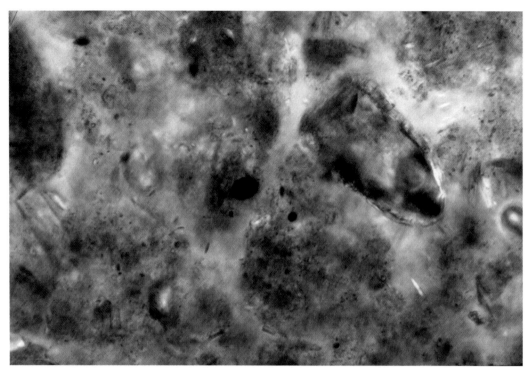

WATLING FIGURE 2 (page 21) Section of mud from Jordan Basin at 250 m depth. This picture is 200 micrometers wide, so five pictures across equals a millimeter. A bullet-shaped tintinnid ciliate (a single-celled organism) that fell from the plankton and was buried in the bottom is visible to right of center. Photograph by Les Watling.

WATLING FIGURE 9 (page 27) A 1985 photograph from the southwest corner of Jeffreys Bank showing two sea pens, a cerianthid anemone, and a witch flounder (*Glyptocephalus cynoglossus*). The tentacle crown of the anemone is about 15 cm across. Photograph by Les Watling.

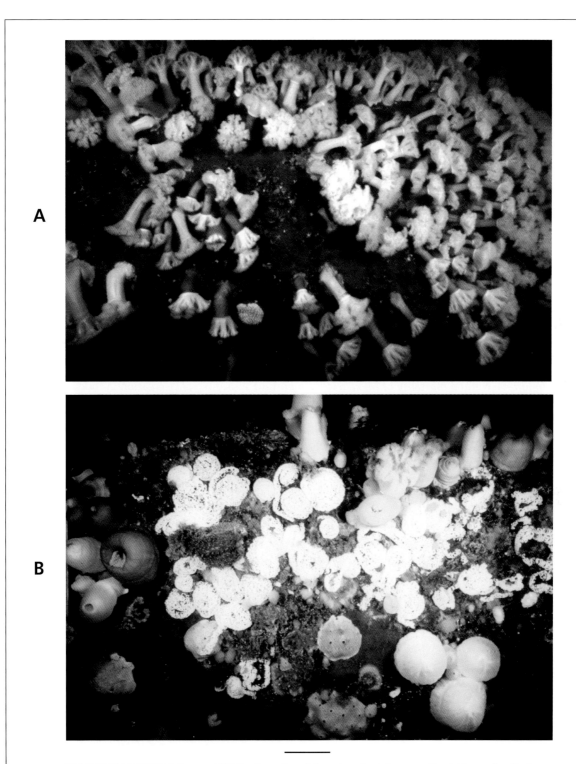

WITMAN FIGURE 3 (page 32) Rock wall at 30 m depth at Ammen Rock Pinnacle, Cashes Ledge. A. Wide angle photograph of dense aggregation of the sea anemone *Metridium senile* that originally covered most of the top of the ledge. B. Close-up photograph of a nearby spot in June 1987, showing patches created by nudibranch (*Aeolidia papillosa*) predation on the sea anemones. One nudibranch is visible left of center, and the sea anemones (colored white, orange, and brown) are contracted in this photograph. Anemones previously occupied the areas covered with white spiraled masses of nudibranch eggs. Bar below photograph indicates 5 cm. Photographs by Jon Witman.

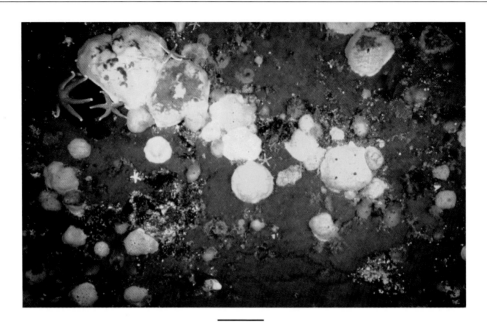

WITMAN FIGURE 4 (page 34) Area of rocky bottom at Ammen Rock Pinnacle (33 m depth) dominated by sponges. The red-orange encrusting sponge is *Hymedesmia* sp. and the orange mounding sponge is *Myxilla fimbriata*. Natural mortality of *Myxilla* is an important source of space creation in rocky subtidal communities in the Gulf of Maine. Note the sponge at upper left that is black and necrotic. The next photograph in the time series indicated that it fell off the wall, creating a patch the same size as the sponge. Two other *Myxilla* mortality patches are visible just left of center and at lower right in this photograph. Bar below photograph indicates 5 cm. Photograph by Jon Witman.

SMOLOWITZ FIGURE 2 (page 48) The New Bedford style scallop dredge, with top removed for illustration. Drawing by Robin Amaral.

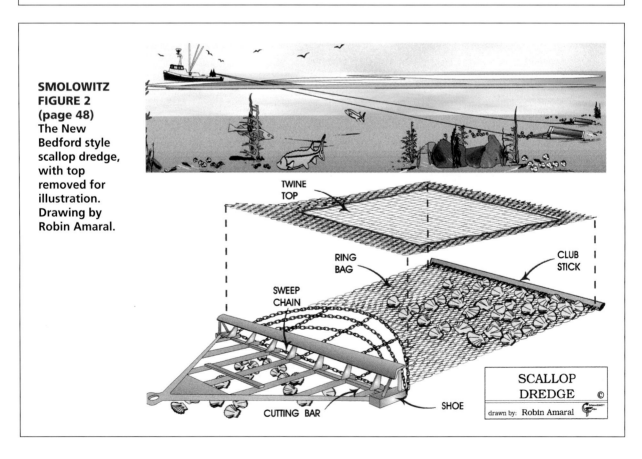

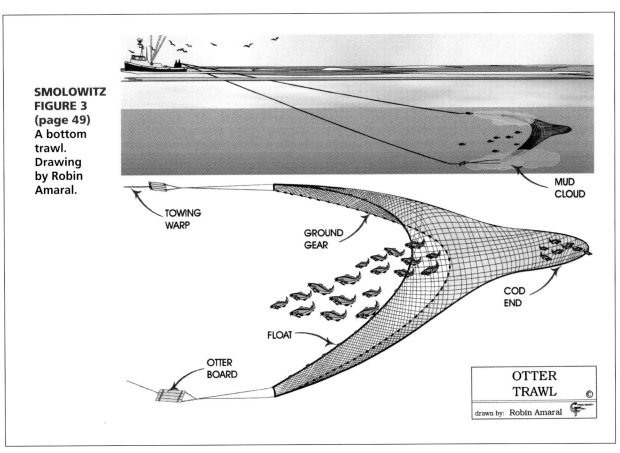

SMOLOWITZ FIGURE 3 (page 49) A bottom trawl. Drawing by Robin Amaral.

MUD CLOUD

TOWING WARP

GROUND GEAR

COD END

FLOAT

OTTER BOARD

OTTER TRAWL ©
drawn by: Robin Amaral

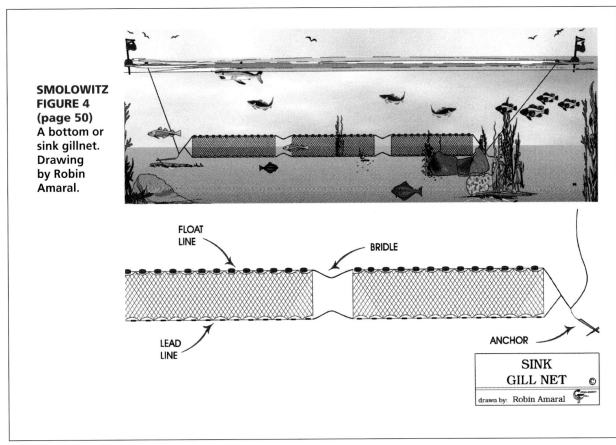

SMOLOWITZ FIGURE 4 (page 50) A bottom or sink gillnet. Drawing by Robin Amaral.

FLOAT LINE

BRIDLE

LEAD LINE

ANCHOR

SINK GILL NET ©
drawn by: Robin Amaral

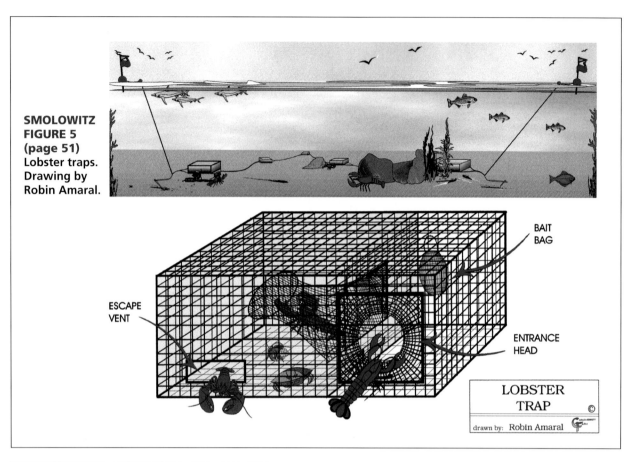

SMOLOWITZ FIGURE 5 (page 51) Lobster traps. Drawing by Robin Amaral.

BAIT BAG

ESCAPE VENT

ENTRANCE HEAD

LOBSTER TRAP ©

drawn by: Robin Amaral

SMOLOWITZ FIGURE 6 (page 52) A bottom longline. Drawing by Robin Amaral.

GANGION

BOTTOM LONGLINE ©

drawn by: Robin Amaral

COLLIE FIGURE 9 (page 61) Photographs of the gravel habitat on northern Georges Bank. A. Gravel pavement in an undredged area, site 20. Abundant hydroids and tubes of the worm, *Filograna implexa*, are attached to the gravel. Visible in the center of the photograph are a horse mussel, northern red anemone, and toad crab. B. Gravel pavement in a dredged area, west of site 17, outside closed area II. There are few attached organisms on the gravel, and few animals apart from burrowing anemones and a juvenile scallop. Photographs by Page Valentine and Dann Blackwood, U.S. Geological Survey.

COLLIE FIGURE 10 (page 62) Photograph of the gravel habitat on northern Georges Bank at site 17, taken in July 1997, 2.5 years after the area was closed to bottom fishing. Sponges, bryozoans, crabs, scallops, and sea urchins show evidence of partial recovery at this site. Photograph by Page Valentine and Dann Blackwood, U.S. Geological Survey.

LEACH FIGURE 1 (page 97) Lemons or stalked sea squirts, *Boltenia ovifera*. These indicators of good cod fishing rarely come up on bottom long-lines any more. Photograph by Jon Witman.